CRIMINOLOGY AND ARCHAEOLOGY

This collection is the product of a collaborative venture between criminologists and archaeologists concerned with the international market in illicit antiquities. It examines the state of regulation in the antiquities market, with a particular focus on the UK's position, but also with reference to the international context.

Looting happens routinely and many countries have rich deposits of cultural material. Antiquities are highly collectable, and there are several prominent international centres for trade. As well as the legitimate face of the antiquities trade there therefore exists an international illicit market in which cultural objects are trafficked for profit in breach of national laws and international conventions.

It is within the complex international and local regulatory context that the essays presented here emerge, focusing upon three areas in particular: the demand for looted antiquities; the supply of cultural artefacts which originate in source countries; and regulation of the international market in antiquities.

Criminology has long been interested in transnational crime and its regulation; archaeology in the destructive consequences of antiquities looting in erasing our knowledge of the past. In the papers presented here both disciplines present new data and analysis to forge a more coherent understanding of the nature and failings of the regulatory framework currently in place to combat the criminal market in antiquities.

Oñati International Series in Law and Society

A SERIES PUBLISHED FOR THE OÑATI INSTITUTE FOR THE SOCIOLOGY OF LAW

Titles in this Series

Social Dynamics of Crime and Control: New Theories for a World in Transition edited by Susanne Karstedt and Kai Bussmann

Criminal Policy in Transition edited by Andrew Rutherford and Penny Green

Making Law for Families edited by Mavis Maclean

Poverty and the Law edited by Peter Robson and Asbjørn Kjønstad

Adapting Legal Cultures edited by Johannes Feest and David Nelken

Rethinking Law, Society and Governance: Foucault's Bequest edited by Gary Wickham and George Pavlich

Rules and Networks edited by Richard Appelbaum, Bill Felstiner and Volkmar Gessner

Women in the World's Legal Professions edited by Ulrike Schultz and Gisela Shaw

Healing the Wounds edited by Marie-Claire Foblets and Trutz von Trotha

Imaginary Boundaries of Justice edited by Ronnie Lippens

Family Law and Family Values edited by Mavis Maclean

Contemporary Issues in the Semiotics of Law
edited by Anne Wagner, Tracey Summerfield and Farid Benavides Vanegas

The Geography of Law: Landscapes, Identity and Regulation
edited by Bill Taylor

Theory and Method in Socio-Legal Research
edited by Reza Banakar and Max Travers

Luhmann on Law and Politics edited by Michael King and Chris Thornhill

Precarious Work, Women and the New Economy: The Challenge to Legal Norms edited by Judy Fudge and Rosemary Owens

Juvenile Law Violators, Human Rights, and the Development of New Juvenile Justice Systems edited by Eric L Jensen and Jørgen Jepsen

The Language Question in Europe and Diverse Societies: Political, Legal and Social Perspectives edited by Dario Castiglione and Chris Longman

European Ways of Law: Towards A European Sociology of Law
edited by Volkmar Gessner and David Nelken

Crafting Transnational Policing: Police Capacity-Building and Global Policing Reform edited by Andrew Goldsmith and James Sheptycki

Constitutional Politics in the Middle East: With special reference to Turkey, Iraq, Iran and Afghanistan edited by Saïd Amir Arjomand

Parenting after Partnering: Containing Conflict after Separation
edited by Mavis Maclean

Responsible Business: Self-Governance and Law in Transnational Economic Transactions edited by Olaf Dilling, Martin Herberg and Gerd Winter

Rethinking Equality Projects in Law edited by Rosemary Hunter

Regulating Deviance: The Redirection of Criminalisation and the Futures of Criminal Law edited by Bernadette McSherry, Alan Norrie and Simon Bronitt

Living Law: Reconsidering Eugen Ehrlich edited by Marc Hertogh

Multicultural Jurisprudence: Comparative Perspectives on the Cultural Defense edited by Marie-Claire Foblets and Alison Dundes Renteln

Changing Contours of Domestic Life, Family and Law: Caring and Sharing edited by Anne Bottomley and Simone Wong

Criminology and Archaeology

Studies in Looted Antiquities

Edited by
Simon Mackenzie
and
Penny Green

Oñati International Series in Law and Society

A SERIES PUBLISHED FOR THE OÑATI INSTITUTE
FOR THE SOCIOLOGY OF LAW

•HART•
PUBLISHING
OXFORD AND PORTLAND, OREGON
2009

Published in North America (US and Canada)
by Hart Publishing
c/o International Specialized Book Services
920 NE 58th Avenue, Suite 300
Portland, OR 97213-3786
USA
Tel: +1 503 287 3093 or toll-free: (1) 800 944 6190
Fax: +1 503 280 8832
E-mail: orders@isbs.com
Website: www.isbs.com

Hart Publishing, 16c Worcester Place, Oxford, OX1 2JW
Telephone: +44 (0)1865 517530 Fax: +44 (0)1865 510710
E-mail: mail@hartpub.co.uk
Website: http://www.hartpub.co.uk

British Library Cataloguing in Publication Data
Data Available

ISBN: 978-1-84113-991-3 (hardback)
ISBN: 978-1-84113-992-0 (paperback)

Typeset by Compuscript, Shannon
Printed and bound in Great Britain by
CPI Antony Rowe Ltd, Chippenham, Wiltshire

Contents

Part IV: Regulation and the Market in Looted Antiquities

Author Biographies

Roger Bland has been Head of Portable Antiquities and Treasure at the British Museum since 2005. From 1994 to 2003 he was seconded to the Department for Culture, Media and Sport, where he advised on the framing and implementation of the Treasure Act 1996 and set up the Portable Antiquities Scheme. In 2000 he became secretary to the Illicit Trade Advisory Panel and advised on the United Kingdom's accession to the 1970 UNESCO Convention in 2002 and also the Dealing in Cultural Objects (Offences) Act 2003.

Neil Brodie graduated from the University of Liverpool with a PhD in Archaeology in 1991 and has held positions at the British School at Athens and the McDonald Institute for Archaeological Research at the University of Cambridge. He co-edited *Archaeology, Cultural Heritage, and the Antiquities Trade* (with Morag M Kersel, Christina Luke, and Kathryn Walker Tubb; 2006) *Illicit Antiquities: The Theft of Culture and the Extinction of Archaeology* (with Kathryn Walker Tubb; 2002) and *Trade in Illicit Antiquities: The Destruction of the World's Archaeological Heritage* (with Jennifer Doole and Colin Renfrew; 2001). Since October 2007 he has been director of the Cultural Heritage Resource at Stanford University, CA, where he is researching the economics and sociology of the antiquities market.

Penny Green is Professor of Law and Criminology at Kings College, University of London where she is Head of Research and Director of the Law School's Research Degree Programme. She has published widely on state crime, state–corporate crime, natural disasters, Turkish criminal justice and politics, transnational crime, and asylum policy. Her current research interests include illegal logging, state violence, environmental harms and looted antiquities (see ESRC-funded evaluation of the impact of the United Kingdom's Dealing in Cultural Objects (Offences) Act 2003, presented in this volume). She is the author of a number of books including *The Enemy Without: Policing and Class Consciousness in the Miners' Strike* (1990); *Drugs, Trafficking and Criminal Policy: The Scapegoat Solution* (1997), *Criminal Justice in Transition: Criminal Policy-Making Toward the New Millennium* 2000, and with Tony Ward, *State Crime: Governments, Violence and Corruption* (2004).

Linda Källman, BA, was at the time of writing her chapter a researcher at The Swedish National Council for Crime Prevention. She contributed to the Council's work on looted antiquities, published as *Crime Goes Underground: Crimes against Historical Sites and Remains* (2007). She was also a key contributor to the book *Cultural Heritage Crime* (2008).

Lars Korsell, jur dr (LLD), is Chief Legal Officer and Head of the Department of Economic and Organised Crime Research at The Swedish National Council for Crime Prevention, an authority under the Ministry of Justice. He has published widely in the fields of white-collar crime and organised crime. In the field of art crime, he was responsible for the study *Cultural Heritage Crime: The Nordic Dimension* (2006). He has also contributed to the work *Crime Goes Underground: Crimes against Historical Sites and Remains* (2007), and has written the second part of the book *Cultural Heritage Crime* (2008).

Gordon Lobay is currently Collections Management and Museum Planning Advisor at the University of Alberta. He leads collections management initiatives and facilitates the movement and certification of cultural property for the University museums. He has a PhD in Archaeology from the University of Cambridge (Homerton College) and wide-ranging excavation experience in Germany, Italy, Tunisia and Ukraine. He has previously held a position at the University of Texas (Institute of Classical Archaeology) and contributed to the project 'Criminalising the Market in Looted Antiquities' with Simon Mackenzie and Penny Green. His research interests focus on archaeological looting, the antiquities trade and the impacts of legal instruments on both the trade in cultural property and the protection of archaeological sites. His current research aims to assess methods intended to reduce the volume of illegal antiquities that reach the art market.

Simon Mackenzie is Reader in Criminology at the Scottish Centre for Crime and Justice Research, University of Glasgow. He has published articles on the criminological analysis of the market in looted antiquities in a number of international journals, and is author of *Going, Going, Gone: Regulating the Market in Illicit Antiquities* (2005), which presented the results of his qualitative research interviewing high-level antiquities dealers in the United Kingdom, the United States, Switzerland, Thailand, Hong Kong and Australia. In 2006 the book was awarded the British Society of Criminology Book Prize. This project was followed by the ESRC-funded evaluation of the impact of the United Kingdom's Dealing in Cultural Objects (Offences) Act 2003 which is presented in this volume.

Kenneth Polk is Professor of Criminology at the University of Melbourne in Australia. Before that he was for many years Professor of Sociology at the University of Oregon. His undergraduate degree was from San Diego State, and his PhD from UCLA. Much of his research over recent years has focused on violence and homicide, including the books *When Men Kill* (1994) and *Child Victims of Homicide* (2001, with Christine Alder). Although now retired from teaching, he continues to do research on art crime, including fraud, theft, and the problem of the international traffic in plundered cultural heritage material.

Tony Ward is Reader in Law at the University of Hull and has research interests in criminology, legal theory, and social epistemology. He is co-author with Penny Green of *State Crime: Governments, Violence and Corruption* (2004) and with Gerry Johnstone of *Law and Crime* (2009), and co-editor, with Bev Clucas and Gerry Johnstone, of *Torture: Moral Absolutes and Ambiguities* (2009).

David Whyte is Reader in Sociology at the University of Liverpool, where he teaches and researches issues of corporate power and regulation and crimes of the powerful, and he has published widely on those subjects in both academic and wider circulation journals. His books include *Unmasking the Crimes of the Powerful* (ed, with Steve Tombs, 2003) *Expanding the Criminological Imagination* (ed, with Alana Barton, Karen Corteen, and David Scott, 2007) and *Safety Crimes* (with Steve Tombs, 2007). His latest book, *Crimes of the Powerful*, will be published in 2009 by Open University Press. He is a board member of the Centre for Corporate Accountability and an advisory board member of Corporate Watch.

Introduction: A Context for the Engagement of Criminology and Archaeology

SIMON MACKENZIE AND PENNY GREEN

THIS COLLECTION IS the product of a collaborative venture between criminologists and archaeologists concerned with the international market in illicit antiquities. Criminology has long been interested in transnational crime and its regulation; archaeology in the pedagogical consequences of antiquities looting. In the chapters presented here both disciplines present new data and analysis to forge a more coherent understanding of the nature and failings of the regulatory framework currently in place to combat the criminal market in looted antiquities.

The international market in illicit antiquities presents a useful case study of a form of transnational crime. Looted antiquities may be defined as those taken illicitly from the ground, or from their place as an integral part of, or attachment to, a temple or other ancient structure (Meyer, 1973; Bator, 1983; Renfrew, 1999). Looting happens routinely (Conklin, 1994; Pastore, 2001; Thosarat, 2001) and many countries, including the United Kingdom (see Bland, chapter five, this volume), have rich underground, or undersea, deposits of cultural material (Stead, 1998).

The list of source countries is long, and serious looting has been recorded for example in Egypt, Italy, Peru, Mexico, Greece, Turkey, Southeast Asia, and China. Antiquities are highly collectable for reasons both of value and of aesthetics, and there are several prominent international centres for trade, most notably London, New York, Paris, Brussels, Hong Kong, Geneva, and Bangkok. The United Kingdom is widely acknowledged to be a significant market for looted antiquities in global terms, both by way of end point in the chain of supply, and as a transit point for looted antiquities which will subsequently leave the country (DCMS, 2000).

The harm looting causes is not immediately obvious to the non-expert. Aside from the incidental destruction of objects deemed subsidiary to the gold, silver, and jewels that attract looters, there is the loss of stratified context and consequent loss of historical record (Burnham, 1975; Renfrew, 1993, 1999). Stratification and context are archaeological terms for the depth at which objects are found (indicating their age) and their relationship to other objects and structures found around them. The association between artefacts *inter se* and their place in the earth in which they are found can add greatly to our knowledge about the human past. The collection of such knowledge and its publication is the essence of archaeology (Coggins, 1969, 1970). The loss of the cultural assets themselves as they travel to overseas markets is, of course, also a detrimental effect caused by looting to source countries. However, this loss is remediable (in theory and occasionally in practice) when a looted and smuggled object is returned to its country of origin. The loss caused to the archaeological record by looting is, on the other hand, irremediable—once context is destroyed, the knowledge it can offer can never be reclaimed (Gill and Chippindale, 1993; Chippindale and Gill, 2000).

The two largest market centres for the sale of antiquities, in terms of volume of trade, are New York and London (Gerstenblith, 1995; Polk, 2000). Antiquities looted from source countries routinely travel to London to be sold by international dealers and auction houses to other dealers, private collectors, and museums (Elia, 1994; Alder and Polk, 2002).

The market therefore operates across national borders. Source states from which looted objects are exported for sale have responded to the problem with a two-pronged legal approach: vesting legislation and export controls. 'State vesting' legislation, as we will call it here, follows a similar model across many source countries: objects over a certain age, usually 100 years old, in the ground are declared to be the property of the state, making their finding and removal a theft from the state (Prott and O'Keefe, 1984). Integral parts of national monuments are often also expressly declared to attract criminal sanction if removed. Export controls usually take the form of licence requirements. Objects of artistic or cultural interest over 100 years old should not be exported without a licence, which will be granted by the state arts or antiquities department (Prott and O'Keefe, 1989; O'Keefe, 1997). Despite these restrictions at source, many countries report widespread looting and unauthorised export of their underground heritage (Brodie, Doole and Renfrew, 2001). Further, due to deficiencies of UK law and practice, these illicit objects have tended to readily enter the London market (DCMS, 2000; O'Keefe, 2000; Polk, 2002).

The failure of the impressive-looking regime of control at source can best be explained by (a) the local context in which regulation is played out in source countries, and (b) the international legal context enjoyed by travelling antiquities.

In terms of local legal and social practices at source, several factors militate against the effectiveness of regulation, leading in practice to a situation in which both sets of legal restraint are routinely ignored by looters and dealers in source countries (Mackenzie, 2005a). The chances of apprehension in the act of looting are, rightly, perceived as negligible. In some countries looting is considered a craft, the skills for this alternative employment being passed down generations of '*tombaroli*' or '*huaqueros*', the local words for tomb robbers in Italy and South America respectively (Paredes Maury, 1996; Ruiz, 2001). Neither is passage of objects out of a source country perceived to be problematic; poorly paid customs officials and the culturally unexceptional nature of 'payment for service', or what western observers would call bribery, undermine the effectiveness of formal export controls. Any cultural restraint on grave-robbing as might be thought likely is often in fact absent due to a certain paradox of respect. This paradox takes the form that, whether the dead are respected or not, their graves often end up fair game for plunder. In some countries the buried are simply not accorded much thought if they are not direct blood ancestors of the present culture, or where they worshipped a different God. This is the case for example where Buddhist objects are found in the now predominantly Muslim Pakistan, and has been brought to public attention most spectacularly in Afghanistan, where the Islamic Taliban destroyed the Bamiyan Buddhas in 2001. In this way, current citizens often feel little connection with the artistic, religious, or bodily remnants of prior occupiers of the land. The other side of the paradox is that where there *is* an ancestral connection between the buried and the living, the latter often consider the grave goods of the former as gifts from their forebears, entombed precisely so as to assist their descendants in times of financial hardship.

The failures and inadequacies of the international treatment of source country legal controls have also been noted in the literature. Once an object is out of a source country, the export restriction which barred its exit may become useless. While it may be assumed that market states would normally enforce the export laws of source states, this is in fact not the case. Export laws are public laws (as are, for example, taxes), and just as one state is not obliged to collect taxes for another, so a breach of a foreign export provision is not something a market country will ordinarily feel obliged to enforce (Merryman, 1986, 1988; Gerstenblith, 2000). In effect, this renders export prohibitions in relation to antiquities a legal form of shutting the stable door after the horse has bolted.[1]

State vesting legislation has in the past rested on a similarly uneasy footing, being at odds with western neo-liberal doxa such as the right to private ownership and freedom of the individual from the unduly wide and imprecise inroads government may make into such perceived fundamentals as property rights and entrepreneurial choices. In spite of this, the answer to the question whether domestic laws against handling stolen property in market states includes property stolen abroad has slowly moved from 'no' to 'yes' in several market states: notably the United States (Gerstenblith, 2002, 2003; Mackenzie, 2005b: 251 fn 4) and also the United Kingdom.

[1] See particularly *Attorney-General of New Zealand v Ortiz* [1983] 2 WLR 809 (HL), affirming [1982] 3 WLR 570 (CA).

In the United Kingdom, the Theft Act 1968 in section 24 made it clear that the offence of handling stolen goods included goods stolen overseas; an inclusion which lives on and is made explicitly applicable to antiquities in the Dealing in Cultural Objects (Offences) Act 2003 (see Mackenzie and Green, chapter eight, this volume). In this respect, then, source country controls are an important element in constituting a theft charge against a buyer of looted property overseas, if not instrumental in preventing the practice of looting in the first place.

This is a good example of the systemic transnational nature of the regulatory effects of legal controls in the antiquities market—a pattern which follows the systemic transnational nature of the market itself. As Michaelowski and Kramer (1987) have observed, there are 'spaces between laws' which in our study might be thought to include the inadequate treatment at home of foreign export laws. There are also, however, 'bridges between laws', where the importance of the existence of a law in one country, such as state vesting, is not in its more obvious domestic effect (that is, in respect of the deterrence of looting, in which it is a demonstrable failure) but in the opportunities it triggers for recognition in the legal processes of other states and prosecutions there which may lead to the seizure and return of looted and illegally exported objects.

What international import/export controls as might remain once we discount the ineffective legal treatment given to source export controls by market states are further tested by the indirect routes often taken by looted objects on their way to market. Objects either travel direct from source to market countries, or pass through one or more 'transit' states. Transit states are functional ports of call for looted antiquities; they perform a laundering role in respect of illicitly obtained objects by freely allowing them entry and then giving them permits when exported. In this way an object looted from China may arrive in the United Kingdom with an export permit from Hong Kong. Although the knowing purchase of looted objects from China is now expressly prohibited in the United Kingdom under the 2003 Act, as is the import of such an object, HM Revenue and Customs has an understandable history of low levels of activity in distinguishing looted objects from legitimately owned ones or fakes, and a dealer in the United Kingdom may safely claim that, while he knows the object to be Chinese, it bears no evidence of looting, and as it came from an international trading port like Hong Kong he had no reason to believe it to be illicit.

It is within this problematic international and local regulatory context that the work presented here emerges. The chapters in the present volume are the outcome of a workshop held at the International Institute for the Sociology of Law in Oñati in 2007. The impetus behind the workshop was to bring archaeologists and criminologists together to discuss the state of regulation in the antiquities market, with a particular focus on the United

Kingdom's position, but also with reference to the international context more generally. It was hoped that a fruitful interdisciplinary discussion might result from the mutual engagement of the disciplines of criminology and archaeology. In particular, it was felt that a discourse which brought together, on the one hand, academics whose 'tools of the trade' were various forms of legal regulation and social control and, on the other, front-line observers of the consequences of the international market in looted antiquities was more likely to articulate successful regulatory strategies.

The important chapters presented here show, we hope, how productive such interdisciplinary discussion can be. They deal in varying degrees with the conceptual theme of harm: an object which has moved to the forefront of contemporary critical criminology, asserted as one of the most salient disciplinary reference points. Many of the chapters illustrate the harm associated with the international market in illicit antiquities. They show that this harm is caused in various ways, intentionally and negligently. Perhaps most importantly, however, the harm which the illicit antiquities market produces emerges from many of the contributions to this volume as being most appropriately identified as systemic. While there are various degrees of intent and negligence at different points in the market for looted antiquities, these legal terms often do not seem to capture the essence of the routine harm caused by a global system in which harms in source countries are driven by demand for objects in sometimes distant market countries; in which looters sometimes depend on the income they make from their illegalities and destroy context as a side-effect of their search for objects valued by the market; in which infrastructure projects do not proceed with appropriate sensitivity to the archaeological record and result in destruction (Källman and Korsell, chapter six, this volume); in which contradictions in moral positions and value judgements are manifest, and deeply entrenched (Ward, chapter two, this volume); in which a range of 'facilitators' profit from their complicity in this international illicit market (Brodie, chapter three, this volume); in which the Internet creates a web of 'always on' instantaneous global connections that allow semi-anonymous trading relations to flourish where distortion or concealment of important declarations about object provenance can be easily performed without appearing unusual (Bland, chapter five, this volume); in which strategies of regulation that focus only on one point in the chain of supply have tended not to succeed in market reduction (Polk, chapter one, Lobay, chapter four, Mackenzie and Green, chapter eight, this volume); and in which the very idea of illicit market control may contain internal contradictions, requiring that thinking about regulation become more sophisticated than has been evident in the usual range of legal and other regulatory interventions which have aimed to punish or persuade those who offend, intentionally or negligently (Whyte, chapter seven, this volume).

Kenneth Polk introduces the collection with an overview of the field in which he has taken a pioneering role in applying criminological theory. This chapter opens the collection by examining the international traffic in illicit antiquities as a criminal market. This approach calls attention to market dynamics in order to help us understand at which points the market is likely to respond to regulatory intervention. Polk revisits key criminological concepts which have developed in his prior writings on this particular 'criminal market'. Among these are a critique of some of the traditional assumptions of deterrence theorists. He finds Braithwaite's models of deterrence more useful than less reflective legalistic views which consider prohibition-type strategies as effective ways to reduce markets. Supply reduction is observed to have an uninspiring history in harm reduction in criminal markets: he suggests that demand-focused initiatives hold more promise.

The chapters which follow this global view of a criminal market fall into three categories, based on particular areas of research within the overall market. These are the *demand* for looted antiquities, the *supply* of cultural artefacts which originate in source countries, and *regulation* of the international market in antiquities.

Tony Ward opens the first category of analysis by drawing on Simmel's phenomenology of value to conceptualise the harm involved in a trade in looted antiquities. He compares and contrasts it with illicit logging, probing the meaning to individual market participants of apparently 'harmful' destruction. Building on classic 'neutralisation' theories in the sociology of deviance, he helps us understand the psychology of participants in harmful criminal markets.

While Ward considers how antiquities dealers neutralise their part in causing distant harm, Neil Brodie examines the ethical dilemmas confronted by archaeologists involved in legitimising looted antiquities through scholarship. Academic archaeologists are often called on to value or authenticate unprovenanced cultural objects, impacting on the market value in the process. In their doing so, Brodie argues that they are complicit in the illicit trade and therefore encourage further looting and destruction at source. In this case study of academic involvement in the illegal trade in ancient manuscripts he finds support for a more expansive take on the controversial proposition that 'collectors are the real looters' (Renfrew, 1993).

Gordon Lobay's chapter is based in a wider research project in which he used US auction catalogues to quantify US import of Italian antiquities around the time of a border control initiative; the US–Italy bilateral agreement. He found only weak support for the agreement in terms of impact on demand in the US: he suggests that the only major effect of the agreement has been in encouraging the publication of previous sale data in auction catalogues. Even this, he argues, is not an especially useful indication of object provenance, and generally his chapter constitutes an indictment of unilateral attempts to control global illicit markets.

The second category of analysis—concerned with supply and source countries—comprises two chapters. The first is Roger Bland's review of the United Kingdom's Portable Antiquities Scheme, which aims to increase the number of finds reported to the authorities. His team at the British Museum have also been monitoring the impact of the Internet on the market in portable antiquities. Although the United Kingdom is usually seen to be a market country in antiquities, Bland points out that it is also a source of antiquities and explores the difficulties involved in regulating this market at source, especially with the growing number of Internet sales.

The second chapter in the 'supply and source countries' section reports a study of crimes against historical sites and ancient remains in Sweden. Lars Korsell and Linda Källman distinguish between two ways in which the destruction of cultural heritage sites can come about: looting, and inadvertent damage as a result of economic development. They come to the provocative conclusion that while the harm caused by the illicit antiquities trade has tended to be attributed to looting, in fact development projects and other forms of land use have had a more significant destructive impact on historical sites in Sweden.

The final section of the book considers the question of market regulation. David Whyte brings a wider perspective to the question of regulation, incorporating historical, theoretical, and criminological observations on criminal markets to argue that a 'paradox' of regulation is that it 'controls' at the same time as it 'enables', becoming a force of legitimation in many instances. This is clearly a significant flaw in the project of regulation conceived as a tool of state intervention in markets. Whyte argues that a better framework is one that sees states and markets as irrevocably intertwined, and regulation emerges from this view as a conceptually highly problematic activity.

Whyte's ideas are developed empirically in the work of Mackenzie and Green, presented as the final chapter in this volume. They explore the development of one particular attempt at demand-oriented regulatory reform—the United Kingdom's Dealing in Cultural Objects (Offences) Act 2003. This chapter reports the findings of a two-year evaluative study of the impact of the Act on both the United Kingdom and the international illicit market. The authors conclude that while the Act may have made some antiquities dealers more cautious in their market activity, their transaction routines have remained largely unchanged. Given the culture of non-enforcement which has accompanied the Act, they argue that the Act as an attempt at market reduction has failed and is unlikely to have any significant impact in the future. A more fruitful harm-reduction approach is proposed which combines international cooperation with a more effective deterrent for market dealing outside any such cooperative schemes.

In this volume we have drawn together several strands of thinking about the issue of looted antiquities which serve a variety of ends in taking the debate forward. At such a relatively early stage in the emerging conversation between criminology and archaeology our main aim has been fairly straightforward: to present a range of chapters which, in addressing some of the key problems in the market, on the one hand, display why the market is an appropriate site of study for criminologists and, on the other, present some theoretical reflection by criminologists on matters such as morality and regulation which may suggest to the archaeological community that criminology can be a productive partner discipline in addressing the looting problem. For colleagues already involved in the study of the illicit antiquities market we think that some of the chapters will be of interest for their development of previous lines of inquiry, while some (for archaeological colleagues, perhaps particularly those by the criminologists Ward and Whyte) will intrigue by introducing a style of thought and writing to the field which may appear new—and, we hope, refreshing. For those new to the subject area, the collection contains key overviews and reflections on the market from some of its established commentators, as well as a range of ideas for further research. We are certain that the essays which follow contain many insights which prove the worth to archaeology of 'thinking with' criminology, and vice versa. Exploring the most effective ways to capitalise on this disciplinary engagement will be an important task for those concerned with reducing the harm associated with the illicit antiquities market.

REFERENCES

Alder, C and Polk, K (2002) 'Stopping this Awful Business: The Illicit Traffic in Antiquities Examined as a Criminal Market' 7 *Art Antiquity and Law* 35.

Bator, PM (1983) *The International Trade in Art* (Chicago, University of Chicago Press).

Brodie, N, Doole, J, and Renfrew, C (eds) (2001) *Trade in Illicit Antiquities: the Destruction of the World's Archaeological Heritage* (Cambridge, McDonald Institute for Archaeological Research).

Burnham, B (1975) *The Art Crisis* (London, Collins).

Chippindale, C and Gill, DJW (2000) 'Material Consequences of Contemporary Classical Collecting' 104 *American Journal of Archaeology* 463.

Coggins, C (1969) 'Illicit Traffic of Pre-Columbian Antiquities' Fall *Art Journal* 94.

—— (1970) 'The Maya Scandal: How Thieves Strip Sites of Past Cultures' October *Smithsonian* 8.

Conklin, JE (1994) *Art Crime* (Westport, CT, Praeger).

DCMS (Department for Culture, Media and Sport) (2000) *Ministerial Advisory Panel on Illicit Trade Report* ['the ITAP Report'], authored by N Palmer, P Addyman, R Anderson, A Browne, A Somers Cocks, M Davies, J Ede, J Van der Lande, and C Renfrew (London, DCMS).

Elia, RJ (1994) 'The World Cannot Afford Many More Collectors with a Passion for Antiquities' 41 *The Art Newspaper* 19.

Gerstenblith, P (1995) 'Identity and Cultural Property: The Protection of Cultural Property in the United States' 75 *Boston University Law Review* 559.
—— (2000) 'Museums, the Market and Antiquities', University of Chicago Cultural Property Workshop, available at http://culturalpolicy.uchicago.edu/workshop/gerstenblith.html (version current at 4 December 2003).
—— (2002) '*United States v Schultz*' 10 *Culture Without Context: The Newsletter of the Illicit Antiquities Research Centre, University of Cambridge.*
—— (2003) 'The *McClain/Schultz* Doctrine: Another Step Against Trade in Stolen Antiquities' 13 *Culture Without Context: The Newsletter of the Illicit Antiquities Research Centre, University of Cambridge.*
Gill, DJW and Chippindale, C (1993) 'Material and Intellectual Consequences of Esteem for Cycladic Figures' 97 *American Journal of Archaeology* 602.
Mackenzie, S (2005a) *Going, Going, Gone: Regulating the Market in Illicit Antiquities* (Leicester, Institute of Art and Law).
—— (2005b) 'Dig a Bit Deeper: Law, Regulation and the Illicit Antiquities Market' 45 *British Journal of Criminology* 249.
Merryman, JH (1988) 'The Retention of Cultural Property' 21 *University of California Davis Law Review* 477.
Meyer, K (1973) *The Plundered Past: the Traffic in Art Treasures* (New York, Atheneum).
Michaelowski, RJ and Kramer, RC (1987) 'The Space Between the Laws: The Problem of Corporate Crime in a Transnational Context' 34 *Social Problems* 34.
O'Keefe, PJ (1997) *Trade in Antiquities: Reducing Destruction and Theft* (London, Archetype).
—— (2000) *Commentary on the UNESCO 1970 Convention on Illicit Traffic* (Leicester, Institute of Art and Law).
Paredes Maury, S (1996) *Surviving in the Rainforest: The Realities of Looting in the Rural Villages of El Peten, Guatemala*, Report submitted to the Foundation for the Advancement of Mesoamerican Studies, Inc, www.famsi.org (version current at 22 March 2002).
Pastore, G (2001) 'The Looting of Archaeological Sites in Italy' in N Brodie, J Doole, and C Renfrew (eds), *Trade in Illicit Antiquities: The Destruction of the World's Archaeological Heritage* (Cambridge, McDonald Institute for Archaeological Research).
Polk, K (2000) 'The Antiquities Trade Viewed as a Criminal Market' September *Hong Kong Lawyer* 82.
—— (2002) *Controlling the Traffic in Illicit Antiquities: Are Criminal Sanctions Appropriate?*, Paper presented at the conference 'Implementation of the UNESCO 1970 Convention' at the Department for Culture, Media and Sport, London, 22 November, Proceedings organised by the Institute of Art and Law and Art-Law Centre, Geneva.
Prott, LV and O'Keefe, PJ (1984) *Law and the Cultural Heritage, Volume 1: Discovery and Excavation* (Abingdon, Professional Books).
—— (1989) *Law and the Cultural Heritage, Volume 3: Movement* (London, Butterworths).
Renfrew, C (1993) 'Collectors are the Real Looters' 46 *Archaeology* 16.
—— (1999) *Loot, Legitimacy and Ownership: The Ethical Crisis in Archaeology* (Amsterdam, Joh. Enschede).

Ruiz, C (2001) 'My Life as a Tombarolo' 112 *The Art Newspaper*, March, p 36.
Stead, IM (1998) *The Salisbury Hoard* (Gloucestershire, Tempus).
Thosarat, R (2001) 'The Destruction of the Cultural Heritage of Thailand and Cambodia' in N Brodie, J Doole, and C Renfrew (eds), *Trade in Illicit Antiquities: The Destruction of the World's Archaeological Heritage* (Cambridge, McDonald Institute for Archaeological Research).

Part I

Criminology and the Market for Looted Antiquities

1

Whither Criminology in the Study of the Traffic in Illicit Antiquities?

KENNETH POLK

INTRODUCTION

CRIMINOLOGY HAS COME late, and with great reluctance, to the study of art crime generally, and the issue of the illicit traffic in antiquities more specifically. This cannot be accounted for by the absence of such crime, either now or in the past. Crimes such as art forgery can be found back through the centuries, as in the case of fraudulent art produced in China as early as the Ming period (1368–1644). Evidence of the plunder of antiquities can be found in tombs from over a thousand years ago in China, and the movement of such material across international boundaries early on became a tradition of victorious armies such as after the conquests of Napoleon, or even earlier with the Romans. Further, the great wealth of the contemporary developed nations has created an insatiable demand for art and antiquities over recent decades, and inevitably accompanying that demand has been the development of criminal activities, including forgery, theft, and the smuggling of illicitly obtained cultural material, to take advantage of that demand.

It is not as if criminology has nothing to offer in terms of analysis, or contributions to discussions of prevention and control, regarding the issue of the illicit traffic in antiquities. In fact, over the years of my involvement with the issue of this traffic, I have become convinced of the central importance of informed criminological research and investigation. To be sure, there is some foundation for such work. John Conklin's (1994) book on art crime has laid out a solid base for others to build upon. Work by professionals in closely related fields has touched on, and supports, further analysis to be undertaken by criminologists. Recently, there have been the beginnings of systematic study of the illicit traffic in antiquities, as can be seen in the book by Mackenzie (2005), a recent investigation carried out in the Nordic countries (Korsell et al, 2006), and research on the impact (or lack of it) of the recent legislation in the United Kingdom which had as its aim the reduction of the illicit traffic in antiquities in and through the United Kingdom (Mackenzie and Green, chapter eight, this volume). In general, however, solid empirically based work using the form of systematic analysis derived from social science is unfortunately rare.

THE TRAFFIC IN ILLICIT ANTIQUITIES EXAMINED AS A CRIMINAL MARKET

From my first writings on this topic, I have argued that a major contribution of criminology to the study of the traffic in plundered antiquities is to describe how this traffic functions in the context of a criminal market. My concern with this arises from a conviction that control strategies depend upon a clear understanding of the dynamics of such markets, and the points at which they are vulnerable to intervention, and, certainly as importantly, other points where interventions are likely to be unsuccessful.

Critical to our understanding of illegal markets is how they function around issues of demand and supply. A criminal market depends upon a demand which in some way is defined as illicit. There are many forms of illegal markets, and many different ways the demand has come to be defined as illicit. A simple illegal market, for one example, is that which evolves around burgled goods. As is true of all such markets, burglary would not occur were it not for the fact that there is a persistent demand for the goods produced by a burglary, most commonly in the form of low-priced goods which flow onto a second-hand market. Burglary would not exist if there were not potential customers, willing to buy items such as household goods, at bargain prices, with no questions asked, 'off the back of a truck'. Such stolen goods markets tend to be highly localised geographically, the material moves rapidly through the market from the initial burglary through middle-men onward to consumers, and those moving the goods tend to have a somewhat wide choice of potential middle outlets for the offloading of goods.

The antiquities market is shaped quite differently. It is mostly (but not entirely) an international market, so that goods are initially plundered from sites often in underdeveloped countries rich in source material in terms of as yet unexplored archaeological sites. These goods then must leave that country for an ultimate country of destination which offers enough wealth to make the effort worth the trouble. For this to happen, some form of smuggling will be necessary, since virtually all source nations now define the removal of cultural material as theft. Further along the chain, a tradition has emerged such that key transit points have evolved, most often in locations with a 'duty-free' history, such as Hong Kong, Singapore, or Switzerland.

Avepens

When the goods transit through these points, papers are generated which give the objects an appearance of legitimacy, in the form of export documents which allow the legal entry of the material into the national sales centres (London, New York, Amsterdam, Brussels, Paris, among others). Once in such centres, and quite unlike most other illicit markets, the sale of the goods (in the case of antiquities) tends to be open and legal.

A further general characteristic of such markets is that it takes considerable time to move goods from starting point to the terminal market location where a consumer purchases the material. Unlike a stolen DVD player which might move through the entire chain in less than 24 hours, cultural material may take months, and often years, to move from initial plunder to ultimate sale. Further, as the goods move closer to the sale point, the market portals become increasingly narrow and specialised, so that there will not be a wide range of options available to the handler anxious to offload the goods.

Detailed analysis over recent years has pointed to the importance of identifying the particular shapes taken for different kinds of illicit antiquities markets. One illustration of the form this takes is in the movement of plundered ceramic material from tombs in China. Typically these objects flow by diverse routes (often dependent upon some involvement of government officials) into such locations as Hong Kong, Macao, or Taipei. Once there, they transit through the various antiquities dealers who function as wholesalers for the international market, moving onward, perhaps in containers, to the various ultimate market destinations. While it often originates in the same country, perhaps in the same initial locations, the traffic in small pieces of jade flows somewhat differently. Its small size makes the transit of the material much easier, and the high cost of the individual items further reduces the sheer volume of the material that must be moved. Therefore, unlike some goods which require a container (and thus the related technologies, including transport carriers), in the case of small jade goods a reasonably large stash of goods can be easily carried, with small risk, by an individual dealer. Furthermore, the demand appears to be more highly localised in Asian locations, which also has an impact on the shape of the illicit market.

Similarly, there has been over recent years a vigorous trade in large stone objects stolen from ancient Khmer sites in Cambodia and Thailand. The sheer size and huge weight of some of these objects poses significant problems for those attempting to arrange the illicit movement of the goods out of their plundered sites onto a market platform. The use of trucks as transport across the borders from Cambodia, for example, has made this traffic vulnerable to official intervention when it has served the interests of countries such as Thailand to engage in such intervention. In this region, as with the previous Chinese examples, there are other kinds of goods available, which dictate a slightly different shape to the illicit traffic. For example, both Thailand and Cambodia produce bronze objects of high quality that are prized on the market. Being smaller, these objects can be moved by different methods than the much larger and bulkier stone objects.

Similar important differences occur in the movement of Pre-Columbian material from Latin America, or Greek, Roman, or Egyptian material from classical areas round the Mediterranean. In each of these, the flow of material depends upon the particular dynamics operating between a demand in developed countries, and the supply from another, probably less well-developed, country. The specific dynamics of each of these will depend upon such factors as the particular problems posed in the movement of the given objects, the vigilance of the source country in terms of surveillance of archaeological sites and known illicit market routes, and the level of willingness in the demand market to accept unprovenanced (that is, without history of ownership), and more importantly, unprovenienced (that is, without disclosure of findspot) goods.

There are, further, important differences between illicit antiquities markets and most of the illegal drug markets (which have been extensively studied by criminologists). For one, drug markets apparently generate huge economic returns far beyond what is obtained from the antiquities trade. More important, however, is the legal status of the goods in the destination countries. While there have been some successes in terms of occasional seizures of illegally imported antiquities into the United States, in that country, and certainly in most market counties, antiquities continue to be sold openly and legally. While fads change over time, and while there is some awareness now in the antiquities marketplace of the future possibilities of a restriction of that legal trade, today, even in the United States, one can purchase openly in the most exclusive of shop venues unprovenienced material from China, Cambodia, Thailand, Egypt, Italy, Turkey, Greece, and so on. Put another way, unlike drug traffic, in the market centres the antiquities trade is not conducted in back alleys or hidden in cars in order to avoid the prying eyes of police, who could be expected to pounce when an illegal deal is observed. As we shall see, this crucial difference between the illicit markets in drugs compared with antiquities exerts a powerful force on the directions that policy and control strategies might take.

Like the traffic in drugs, however, many countries are forced to address the issue that some of the trade involves domestic as well as international dimensions. In the United States, for one example, there continues to be a vigorous traffic in material plundered from Native American heritage sites. In the United Kingdom, there is a busy trade in Roman objects from the period when Rome occupied Britain. There is, of course, a parallel here between antiquities and drugs, since in many countries, a major supply of marijuana originates in domestic suppliers of the material. Again, while in most countries the preparation, movement, and sale of domestic drugs will be illegal (and thus must be kept out of the sight of authorities), the legal status of domestic antiquities varies but a common dynamic is that the goods can be found in what appears to be the legitimate marketplace. The vulnerability of domestic antiquities in the United States or the United Kingdom to official intervention depends upon a number of circumstances. In the United Kingdom, for example, while using a metal detector continues to be quite legal in searching for Roman (and other) antique material, if that search took place on private land without the permission of the landowner, then seizure of the material, and arrest of the offenders, becomes possible (for an example, see the account of the affair of the Salisbury Hoard as described by Stead, 1998; see also Bland, chapter 5, this volume) In the United States, for a different example, over recent years there has been an increased focus on the protection of cultural material of Native American origin, including a number of arrests of offenders who have illegally extracted such objects.

THE FIRST OBSESSION: THE FOCUS OF POLICY ON PUNISHMENT AND DETERRENCE

My purpose in filling out this description of the shape and forms that are taken by the various illicit antiquities markets has been to draw upon that analysis to focus on the question of what steps might be taken in terms of prevention and control. From my initial forays into this issue, I have been disappointed by the continued reliance, to the point of obsession, of many of those shaping policy around the traffic in antiquities, on crude forms of punishment and deterrence. The criminological literature has numerous examples of the failure of public policy attempts to restrict illicit markets using these processes. Among the most notable of these was the attempt in the United States in the early twentieth century to prohibit the consumption of alcohol. In common with many such attempts, it was inherently a strategy based on the restriction of *supply* by means of criminal laws aimed at production and sale of alcoholic beverages. The fact that demand remained exceptionally high throughout the period of Prohibition assured not only that alcohol use continued, but that in addition large networks of criminal activity were created to supply that demand, these networks remaining in place, seeking new outlets, when the failed supply prohibition strategy was repealed.

An even more spectacular failure, although this view is contentious in some quarters, has been the so-called 'war on drugs' which has been waged now for some decades. Like Prohibition, it has been fundamentally a strategy based on supply reduction, including attempts to close borders with ever-greater vigilance over time, and increasingly direct intervention by developed nations (especially the United States) in supply nations in an attempt to eradicate supplies at the source. While there have been some remarkably large 'busts' of drug networks, and at times Draconian punishments (including capital punishment in some of the Southeast Asian countries), a crude gauge of the lack of success of this long-running 'war' is that despite the occasional 'successes', on the streets there appears to remain a large supply of illicit drug material available for young people in most developed countries. In the view of many criminologists, this is a result fundamentally of a misguided attempt to restrict an illicit market by means of restriction of supply when demand remains high.

Despite that record, many of the public policy initiatives created in an attempt to restrict the traffic in illicit cultural material share with the drug initiatives a reliance on supply restriction strategies founded in deterrence. Virtually all of the source countries have for many years progressively tightened their laws regarding their cultural heritage, so that now it is most commonly the case that the extraction of such material without authorisation is defined as a form of theft. This step has proved important, since the earlier reliance on mere export restriction had little effect, given that when the facts can be proven, many of the developed nations are willing to step in and prosecute individuals in such developed countries if it can be proven that goods have been stolen in the source country.

There are certainly indications that the leading market nations are being roused to action. In the United Kingdom, there was in 2003 the implementation of a Dealing in Cultural Objects (Offences) Act which at least had the policy intent of bringing some control to the market in illicit antiquities (Mackenzie and Green, chapter eight, this volume). In the *Schultz* case in New York (see Gerstenblith, 2002), which resulted in the successful prosecution, conviction, and jailing of a leading US antiquities dealer in 2002/03, the courts made clear that serious penalties might be applied if the theft of antiquities can be proven, even if that theft occurred in a foreign country. In another recent (2008) US case, federal agents raided a number of galleries and museums in the Southern California area as part of a five-year investigation into allegations of theft of looted antiquities from Thailand, Myanmar, China, and Native American sites (Wyatt, 2008). There have been, as well, a number of international conventions which have the intent of bringing the traffic in cultural heritage material under some control (a brief summary of some of these, including the UNESCO Convention of 1970, can be found in Renfrew, 2006).

It would be foolish to argue that there is no role in the control of illicit antiquities for deterrence in the form of penalties found in the criminal laws, or perhaps in the opportunities for civil redress in other laws, regulations, and conventions, and that steps such as these are unimportant. If they do nothing else, such laws and conventions send a message about a moral stance being taken by the various governments.

As I have said many times elsewhere (Alder and Polk, 2005, 2007), the reasons for seeking a wider set of policy approaches rest in the clear limits of deterrence which can be found in the empirical record of such laws, as well as an understanding of the theoretical factors which limit the effectiveness of deterrence. As is the case with drug enforcement, there seems ample empirical evidence for the failure of deterrence to restrict significantly the antiquities traffic. Despite its intent, according to the extensive evaluation carried out by Green and Mackenzie, the Dealing in Cultural Objects (Offences) Act 2003 in the United Kingdom '... appears to have been ineffective in achieving any substantial effect on the trade in illicit antiquities' (Mackenzie and Green, chapter eight, this volume). Even when the *Schultz* case was being conducted in New York (upon conviction Schultz was sentenced to 33 months in prison), I found a large supply of antiquities from various parts of the world on offer in antiquities galleries in that same city.

From a theoretical perspective, according to what is argued, deterrence will only have an effect where there is a perception there is a reasonable chance that penalties will be applied, and that the penalties will be both swift and serious in their effect. These conditions are hardly met when the purchase of antiquities in market centres (where the critical demand originates) is defined as legal, or when limits placed on such purchases are easy to evade (as in the case of the UK law). Put simply, the illicit traffic in antiquities will continue until we can find ways to strengthen the impact of deterrence-based strategies, and/or we find other means of discouraging the demand for such antiquities.

THE SECOND OBSESSION: THE FOCUS ON OBJECTS (AND THEIR RETURN) RATHER THAN THE PROTECTION OF CULTURAL HERITAGE SITES

A second general problem that is found in discussions of cultural heritage policy is the emphasis given to the return of pillaged objects, at the expense of analyses of ways to protect the cultural sites which have yielded up these treasures. To be sure, there are important discussions that are, and should be, taking place about the origins of illicitly exported cultural objects, and the return of these to some home context. Many of these discussions are heavily laden with political overtones. One of the most notable examples consists of the Elgin/Parthenon Marbles, which came into the possession of the British Museum in the nineteenth century; their return has been a point of contention between the United Kingdom and Greece for decades. Such disputes can take many forms: for example, arguments about the return of human remains of indigenous persons removed often over a century ago, but now being claimed as local indigenous populations gain some amount of access to the political process. Some countries have been especially vocal in making claims for return of cultural material which they view as stolen, including Italy and Egypt. At times such claims are relatively straightforward, since they involve documented material that has been stolen in recent years (and thus after both the UN Conventions and the stolen property laws of the source nations eased the legal problems of return). In other notable cases, the material may not be clearly documented in terms of its origins, and the date of the extraction may be far from clear (and thus the legal status of the claim for return becomes clouded and problematic).

THE MAIN TARGET: PROTECTION OF CULTURAL HERITAGE SITES

The major focus of policy and discussion around the issue of protection of illicit traffic must be the protection of cultural heritage sites. The question here is whether we focus on objects (and thus spend our energies on the return problem) or whether we are able to protect the sites so that the priority of return is reduced somewhat as an issue. The immediate difficulty, of course, is that in the current climate it is impossible to assure physical protection of sites, a proposition amply demonstrated in the current conflicts in Iraq (Polk and Schuster, 2005) and Afghanistan (van Krieken-Pieters, 2006). If powerful nations are not even able to protect their troops, they are hardly in any position to devote much in the way of resources to cultural heritage sites.

A different approach to site protection is to create an antiquities market where there is no place for unprovenienced objects (as suggested above, we follow here the suggested distinction between 'provenance', which concerns the ownership history of an object, and 'provenience', which concerns the availability of a full archaeological history for the object: for discussion, see Lapatin, 2002). If potential consumers refused to purchase, and dealers refused to handle, material that did not have proper provenience, then the absence of demand would see the withering away of illicit traffic in antiquities and then the reduction in the plunder of cultural heritage sites.

The problem today is that since the sale of antiquities in the market centres tends to be an open and legal activity, since consumers are either unaware of or unconcerned about provenience, and since it is the common practice of dealers not to provide either provenance or provenience information, the demand for cultural heritage material which has been plundered continues.

In many respects the continued ignorance of both provenance and provenience of objects exposes consumers to huge risks that one might think would create at least some caution. It goes without saying that one of the major risks of not having solid provenience information is that the objects might not be authentic. In the infamous case of the Snake Goddess in the collection of the Museum of Fine Arts in Boston, Lapatin (2002) makes the point that a major element in the purchase of this object (which the evidence today says is not authentic Minoan but a fake produced in Crete roughly 100 years ago by persons close to the archaeology of the region) was the knowing willingness of those close to the museum to buy objects which were unprovenienced. Further, buying material from the Classical world where the provenance is unclear between mid-1930 and mid-1940 might result at a very minimum in a lawsuit and seizure of the material as Nazi loot.

Because there continues to be a poorly controlled legal market for antiquities, the consequent forces of demand result in a flow of material out of plundered sites and then the availability of desirable objects in that market. These objects become the focus for intense debate about who should be able to own them, and the conditions of that ownership. Recent years have seen the re-emergence of powerful voices concerned with the proper preservation and display of such material, especially from some of the leading museums. Typically such arguments focus on objects, and questions such as 'who owns antiquities?' (for examples, see Gibbon, 2005; and Cuno, 2008), all too conveniently avoiding the issue of the role of the market in the destruction of archaeological context. A common form of such discourse is to argue that 'of course, no one sanctions the destruction of heritage sites but once the damage has been done, and the objects find their way (magically?) to the market, then do we not have a duty to preserve and treasure such objects (especially in the major collections)?'. My view is that these arguments result from a blind focus on objects, and would be much more persuasive if the same authors were as concerned for actual and concrete ways of contributing to the protection of context. Without that, support for the acquisition of objects, because this maintains demand, will have as its major result the continued destruction of cultural heritage sites.

THE OWNERSHIP GAP PROBLEM: LOCATING ACTION POLICIES

It is not necessary to rely solely upon some altruistic motive around protection of antiquities to work towards a market of buyers and sellers who are concerned and knowledgeable about issues of both provenience and provenance. The difficulty I have found is not so much an awareness of the potential importance of strategies of increasing consumer concern with provenance and provenience, but that it is unclear where campaigns to increase awareness might be located, and what groups or organisations have a strong constituent motivation to provide leadership.

Criminology can play a role in formulation of policies to control the illicit traffic in antiquities by identifying policies which are likely *not* to work (deterrence-based approaches aimed at supply reduction) and a potentially more fruitful direction that might be considered (demand reduction programmes based on persuasion aimed at market buyers). Thus, criminology can draw upon previous research and scholarship to point out the limitations of public policy based in deterrence, especially aimed at fruitless attempts at supply reduction where demand remains high. When we shift the focus to demand reduction, and seek approaches that are outside of traditional deterrence strategies, we find that criminology quickly finds itself on territory either outside of, or at best at the outer boundaries of, its disciplinary reach.

In some of my earlier writings (Alder and Polk, 2005, 2007), I pointed out that a possible direction might be found in the works on 'restorative justice' and 'responsive regulation' found in the writings of Braithwaite (1985, 2002). Closer examination reveals, however, that these ideas are at best a starting point for the problem we are examining here. The restorative justice programmes, as found in such areas as juvenile justice, are still located firmly within the justice system, and tend to require the close cooperation of police and the courts. The responsive regulation approaches, particularly those that focus on 'persuasion rather than punishment', are somewhat closer to our conception of effective strategies for the antiquities market, but even here much of the existing work presumes the existence of known regulatory agencies, and the regulatory options they face (such as an occupational health and safety agency). In these regulatory environments, the responsible agency is defined in law, and the analysis consists of attempts to widen the regulatory options considered by that agency.

The illicit traffic in antiquities poses quite a different problem. Few cases ever reach the criminal justice system, so that any strategy based in justice, even an innovative form of justice (such as 'restorative justice') is likely to have little, if any, impact on this illicit traffic. If the policies are to reside outside of the justice system, the question arises regarding the location and 'ownership' of such policies. The issue here is that there not only is no specific regulatory agency that claims ownership and responsibility for policy over the illegal traffic, there is also no law that identifies where such ownership might reside, especially if the focus is to be on persuasion rather than punishment. Put simply, once the criminologists have demonstrated that punishment as found in the criminal justice system is not effective in reducing the traffic, it seems reasonable to argue for a shift from punishment to persuasion. The problem then arises as to who will do the persuading, or where that persuasion should be positioned. While criminology as a field can be an important part of any solution, it in all probability will not provide the major institutional locus or impetus for the needed social change.

We can also cite locations where there is likely to be opposition to attempts to bring about a new approach to market buying, especially one that is created around a requirement for adequate provenience information as a pre-condition of sale. Antiquities dealers, while they often give lip service to the protection of cultural heritage, cannot be expected to be enthusiastic about pushing a market strategy that will so radically change (and potentially reduce) buyer purchasing. Similarly, in my early working through of the issue, it seemed to me that the educational programmes of the major public museums were a logical place to locate such efforts. Except, of course, it transpires that it is precisely these institutions which have over the years amassed huge collections of material that is both unprovenanced and unprovenienced. While there might be a few isolated curators who are committed to the task of reducing current illicit traffic, the back rooms of the large public institutions are filled with material in relation to which analysis of provenance and provenience information might result not just in embarrassment, but also support for claims of repatriation of the material.

There are a number of locations where there is likely to be some willingness to provide leadership for demand reduction activities. Archaeology is a discipline heavily affected by the looting of heritage sites, and is a field that in the past has provided important leadership for changing public attitudes, and policies regarding cultural heritage. Some of the best writings regarding the looting issue have been done by archaeologists, including some of the clearest writings about the workings of the illicit antiquities market. At the same time, it would be important to recognise the limits of the enthusiasm of that discipline for this issue, since time spent on the prevention of looting is time taken away from the 'real' tasks of archaeology, that is, the investigation of the sites themselves.

Most developed countries have created a national-level agency which has responsibility for the protection of cultural heritage. While in the past much of the work of these agencies has been the protection of cultural heritage within the given country (and the pursuit of objects that have been illegally exported, as illustrated by the actions of the Italian government), these units logically are some of the best placed to play a key role in the development of policies and programmes directed at altering antiquities market behaviour to reduce demand in the major market nations.

International cultural heritage bodies, too, might play a crucial role. In the past, key developments in terms of agreements and conventions have come from organisations such as UNESCO. Similarly, the International Council of Museums (ICOM) has provided important institutional leadership in the promulgation of policies for the protection of cultural heritage, including the development of acquisition practices that prohibit the purchase of objects that lack proper provenience by member museums.

Much inventive thinking will be required to develop proposals to change market purchasing practices. At one level, more effective legislation is needed which is aimed at demand reduction. Some legislation of necessity will be based in deterrence, and could include regulations that make it illegal either to sell or to purchase material that does not have proper provenience, as well as civil regulations that make it easier for nations that have suffered from looting to regain their possessions. While such legal provisions obviously will have to have more bite than the UK Dealing in Cultural Objects (Offences) Act 2003, there are other more effective models, for example, the criminalisation by nations such as the United States and the United Kingdom of dealing in antiquities looted from Iraq and Afghanistan. Civil remedies that provide for seizure of objects that are not properly provenienced would also send a powerful message to the antiquities market.

I would suggest that supporting these legal strategies should be inventive practices aimed at expanding on Braithwaite's idea of 'persuasion'. Thus, national and international cultural heritage bodies might cooperate in organising, along with archaeologists, criminologists, art historians, and legal scholars (among others), systematic educational programmes such as seminars and workshops located in the major market centres such as New York, London, Brussels, and Paris (among others). These educational initiatives could be aimed at informing the art market, including dealers and purchasers, of the definition, and importance, of provenience, and of the impact of the various laws and regulations on market behaviour.

THE RESISTANCE OF CRIMINOLOGY TO THESE ISSUES

A final issue to be addressed is the puzzle regarding what appears to be the slowness of criminology to take up the study of the issue of looting of cultural heritage material, and the analysis of the consequent illicit traffic. It has always seemed to me that the study of this form of trafficking should be of considerable interest to the field of criminology. The interaction between demand and supply, the nature of the international routes in the development of traffic patterns, and the possibilities for studying various policy approaches to the control of illicit antiquities as a form of illegal market, all appear to relate to central issues within the field. Furthermore, there is a clear urgency in terms of the need for information since the capacity for devastation of cultural heritage sites has increased so dramatically.

Yet, the number of research scholars within criminology for whom this is a central interest is just a bare handful, and the research output to date has been limited. To be sure, the topic of the illicit traffic in antiquities is well removed from the traditional core of interests in street crime, and on the impact such crimes have on the criminal justice system, that has long been central to criminology. Further, if the 'true' concerns of criminology are to be found in the workings of the criminal justice system, then the exceptional rarity of 'offenders' in the antiquities market, at least in the market centres, is notable.

This form of crime would seem to fit well within discussions of white-collar crime generally, and analysis of this form of crime is by now well established in the field. Furthermore, there tends to be reasonable concern with issues of transnational crime, since these pose particular, and often important, problems in our thinking about crime and criminal justice. The few works available suggest that there is much that criminology could learn from study of this form of illicit traffic, one of the best examples being the failure of the recent UK Act to address dealing with cultural objects, and the careful documentation of why the results of this Act are so far from what might have been anticipated.

There are, to be sure, some profound theoretical and methodological issues that confront those attempting to initiate work in this field. Crime involving widespread international traffic patterns can be both difficult and expensive to study. Even developing a simple conceptual model of the pathways followed by one type of object can involve overwhelming practical obstacles, especially in terms of translating such models into empirical research.

Nonetheless, it is my view that criminology provides analysis and information critical to the development of comprehensive and effective strategies for the control of the illicit traffic in cultural heritage material. From the analysis of the market dynamics, the findings of criminology strongly suggest that any solution to the problem will require processes which are able to reduce demand in the market centres. These processes call for a mix of both deterrence and innovative persuasion. Certainly, the urgency of the issue must be underscored. Plundered cultural heritage sites are destroyed for ever, and their knowledge lost to future generations. Criminology in our view, can, and should, continue to provide directions for the prevention and control of this form of illicit traffic.

REFERENCES

Alder, C and Polk, K (2005) 'The Illicit Traffic in Plundered Antiquities' in P Reichel (ed), *Handbook of Transnational Crime & Justice* (London, Sage), pp 98–113.

—— (2007) 'Crime in the World of Art' in HN Pontell, and G Geis (eds), *International Handbook of White-Collar and Corporate Crime* (New York, Springer), pp 347–57.

Braithwaite, J (1985) *To Punish or Persuade: Enforcement of Coal Mine Safety* (Albany, NY, State of New York Press).

—— (2002) *Restorative Justice and Responsive Regulation* (New York, Oxford University Press).

Conklin, JE (1994) *Art Crime* (London, Praeger).

Cuno, J (2008) *Who Owns Antiquity: Museums and the Battle over Our Ancient Heritage* (Princeton, NJ, Princeton University Press).

Gerstenblith, P (2002) 'United States v Schultz', *Culture Without Context* Issue 10, Spring, pp 27–31.

Gibbon, KF (ed) (2005) *Who Owns the Past? Cultural Policy, Cultural Property and the Law* (New Brunswick, NJ, Rutgers University Press).

Korsell, L, Hedlund, G, Elwer, S, Vesterhav, D, and Heber, A (2006) *Cultural Heritage Crime – The Nordic Dimension* (Stockholm, The Swedish National Council for Crime Prevention).

Lapatin, K (2002) *Mysteries of the Snake Goddess: Art, Desire and the Forging of History* (Cambridge, MA, De Capo Press).

Mackenzie, S (2005) *Going, Going, Gone: Regulating the Market in Illicit Antiquities* (Leicester, Institute of Art and Law).

Polk, M and Schuster, AMH (eds) (2005) *The Looting of the Iraq Museum, Baghdad: The Lost Legacy of Ancient Mesopotamia* (New York, Harry N Abrams).

Renfrew, C (2006) *Loot, Legitimacy and Ownership: The Ethical Crisis in Archaeology* (London, Duckworth).

Stead, IM (1998) *The Salisbury Hoard* (Stroud, Tempus Publishing).

van Krieken-Pieters, J (ed) (2006) *Art and Archaeology of Afghanistan: Its Fall and Survival.* (Leiden, Brill).

Wyatt, E (2008) 'Four California Museums Are Raided', *New York Times*, 26 January, p 3.

Part II

Demand for Looted Antiquities

2

Antiquities, Forests, and Simmel's Sociology of Value

TONY WARD

I MUST ADMIT that before I was invited to participate in the Oñati workshop from which this book derives, I had taken only a passing interest in the subject of antiquities. I had, however, collaborated with Penny Green in studying some other illegal or ethically dubious forms of international trade, particularly that in the products of illegal or unsustainable logging (Green, Ward, and McConnachie, 2007), and it struck me that there was at least one interesting theoretical question common to the study of this trade and of that in antiquities. That is the issue I want to explore here.

Both the looting of antiquities and the destruction of forests involve damage to insentient objects which are highly valued by some people, in ways not reducible to economic value. Such crimes (and the question whether they should be labelled as crimes at all) pose a challenge to those forms of critical criminology, or studies of social harm, which look beyond legal definitions of crime and seek to ground their approach in some kind of sociology of morality. Damage to objects or plants does not fit easily either into a human rights-based approach (Green and Ward, 2004) or into one derived from the moral phenomenology of Lévinas (Bauman, 1993; Mackenzie, 2006). The criminological question, in other words, is not so much how some people come to have an attitude of moral indifference or aggression towards other human beings (Pemberton, 2004), but why some people feel free to act destructively towards features of the material world to which other people attach great intrinsic value. What would appear to be lacking or neutralised in such cases is not (or not only) empathy, but some other kind of moral emotion or evaluative attitude. To identify what this is involves an investigation of the phenomenology of value.

The classic work on the phenomenology of value within the sociological canon is that of Georg Simmel, particularly the first chapter of his *Philosophy of Money*.[1] Simmel substantially revised this chapter in the second edition

[1] I am indebted to Peter Young for pointing out the relevance of Simmel's work to my concerns.

(1907), which is the one translated into English (Simmel, 2004). In her recent commentary on *The Philosophy of Money,* Natalia Cantó Milà (2005) argues that the theory of value is the central theme of the book. While Simmel's argument is not exactly a model of clarity, he seems to me to have been addressing exactly the question that I want to explore in relation to both antiquities and timber. That is: how can we take the idea of intrinsic, non-economic, values seriously and at the same time understand them sociologically, as human constructs that are not inherent in the world independently of human perception? What I want to consider, very tentatively, is how far Simmel might help us to understand crimes against the environment and cultural artefacts, and how far an understanding of such crimes might help us to clarify and revise Simmel's theory as a tool for social scientists a hundred years on.

THREE KINDS OF VALUE

Cantó Milà suggests that we should understand Simmel's work as a dialogue with a number of his contemporaries, particularly Karl Marx and the neo-Kantian philosopher Heinrich Rickert, with whom Simmel exchanged many letters. While Simmel regarded his investigations of value in some respects as complementary to Marx's, he rejected the idea that the average labour power required to produce a commodity could provide an objective measure of value independently of its price on the market. For Simmel, it was through exchange rather than production that values were 'objectified' (for a critique of Simmel's argument see Kamolnick, 2001). More important for our purposes is Simmel's dialogue with Rickert and other neo-Kantian thinkers. Rickert maintained that values had a transcendental validity independent of the human mind (Hughes, 1979: 191). Simmel, by contrast, maintained a 'relativist'[2] position, according to which the 'objective' validity of any statement of value could be established only by reference to some other value, leading (as he acknowledged to Rickert) to an infinite regress or a vicious circle (Cantó Milà, 2005: 115). At the same time, he acknowledged that people *experienced* moral and aesthetic values (unlike mundane economic value) as objective and absolute. What Simmel needed, therefore, was a relational explanation of why some values appear absolute (ibid).

The Philosophy of Money begins by discussing the phenomenology of value—the place of value in the structure of consciousness—before moving on to investigate social relations of exchange and the psychological effects of a money economy. Value, for Simmel, emerges in a process of differentiation by which the flux of experience is divided into the self-awareness of a subject and her awareness of a number of distinct external objects. Among

[2] Cantó Milà prefers the term 'relationist' which avoids connotations of scepticism.

those external objects, some stand out because the subject desires them but recognises them as attainable only by some degree of effort. Value shapes our perception of the salient features of the world and orients our actions towards it (here as elsewhere, there is an affinity between Simmel's work and the much more recent philosophy of McDowell, 1998). Thus a forest will appear different to a hunter, a botanist or a tourist (or a logging company) as each will pick out different features from the 'indivisible unity' of the forest, giving salience to objects that their respective interests render valuable (Simmel, 1900: 579).[3]

Valuable objects, according to Simmel, are characterised by a degree of *distance* from us—we have to do more than simply reach out for them or breathe them in—and by the fact that some form of *sacrifice* is necessary in order to attain them, either in the form of effort or of some other object which we give up in exchange. It is through social relations of exchange that the values people subjectively attach to objects come to be measured against each other and thereby take on an objective social existence. These socially objective values are ultimately reduced to one common denominator: money.

Simmel also identifies two forms of non-economic value. One is aesthetic value. An object, such as a tree or a sculpture, has aesthetic value for a subject who can enjoy the mere contemplation of the object without desiring to use or consume it in any way (Simmel, 2004: 73–75). Simmel speculates that aesthetic enjoyment might be explicable in terms of what would now be called evolutionary psychology—that it is derived from emotional responses to the environment that served practical ends at some earlier stage in the life of the species. Although aesthetic value is quite distinct from economic value, their common feature, according to Simmel, is the distance between the subject and the object. In the case of aesthetic value this is manifested both in the 'reserve and remoteness' of the subject's contemplative relation to the object (which may be overcome in very intense aesthetic experience, when the division between subject and object seems to dissolve) and in the remoteness of aesthetic pleasure from the 'primitive enjoyment' which it sublimates (ibid: 73). The influence of this idea is apparent in Benjamin's concept of the 'aura' of nature or of a work of art, which is also associated with a literal or metaphorical sense of distance from the object (1936: 5). An authentic antiquity or old work of art has an 'aura' associated with its distant origins and unique history, unlike a replica, which from a purely aesthetic point of view might be indistinguishable from it.

The other form of value discussed by Simmel is the kind that appeared to Rickert and others to be absolute. It is the value we perceive when 'we sense that objects, people and events are not only appreciated as valuable by us,

[3] Simmel's use of this example strikingly foreshadows Halsey's (2006) analysis of textual constructions of an Australian forest.

but would still be valuable if no-one appreciated them' (Simmel, 2004: 67). Among the objects to which Simmel attributes this kind of value are human virtues and emotions and 'the fact that, regardless of man, nature moves according to reliable fixed norms, that the manifest natural forms are not incompatible with a more profound unity of the whole, that nature's mechanism can be interpreted through ideas and also produces beauty and grace' (ibid). We experience these values in the form of 'a claim or demand' which is neither 'imposed by ourselves on ourselves', nor a quality of the object:

> it is a third category, which cannot be derived either from subject or object, but which stands, so to speak, between us and the objects ... It is not a particular quality of the objects of valuation, but consists rather in the significance that the objects have for us as subjects through their position in the order of [an] ideal realm. (ibid: 68)

The last passage sounds rather mysterious, but I think we can see what Simmel is getting at by considering the examples of antiquities and forests. In the case of antiquities, what is considered to be lost when they are looted is not simply the particular objects, but the 'stratified context' in which they were found, and from which information about the past can be inferred, as well as their place as 'cultural assets' of a particular country (Mackenzie, 2005a: 251). Watson and Todeschini (2006: 47) claim that 'virtually half the history of Greek, Etruscan and Roman culture has been stolen from us' by tomb robbers and dealers. The value of what is 'stolen' in this sense inheres not in any particular objects, but in their relationship to other objects and events which form part of a totality (the history of a civilisation or the culture of a country) and to the forms of knowledge (archaeology and cultural or national history) through which those totalities are apprehended. Similarly in the case of forests—a particular case of Simmel's own example of the value of nature—what is damaged by logging is not just particular trees but an entire ecosystem which is apprehended through various scientific and cultural discourses as a harmonious and valuable totality. Eder (1996: 177) goes so far as to argue that the combination of aesthetic and scientific discourses assimilates the self-organisation of nature to the 'idea of a divine order'.

The metaphysical overtones of Simmel's term 'ideal realm'—which might not be out of place in respect of some forms of environmentalism—can be avoided by substituting a more neutral term like 'conceptual scheme'; but not just any conceptual scheme will do. A conceptual scheme will lend 'a peculiar ideal dignity' to the objects it represents only if it is perceived as 'valid and significant' because it possesses 'a logical sense, an inner structural validity' (Simmel, 2004: 67). Simmel is not very clear about where this 'ideal dignity' derives from, but it can be explained fairly straightforwardly by a combination of: (1) an assumption that knowledge or understanding of the relevant domain of objects is worth having; (2) a belief that a particular conceptual scheme does provide valid knowledge, or a coherent understanding, of its domain; and (3) the portrayal of objects and relations within the conceptual scheme in such a light that they tend to arouse feelings such as wonder, which, as Midgley (1989) argues, involves a kind of love. From this there arises the sense that the knowing subject is entering into a relationship with the objects of knowledge which is suffused with positive emotion, and it is this relationship, not just the objects themselves, that the subject values.

The human mind has, according to Simmel, a capacity to separate itself from its ideas and objectify them, and hence our conceptual schemes are often projected onto a metaphysical 'ideal realm', as they were by the neo-Kantians. This tendency is probably less pronounced in contemporary culture than it was in Simmel's Germany. Contemporary archaeology, from my limited knowledge of it, seems more prone to the opposite problem, in that practitioners' awareness of the theory- and value-laden nature of their knowledge claims drives some of them towards an untenable epistemic relativism (Boghossian, 2006: 1–5; Wylie, 2007). But even if Carver (1996: 46) is right to argue that 'the past cannot be "known" but only "modelled"', a compelling narrative or 'model' of the past could still have the kind of value Simmel discusses. Archaeological narratives are also linked to ideas of national and ethnic identity, which have been a major driving force behind the legal protection of antiquities (Dawson, 2007).

In contrast to aesthetic appreciation, the 'claim' which such values make upon those who are sensitive to them does not depend upon the direct perception of a particular object. People can value rainforests on the other side of the world, or artefacts buried and unseen for millennia. People can therefore have interests in the preservation of these objects without owning them or even having a legal or customary right of access to them. The setting back of those interests by the destruction or theft of the valued objects may be as harmful to the people concerned as everyday vandalism and theft, but in more diffuse and less obvious ways.

VALUE, OBJECTIVITY, AND IRONY

Was Simmel affirming the intrinsic value to be found in art, nature, and so forth, or was he debunking it? For Bauman, Simmel is to be celebrated for his 'audacious de-sacralization (desecration?) of values', brutally bringing them down from their ideological pedestal (1991: 186). This is, I think, a one-sided reading, and neglects what Simmel has to say about aesthetic and other values that are not, in any direct way, a reflection of desire. As I read him, Simmel invites us to dispense with a metaphysics that attributes to values an 'absolute' existence independent of human perception, while at the same time taking seriously the phenomenology of value experience which suggests to us that value is in some sense part of the external world. That way of putting it is, in fact, a paraphrase of McDowell (1998: 129), who seems to me to be saying something very similar to Simmel, albeit in a different philosophical idiom.

McDowell (1998: Essay 7) provides a helpful analogy in thinking about the 'intrinsic' value of objects: namely that values are in some respects like colours. (Simmel (2004: 63) rejects any such analogy for the general run of values, but adds that there are cases 'where the psychological facts appear to lead to an opposite view'.) An object's being red consists, according to McDowell, simply in its disposition to appear red, under certain conditions, to people with normal colour vision (1998: 133). Such a property is 'subjective' in the sense that it cannot be understood without reference to subjective experience (in contrast to, say, radioactivity) but it is objective in the sense that it is a real, not an illusory, property of red objects. Similarly, an object is valuable (in a moral or aesthetic sense) if it is disposed to appear valuable to people who have been habituated into a certain widely shared way of perceiving and relating to the world. As McDowell points out, the analogy is not exact, because usually when we say that something is valuable we mean not only that it tends to elicit a certain response but that it *merits* such a response (1998: 143). Such a judgement can only be made from within the relevant evaluative outlook.

A social scientist can, of course, record the fact that certain things are valuable to certain people without sharing those valuations. An anthropologist, for example, can record that cows of a particular colouring have a special aesthetic value for the Dinka (Leinhardt, 1973). To *understand* an evaluative category of this sort involves more than simply observing correlations between the colours of cows and favourable reactions by humans (Winch, 1990: 115). The anthropologist must presumably learn to *see* cows in a way that is close enough to how the Dinka see them to be able to grasp what it is about certain cows that makes them beautiful to the Dinka, even if he gains no aesthetic pleasure from looking at them. And he must have *some* aesthetic sense to understand what it means to see something as beautiful (Winch, 1990: 88). He need not, however, share the particular aesthetic values of his subjects.

I do not, however, think that this is all that Simmel is doing in his discussion of the value of nature or moral virtue, nor that it is what criminologists are doing when they identify looting or logging as crimes or social harms. In the case of Simmel, much of the point of his critiques of the money economy and of metropolitan life (Simmel, 1971) would be lost if he did not regard these phenomena as corroding people's ability to respond to genuine, non-monetary values. In our case as criminologists, there would be little point in studying looting or logging as crimes or harms if we did not regard them as harming something genuinely valuable.

At the same time, Simmel also encourages us to adopt a certain ironic distance from the modern valuation of nature and antiquities. Rather obviously, the value attached to primeval forests is a reaction against the pace and pressure of urban life (*cf* Simmel, 1971; Thomas, 1983; Macnaghten and Urry, 1998), and—particularly where forests are relatively close to cities—this gives them an economic value as tourist attractions. With regard to antiquities, Simmel hints at something more subtle and paradoxical. Antiquities often end up in museums, typically in the heart of great cities. Again, these might seem like havens from the bustle of urban life, as well as lucrative tourist attractions. For Simmel, however, the accumulations of material culture in the metropolis tend to overwhelm the individual: a 'hypertrophy of objective culture' merely accelerates the 'atrophy of individual culture' (Simmel, 1971). (In late modernity we might see the media rather than the metropolis as the main culprits in this process: Lash, 2005.) Simmel insists that the superficial and distorted nature of most individuals' knowledge of 'their' culture does not diminish the intrinsic value of that cultural heritage: 'The insignificance or irrationality of the individual's share leaves the substance and dignity of mankind's ownership unaffected' (2004: 449–50). In Benjamin's (1936) terms, Simmel appears to celebrate the 'cultic value' of cultural objects to specialists and connoisseurs as opposed to their 'exhibition value', and it is debatable how exactly this value benefits 'mankind' at large.

There is another irony implicit in Simmel's 'sacrificial' theory of value. When we demand that antiquities or trees be preserved for the sake of their intrinsic value, we are demanding that something be sacrificed to preserve them—the economic value to be derived from digging them up or cutting them down. But in doing that we are putting our sense of intrinsic value onto the scale of economic value, however much we may protest that the archaeological heritage is literally 'priceless'.[4] In fact, the demands of conservation create new forms of economic value, such as that attached to provenance in the case of antiquities (Mackenzie, 2005a) and certification in the case of timber. The rise of 'ethical consumerism' is a phenomenon Simmel would surely have relished. The central irony, or paradox, of Simmel's analysis is that the social relations that 'objectify' values simultaneously 'relativise' them.

Simmel is also an ironist in Rorty's (1989) sense that he remains committed to certain values while recognising those values as historically

[4] 'The archaeological heritage has nothing to do with productive use, however defined, and certainly nothing to do with money. It is meant to be—in the fullest and best sense—*useless*; it is also *price*less rather that *worth*less. This principle is one to which all archaeologists would no doubt happily subscribe.' (Carman, Carnegie, and Wolnizer, 1999). Compare Shelbourn (2008: 209) praising a US law which 'seeks to look at the real value of what has been lost' by relating penalties to the financial costs of retrieving information lost as a result of a violation.

contingent. Like Simmel, I want to affirm that some things *are* intrinsically valuable—valuable in themselves, not as a means to an end—but only to human beings who, as a matter of contingent historical fact, are disposed to value them. The source of value lies not in the things themselves, but in the relationship between those things and the people who value them. While Simmel affirms the importance of intrinsic values, he also 'desacralises' them; there is no room here for what the neo-Kantian legal philosopher Radbruch (cited by Friedmann, 1967: 194–95) called 'transpersonalism', the valuing of cultural achievements above human life.

CRIMINOLOGICAL IMPLICATIONS

The forms of conduct that criminologists study generally have two characteristics. They are harmful, that is they set back some interest of other people (Feinberg, 1984), and they are deviant, that is they violate a norm to which the actor is under significant social pressure to conform. There are, of course, forms of 'crime' that lack one or other of those characteristics (victimless crimes and infringements of rules 'honoured in the breach') but they are seen as anomalous. A third characteristic of many crimes is that the norms they violate, and/or the harm they inflict, are invested with some degree of moral emotion by the actors themselves. They may feel shame or guilt at violating the norm, they may have temporarily or permanently neutralised feelings that such violations would have aroused in them in the past, or they may take pleasure from the transgressive nature of their conduct. They may empathise with the victim, they may have 'edited' feelings of empathy they would otherwise experience (Mackenzie, 2006), or they may exult in the victim's suffering. The nature of these moral emotions is one of the main objects of criminological enquiry. In simple terms, 'how can you do that?' and 'how does that make you feel?' are among the questions that laypeople and criminologists alike tend to ask of the perpetrators of harmful and deviant acts.

In the case of the destruction of forests or the looting of antiquities, the moral emotions into which we need to enquire are rather more complex, and possibly less universal, than in most forms of crime. Nearly every conscious human being can feel pain, and nearly everyone has some possessions; so anyone who has the capacity for empathy at all should be able to empathise with another's physical pain, or distress at the loss of a valued possession. It is at least conceivable, however, that some people are entirely insensitive to the intrinsic value of natural and cultural objects, and neither feel distress at their destruction nor are able to empathise with the distress felt by others. Or it may be that such feelings are a 'luxury' that gives way (even) more readily than ordinary empathy to the pressure of economic need.

For example, there is a longstanding conflict over illegal logging in Mexico's Monarch Butterfly Biosphere Reserve. Thompson (2004) reports that local people involved in logging refer to the butterflies as 'worms'. The loggers 'spoke with contempt for a society they say cares more about the butterflies than about their families. This land belongs to them, they say, and they would not surrender their rights to a presidential decree, much less forsake the needs of their children for bugs'. It is unlikely that this attitude represents some pathological criminal trait,[5] and more likely that it is a response to circumstances which dictate that economic survival takes precedence over other values.

It seems, however, that some perpetrators of this kind of crime or harm are very far from being complete philistines. For example Pendleton (1997) writes that Canadian loggers almost universally felt a sense of grief at killing trees they knew to be several centuries old, but had to suppress such feelings in order to do their job. Felling such trees was a difficult and dangerous task, and it seems that for the elite of forestry workers who did this job, their identity was bound up with a certain respect for the trees, as well as with the ability to kill them (much as some hunters might feel toward their game). In the field of antiquities, Mackenzie's (2005b) research indicates that most of the dealers he interviewed, and a certain type of collector, have a very strong sense of the aesthetic value of the objects they acquire, and relatively little regard for their value as sources of archaeological knowledge:

> *I'm interested in them for aesthetic reasons: for beauty, for learning, for the awe and inspiration that beauty inspires, and not for archaeological reasons ... Archaeology is a non-humanistic discipline... This is what will live.* ('New York Dealer 2', quoted by Mackenzie, 2005b: 196–97; original italics).

There is, however, an important difference between these two examples. In Pendleton's (1997) study, both the forestry workers and the conservationists shared a sense of the value of ancient trees, but the workers enabled themselves to violate that value by claiming they were 'only doing their job'. What Mackenzie's study seems to show is a genuine conflict between incommensurable values. The dealers' sensitivity to the aesthetic value of antiquities—which of course can be appreciated only when they are out of the ground—conflicts with the archaeologists' interest in their 'ideal value' as resources in constructing a narrative of the past.[6] This kind of deep conflict between an offender's values and those that their acts are condemned for infringing is just what Matza (1964) found to be generally absent among

[5] When I gave a version of this paper in Mexico, a member of the audience suggested (apparently without irony) that the peasants' insensitivity to transcendent values might best be understood by applying the theories of Lombroso. Needless to say, this is not what I had in mind.

[6] Halsey notes a parallel conflict between 'concerns with the biological integrity of a region [and with] its *aesthetic* appeal' in his account of Australian forest management (2006: 163).

juvenile delinquents who, he thought, 'evaded rather than radically rejected' legal norms (1964: 60). This raises an intriguing question about Mackenzie's (2005b) sophisticated reworking of Matza's theory of neutralisation as an explanation of the dealers' deviant behaviour. Since the dealers he interviewed 'seem genuinely to believe in the righteousness of their actions' (2005b: 217), what is it that they need to 'neutralise' in order to make their deviant actions possible? They know, of course, that their acts are illegal (ibid: 195), but might they not, quite simply and genuinely, regard those particular laws as illegitimate and not morally binding upon them? There is no *rational* inconsistency in 'radically rejecting' the legitimacy of particular laws while accepting and abiding by most other laws. As I understand Mackenzie's argument, he assumes that the dealers have a sense of 'loyalty' to 'law' in the abstract, which they 'neutralise' by appealing 'to the higher loyalties of artistic appreciation and object preservation' (2005b: 205). My question is: how do we know that antiquities dealers and other high-status offenders have any such abstract reverence for law in the first place?

Lest I give the impression of being sympathetic to the dealers, I hasten to add that their behaviour strikes me as highly objectionable not merely on legal grounds but on grounds of distributive justice. They provide a source of aesthetic pleasure for themselves, for an elite of very wealthy collectors, and in some cases for visitors to museums in rich countries, at the expense of what it seems reasonable to regard as the common heritage of humanity, as well as of particular nations and cultures. This argument raises some difficult questions: there is an obvious tension between universal and particular claims to the archaeological heritage, and as I have mentioned, Simmel's analysis suggests a certain scepticism as to how widely the 'substance and dignity of mankind's ownership' is shared in modern culture. It also suggests, however, that the more widely appreciation of the archaeological (or the ecological) heritage is diffused in civil society, the more it will take on the nature of an objective value and the harder it will be for economic actors to deny or neutralise its moral force.

REFERENCES

Bauman, Z (1991) *Modernity and Ambivalence* (Cambridge, Polity).

—— (1993) *Postmodern Ethics* (Cambridge, Polity).

Benjamin, W (1936) 'The Work of Art in the Era of Mechanical Reproduction' (www.marxists.org/reference/subject/philosophy/works/ge/benjamin.htm).

Boghossian, P (2006) *Fear of Knowledge: Against Relativism and Constructivism* (Oxford, Oxford University Press).

Cantó Milà, N (2005) *A Sociological Theory of Value: Georg Simmel's Sociological Relationism* (Bielefeld, transcript Verlag).

Carman, J, Carnegie, GD, and Wolnizer, PW (1999) 'Is Archaeological Evaluation an Accounting Matter?', 73 *Antiquity* 143.

Carver, M (1996) 'On Archaeological Value', 70 *Antiquity* 45.
Dawson, NM (2007) '"National Antiquities" and the Law', 28 *Journal of Legal History* 57.
Eder, K (1996) *The Social Construction of Nature* (London, Sage).
Feinberg, J (1984) *Harm to Others* (New York, Oxford University Press).
Friedmann, W (1967) *Legal Theory,* 5th edn (London, Stevens).
Green, P and Ward, T (2004) *State Crime: Governments, Violence and Corruption* (London, Pluto).
Green, P, Ward, T, and McConnachie, K (2007) 'Logging and Legality: Environmental Crime, Civil Society and the State', 34 *Social Justice* 94.
Halsey, M (2006) *Deleuze and Environmental Damage: Violence of the Text* (Aldershot: Ashgate).
Hughes, HS (1979) *Consciousness and Society: The Reorientation of European Social Thought 1890–1930* (Brighton, Harvester).
Kamolnick, P (2001) 'Simmel's Legacy for Contemporary Value Theory: A Critical Assessment', 19 *Sociological Theory* 65.
Lash, S (2005) 'Lebenssoziologie: Georg Simmel in the Information Age', 22(3) *Theory, Culture & Society* 1.
Leinhardt, G (1973) Excerpt from *Divinity and Experience: The Religion of the Dinka,* in M Douglas (ed), *Rules and Meanings* (Harmondsworth, Penguin).
Mackenzie, SRM (2005a) 'Dig A Bit Deeper: Regulating the Illegal Antiquities Market', 45 *British Journal of Criminology* 49.
—— (2005b) *Going, Going Gone: Regulating the Market in Illicit Antiquities* (Leicester, Institute of Art and Law).
—— (2006) 'Situationally Edited Empathy: an Effect of Socio-economic Structure on Individual Choice', 14 *Critical Criminology* 265–85.
Macnaghten, P and Urry, J (1998) *Contested Natures* (London, Sage).
Matza, D (1964) *Delinquency and Drift* (New York, Wiley).
McDowell, J (1998) *Mind, Value and Reality* (Cambridge, MA, Harvard University Press).
Midgley, M (1989) *Wisdom, Information and Wonder* (London, Routledge).
Pemberton, S (2004) 'A Theory of Moral Indifference' in P Hillyard, S Tombs, C Pantazis, and D Gordon (eds) *Beyond Criminology: Taking Harm Seriously* (London, Pluto).
Pendleton, MR (1997) 'Beyond the Threshold: The Criminalization of Logging', 10 *Society and Natural Resources* 181.
Rorty, R (1989) *Contingency, Irony and Solidarity* (Cambridge, Cambridge University Press).
Shelbourn, C (2008) '"Time Crime"—Looting of Archaeological Resources and the Criminal Law on England and the United States', *Criminal Law Review* 204.
Simmel, G (1900) 'A Chapter in the Philosophy of Value' 5 *American Journal of Sociology* 577, www.brocku.ca/MeadProject/Simmel/Simmel_1900.html (accessed 20 June 2008).
—— (1971) 'The Metropolis and Mental Life' in D Levine (ed), *On Individuality and Social Forms* (Chicago, IL, University of Chicago Press).
—— (2004) *The Philosophy of Money,* trans T Bottomore and D Frisby, 3rd edn (London, Routledge).

Thomas, K (1983) *Man and the Natural World: Changing Attitudes in England 1500–1800* (Harmondsworth, Penguin).
Thompson, G (2004) 'Illegal Loggers Destroying Lacandon Rainforest in Mexico' *New York Times*, 6 June.
Watson, P and Todeschini, C (2006) *The Medici Conspiracy: The Illicit Journey of Looted Antiquities from Italy's Tomb Raiders to the World's Greatest Museums* (New York, Public Affairs).
Winch, P (1990) *The Idea of a Social Science and Its Relation to Philosophy*, 2nd edn (London, Routledge).
Wylie, A (2007) 'Critical Distance: Stabilizing Evidential Claims in Archaeology', Paper presented at the British Academy conference on 'Enquiry, Evidence and Facts', 14 December.

3

Consensual Relations? Academic Involvement in the Illegal Trade in Ancient Manuscripts

NEIL BRODIE

INTRODUCTION

OVER THE PAST two decades, a large number of previously unseen ancient manuscripts and other inscribed objects have appeared on the international market. Although this material is often characterised as unprovenanced, the modern country of origin of a manuscript can usually be deduced from the physical nature of the document and the style, language, and content of its text. Thus it is known that most are from Iraq or Afghanistan, although some, most famously the Gospel of Judas, are from other countries (in the Gospel's case, Egypt). They have usually been excavated and exported in contravention of national laws. The academic response to these manuscripts is divided. Some scholars view them as a legitimate resource for historical research. Others feel that their historical value is reduced and perhaps compromised by the loss of archaeological context entailed by the destructive manner of their excavation, and fear that the acquisition and publication of such manuscripts might encourage further destructive excavation of what is at the moment still safely buried material. This difference in opinion has been expressed through debate at academic meetings and in the literature, although to date the debate has focused largely on what effects the manuscripts trade might have on scholarship. Little or no attention has been paid to the criminal relations of the trade and their possible social consequences. This chapter considers the debate over the manuscripts trade in more detail, before offering an outline account of the criminal relations of the trade and considering what might be the appropriate scholarly response to criminally traded material. Finally, it is argued that the criminality of the trade is a subject excluded from academic archaeological discourse, and some thought is given to the negative implications of that exclusion for criminological research.

Two examples, one from Afghanistan and one from Iraq, are enough to demonstrate the scale of the problem. Bactrian was the language spoken in northern Afghanistan until at least the ninth century AD. Before 1993 only a few Bactrian inscriptions were known, but since then 'the corpus of Bactrian documents has grown to about 150, most of which appeared on the international art market via the bazaar of Peshawar' (Sims-Williams, 2004: 3). These Bactrian documents are all unprovenanced in that their ownership histories are not known (or, at least, have not been made public), and nothing is known about the circumstances or contexts of their discoveries. The second example, Aramaic incantation bowls, date from the seventh and eighth centuries AD. They are hemispherical or flat-based bowls with Aramaic inscriptions written in ink on their inner surfaces. They have been known since the mid-nineteenth century, and by 1990 something like 1,000 had been documented. All those with a reliable archaeological context had been found in Iraq. During the 1990s, however, many hundreds of previously unknown bowls began to appear in private collections, although again, like the Bactrian documents, nothing is known of their find contexts. It has been estimated that since 1990 the size of the known corpus of Aramaic incantation bowls has doubled (Brodie, 2008: 44–48).

Some unprovenanced manuscripts have been bought by public institutions, but most come to light in private collections, where they are studied and published by university-based scholars. Table 3.1 lists collections of manuscripts that have recently been published or are being studied by scholars at major universities, and thought by those scholars to be from Iraq or Afghanistan.

Academic study of unprovenanced manuscripts often proceeds with the support of public money. For example, in the United Kingdom, the Arts and Humanities Research Council has supported research into privately held Bactrian manuscripts from Afghanistan and Aramaic incantation bowls from Iraq; in the United States the National Endowment for the Humanities has funded research into Buddhist manuscripts from Afghanistan; and the Australian Research Council has done likewise.

The description of these manuscripts as unprovenanced really means that they have no ownership history, or, to put it more bluntly, no information is publicly available as to how they passed from their countries of origin onto the international market and into private hands. Sometimes they are simply said to have 'appeared' (Braarvig, 2000), but in the absence of any evidence to the contrary it is often supposed that they have recently been excavated clandestinely and exported illegally from the country of origin. The alternative supposition—that large collections of important manuscripts have been languishing unseen and unsuspected by the academic community for several decades or more in private collections—is not credible. Only a foolish collector would spend a large sum of money on material without knowing its character and being sure of its authenticity,

Table 3.1. Recently Appeared Manuscripts or Other Inscribed Objects from Afghanistan and Iraq that are being Studied by University Scholars

Collection	Language/script of documents	Probable country of origin	University	Primary reference
Schøyen	Kharosthi	Afghanistan	Washington	http://depts.washington.edu/ebmp/manuscripts
	Brahmi	Afghanistan	Coordinated through Oslo	Braarvig, 2000
	Aramaic	Iraq	University College London/ Hebrew	http://www.schoyencollection.com/magical.htm
	Cuneiform	Iraq	Chalmers	Friberg, 2007
	Cuneiform	Iraq	School of Oriental and African Studies	http://www.schoyencollection.com/infopub.htm
Khalili	Bactrian	Afghanistan	School of Oriental and African Studies	Sims-Williams, 2000
	Aramaic	Afghanistan	Hebrew	http://www.khalili.org/research-ic-aramaic.html
	Arabic	Afghanistan	Cambridge	http://www.khalili.org/research-ic-stud-v.html
Rosen	Cuneiform	Iraq	Cornell	http://cuneiform.library.cornell.edu/about.php
Moussaieff	Aramaic	Iraq	Southampton	Levene, 2003
British Library	Kharosthi	Afghanistan	Washington	Salomon, 1999
Senior	Kharosthi	Afghanistan	Washington	Salomon, 2003

and ensuring appropriate conservation after purchase. Identification, authentication, and conservation all require professional expertise, and so would alert interested scholars. The existence of the Gnostic Gospel of Judas, for example, was known to Coptic scholars for at least 20 years before its first public acknowledgement in 2006. There do not appear to have been any equivalent long-term rumours of previously unknown Afghan or Iraqi manuscripts, implying that most have only recently been taken out of the ground.

ACADEMIC EXPERTISE AND THE MANUSCRIPTS TRADE

Because identification and conservation are expert activities, academic involvement with dealers and private collectors is quite routine. Martin Schøyen, for example, bought his first 108 Buddhist manuscript fragments from a London dealer, for whom they had been described by a leading academic expert (Braarvig, 2000: xiii). The successive dealers in possession of the Judas Gospel after 1983 all found willing academic partners (Brodie, 2007). Presumably some academics receive payment when their time and expertise are put at the disposal of the trade, although most are probably more concerned to gain access to previously unknown material—'scholarly gold' as Jens Braarvig of Oslo University termed it (NRK, 2004).

The academic identification and, particularly, translation of an ancient manuscript establish its historical interest and scholarly importance, and so provide the criteria of rarity that allow it to be assigned a monetary value. Thus academic intervention is crucial for price formation and makes a positive impact on the market. For example, translation of the texts on Aramaic incantation bowls increases their market value tenfold (Brodie, 2008: 47). The Swiss dealer Frieda Tchacos-Nussberger has said she paid something in the region of $300,000 for the group of papyri containing the Gospel of Judas when she bought them in April 2000 (Cockburn 2006, 93), although at the time of the transaction neither she nor the vendor knew that one of the documents was the historically attested but lost Gospel. Upon acquiring the papyri, Tchacos-Nussberger's first action was to deposit them with the Beinecke Library at Yale University for preliminary study and identification, where it was recognised that one of the texts was in fact the Gospel. In August 2000, the manuscripts were returned to Tchacos-Nussberger, and by the end of February 2001 she had sold them to the Maecenas Foundation of Switzerland for $1.5 million and half of any proceeds that might accrue from the commercialisation of the Gospel (Gugliotta and Cooperman, 2006; Felch and Frammolino, 2006). Thus within 11 months of buying the papyri she had turned a profit of more than $1.3 million, or 400 per cent. Part of this, probably the major part, must have been due to the Beinecke Library's identification of the Gospel.

The routine suppression of provenance also facilitates the entry onto the market of fakes, and there are now thought to be many inscribed artefacts on the market or in collections that might be either completely fake, or have been augmented in historical and thus monetary value by the addition of a fake inscription. Eric Meyers of Duke University, for example, has suggested that between 30 and 40 per cent of all inscribed materials in the Israel Museum might be forged (Byle, 2004: 52). Fears about fakes might be expected to depress the market, but again, the deployment of academic expertise to weed them out helps to sustain market confidence.

Simple microeconomics would suggest that the scale of looting correlates positively with the size of the market, so it is argued, not unreasonably, that the academic underpinning of the market acts indirectly to stimulate looting. For this reason, the ethical guidelines of many professional organisations now caution against direct involvement. Article 2 of the Archaeological Institute of America's (AIA) Code of Ethics, for example, states that members should:

> Refuse to participate in the trade in undocumented antiquities and refrain from activities that enhance the commercial value of such objects. Undocumented antiquities are those which are not documented as belonging to a public or private collection before December 30, 1970, when the AIA Council endorsed the UNESCO Convention on Cultural Property, or which have not been excavated and exported from the country of origin in accordance with the laws of that country.

THE ACADEMIC PUBLICATION OF UNPROVENANCED MANUSCRIPTS

Not all academics are involved with the manuscripts trade to the extent that they will collaborate with dealers and collectors, but even among those who are not so involved (who constitute the majority), there is debate over whether or not unprovenanced manuscripts (and in fact unprovenanced archaeological artefacts generally) are appropriate objects of academic study and publication. There are two arguments made against study and publication of unprovenanced artefacts, although both are disputed. The first is that the historical value of an unprovenanced artefact has been lessened by the loss of contextual information caused by the unscientific and unrecorded methods of its excavation. The second is that the academic publication of an unprovenanced artefact provides information and a provenance that might increase its monetary value, thus indirectly supporting the market and provoking further looting.

Because of the problems that are believed to be associated with the academic publication of unprovenanced artefacts, some professional organisations, notably the AIA and the American Schools of Oriental

Research (ASOR), have adopted policies forbidding the first publication of unprovenanced artefacts in their journals.

The AIA policy is as follows:

> As a publication of the Archaeological Institute of America, the *American Journal of Archaeology* will not serve for the announcement or initial scholarly presentation of any object in a private or public collection acquired after December 30, 1973, unless its existence is documented before that date, or it was legally exported from the country of origin. An exception may be made if, in the view of the Editor, the aim of publication is to emphasize the loss of archaeological context. (Norman, 2005)

The ASOR policy is that:

> ASOR members should refrain from activities that enhance the commercial value of ... artefacts [illegally excavated or exported from the country of origin after 1970] and thus contribute indirectly to the illicit market, for example, publication, authentication, or exhibition. ASOR publications and its annual meeting will not be used for presentations of such illicit material. (ASOR, 2006)

In view of the large quantities of cuneiform tablets that were being smuggled out of Iraq, ASOR modified its policy in 2004 to allow publication and presentation of such material at ASOR meetings provided 'the State Board of Antiquities and Heritage of Iraq (SBAH) gives its consent' and that the 'materials to be published are returned to Iraq and are in the ownership and custody of the SBAH'. For such publications, ASOR also requires that information known 'concerning the acquisition or appearance of the texts in the United States should also be included' (ASOR, 2006).

Not all scholars agree that unprovenanced artefacts should not be published, and a reply took shape in 2006 when the Biblical Archaeological Society (BAS) mounted on its website a statement of concern about non-publication (BAS, 2006), said to have been drafted by Lawrence Stager of Harvard University (Eakin, 2006). By July 2007 the statement had attracted 157 signatures. As described above, one of the arguments against studying unprovenanced artefacts is that unrecorded excavation destroys contextual information and so reduces their historical value. Ancient manuscripts are often seen to be a special case, however, because it is argued that the importance of the written information they contain is to some extent independent of context (Braarvig, 2004: 36; Finkel, 2004: 42), and the debate over the publication of unprovenanced artefacts has been sharpest for manuscripts and other inscribed objects. So, paragraph 2 of the BAS statement reads:

> We also recognize that artefacts ripped from their context by looters often lose much of their meaning. On the other hand, this is not always true, and even when it is, looted objects, especially inscriptions, often have much of scholarly importance to impart.

Furthermore, the examples of important unprovenanced artefacts provided in paragraph 4 of the BAS statement to support its arguments are all manuscripts (the Dead Sea Scrolls, the Nag Hammadi Codices, the Gospel of Judas, and the Wadi Daliyeh papyri), and the majority of signatories are philologists of one stripe or another.

Paragraph 3 of the BAS statement claims that not all unprovenanced artefacts are looted—some are chance finds or from old family collections—although it offers no corroboration. Paragraph 6 claims that publication in the academic literature of research conducted on unprovenanced material has little or no effect on looting. This claim might, in fact, be true—for manuscripts at least. If direct academic involvement with the manuscripts trade is as pervasive as it appears, with pre-publication services of identification and authentication crucial for price formation, then subsequent publication of unprovenanced material in the academic literature may have little further effect on price and thus the trade.

THE ACADEMIC JUSTIFICATION FOR ACQUIRING AND PUBLISHING ILLEGALLY TRADED MANUSCRIPTS

Notwithstanding the BAS claim that not all unprovenanced artefacts have been looted, there is not really any doubt, even among people who own and study them, that most recently 'appeared' ancient manuscripts have probably been moved illegally out of their country of origin. The scholarly justification offered for acquiring, studying, and publishing them despite their illegal provenance is one of 'rescue'—the historical information they contain is rescued for posterity. Thus paragraph 7 of the BAS statement says that:

> important artifacts and inscriptions must be rescued and made available to scholars even though unprovenanced. When such objects have been looted, the antiquities market is often the means by which they are rescued, either by private party or a museum. To vilify such activity results only in the loss of important scholarly information.

In a 2005 letter to the journal *Science*, David Owen of Cornell University wrote about cuneiform tablets recently looted from archaeological sites in Iraq that:

> From my perspective, any and all such written documentation must be rescued, recorded, preserved and published. Only then will we be able to save even a small part of what has been destroyed by the looters. (Owen, 2005)

(Two years earlier it had been reported that the US collector Jonathan Rosen had donated a collection of 1,500 cuneiform tablets assembled during the 1990s to Cornell, in return for 'a significant tax break' (D'Arcy, 2003)).

Sometimes the trope of rescue acquires a more tangible form. Writing the introduction for the first volume of the Schøyen Collection of Buddhist manuscripts, Braarvig indicated that the manuscripts were 'found recently in Afghanistan by local people taking refuge from the Taliban forces in caves near the Bamiyan valley, where an old library may have been situated or possibly hidden'. He went on to say that 'Local people trying to save the manuscripts from the Taliban were chased by them when carrying the manuscripts through passes in the Hindu Kush to the north of the Khyber Pass' (Braarvig, 2000: xiii). Schøyen himself, when interviewed on Norwegian radio, expanded: the manuscripts had been smuggled out of Afghanistan by refugees fleeing the Taliban regime, and he had mounted a 'rescue operation' to save them (Lundén, 2005: 3–4). Braarvig later congratulated Schøyen for saving this material through a series of purchases 'as a consistent whole from destruction' (Braarvig, 2004: 37).

In 2004, the Norwegian Broadcasting Corporation (NRK) television programme *Skriftsamleren* (*The Manuscript Collector*) questioned this story (NRK, 2004; Lundén, 2005). Through research on the ground in Afghanistan the programme discovered that the caves in the area of Bamiyan had been thoroughly looted long before the Taliban came into power in 1998, and that the manuscripts had most likely been discovered in a cave near Zargaraan, a small town east of Bamiyan, several years earlier in 1993. Schøyen's story of rescue from the Taliban did not hold up. The programme also discovered that at least two and perhaps three more manuscript fragments in the Schøyen Collection were from the collection of the Kabul Museum. Perhaps 300 had not actually come from Afghanistan at all, but had probably been discovered in a cave near Gilgit in Pakistan (Lundén, 2005: 4–5; Omland, 2006: 233–35). Braarvig's 'consistent whole' was an illusion. In 2005 Schøyen returned the Gilgit material to Pakistan. Nevertheless, the Schøyen Collection continues to adhere to its story of rescue from the Taliban.[1]

The programme *Skriftsamleren* also investigated the acquisition in 1994 by the British Library of about 60 Kharosthi manuscript fragments thought to have been discovered in Afghanistan, arguing that the act of 'rescuing' unprovenanced manuscripts can in fact stimulate further looting (Lundén, 2005: 7–8; Brodie, 2005)., An internal British Library memo shows that, at the time of acquisition, staff had been aware that the material 'might have been smuggled out of an Asian country' but that nevertheless 'in the interests of scholarship' the British Library should acquire and conserve the manuscripts (Brodie, 2005: 6). However, *Skriftsamleren* offered a less sanguine account. A London-based smuggler interviewed by the programme claimed that before the British Library acquisition there had been no real

[1] http://www.schoyencollection.com/Buddhism.htm, accessed 25 October 2007.

market for Afghan manuscripts, but that the acquisition alerted private collectors to their existence, value, and availability. Once private collectors took notice, the artefact hunters on the ground in Afghanistan began to look for them. A Pakistani shepherd interviewed on the programme told of the resultant devastation, with hundreds of manuscript fragments left behind on the surface of the ground. The British Library has not been able to confirm or to deny the *Skriftsamleren* account, presumably because it has no real grasp on the provenance of the material in question.

The academic debate over unprovenanced ancient manuscripts looks set to continue, but to date it has focused on what in the long run might pose the greatest threat to scholarship, with opinions divided over whether or not acquisition and publication are likely to lead to more looting, and thus destruction of historical information, or whether they are justified by the quality of historical information contained in the material in question. What is missing from the debate, however, is any real consideration of the fact that the trade in unprovenanced manuscripts is illegal. No one is under any illusions about the illegal origins of these unprovenanced manuscripts, but the social harm that might be caused by their criminal trade is not something that impinges upon the academic consciousness (or conscience).

THE CRIMINAL RELATIONS OF THE MANUSCRIPTS TRADE

Most countries, including Iraq, Afghanistan, and Egypt, exert some degree of state control or ownership over undiscovered archaeological objects, including manuscripts. Thus Afghanistan has had a law prohibiting the unauthorised export of artefacts since 1958 (Prott, 2006: 195), and a series of similar laws in Iraq dates back to 1974 and before that to the period of the British mandate (Foster, Foster and Gerstenblith, 2005: 217). Thus the unauthorised export of ancient manuscripts constitutes an illegal trade. The academic view of this illegal trade seems to be that it proceeds in a socio-economic vacuum. It is considered a relatively benign phenomenon, providing a small income for the people who dig the manuscripts up, a larger income for the people who smuggle them and sell them, and perhaps also an income supplement for some corrupt border guards or bureaucrats, but beyond that nothing. There is no thought as to how the 'dirty money' generated through such transactions might percolate through wider and more diverse criminal networks, or how the transactions themselves might be used to 'clean' dirty money obtained through other criminal enterprises. Having said that, it is difficult to obtain reliable information about the criminal relations of the manuscripts trade because provenances are occluded and the crimes are often committed in (what are from the academic perspective) remote locations. Nevertheless, the manuscripts trade is part of the larger illegal trade in archaeological artefacts, and claims of criminality are often made about the artefacts trade. Such claims cannot always be substantiated, but sometimes, someone who must be assumed to be a 'credible witness', a person whose position or experience endows his or her first-hand reporting with some degree of authority, makes a statement that might be taken seriously. Occasionally, it is possible to construct a tenuous triangulation between the observations of different witnesses.

In Afghanistan, it has been reported that the money used to purchase artefacts might derive from the sale of opium, and that the money obtained from antiquities sales might be used to purchase arms. Such links in illicit commodities are regularly observed in the criminological literature on criminal markets (see for example, Naylor, 2005; Sheptyki and Wardak, 2005). As early as 1996, for example, Nancy Dupree of the Society for the Preservation of Afghanistan's Cultural Heritage (SPACH) reported that Mujahideen commanders in Afghanistan were digging up artefacts to sell, particularly in the region of Hadda (Dupree, 1996: 47). In 1998 she reported that bulldozers were being used to dig out the site of Ai Khanoum 'under financial agreements with ruling commanders', and that authorities in Badghis were levying a 20 per cent tax on the sale of artefacts (Dupree, 1998). In 2002, the Director General of Afghanistan's National Institute of Archaeology, Abdul Wasey Feroozi, was quoted as saying that 'In the western district of Paghman alone, more than four or five areas have been illegally dug by commanders. These men have trucks, they have equipment and they have guns' (ABC, 2002). When in 2003 a UNESCO mission was sent to investigate reports of illegal digging at a previously unknown site at Kharwar in central Afghanistan, it was turned away by local warlords. Jim Williams (of the Kabul UNESCO office) complained that 'It's being excavated by criminals. They're the same people, the drug barons, the warlords, who are causing all Afghanistan's problems' (Astill, 2003).

Perhaps the most reliable eye-witness reporting is by the British writer and ex-diplomat Rory Stewart, who in 2002, soon after the fall of the Taliban, walked west–east across Afghanistan from Herat to Kabul (Stewart, 2004). Arriving at Jam, about 380 km east of Herat and the site of a twelfth-century minaret and extensive archaeological remains, the local military commander told Stewart that he and his men had arrived there a year earlier to dig, and that a few hundred more people travelled there to dig from nearby villages (Stewart, 2004: 170). The artefacts were sold to traders from Herat (Stewart, 2004: 168), and from Herat were moved over the border into Iran. Stewart claimed that the governor of Herat profited from the trade, although did not make much from it compared with the profit from other contraband (Stewart, 2004: 176).

It has also been reported that illegally excavated artefacts might be caught up in criminal networks that extend to countries outside Afghanistan. In 2001, the *New York Times* interviewed one Robert Puffer, who claimed to be a 'go-between' for antiquities dealers and who said that smugglers routinely did business with a former interior minister of Pakistan, who was an avid collector of Afghan antiquities (Bohlen, 2001). The story received some confirmation from London antiquities dealer Johnny Eskenazi, who in 1996 visited a 'powerful politician' in Pakistan to view high-quality Afghan antiquities the politician was offering for sale for US$10 million (Eskenazi, 2002). Eskenazi suggested that such politicians could launder money made from the drugs trade by buying and selling antiquities, and Robert Kluyver (of SPACH), from his different perspective, has claimed likewise (Kluyver, 2001). The sums of money generated by the manuscripts trade, or at least the artefacts trade more generally, are not large compared with those from the drugs trade, but neither are they inconsequential. It was widely reported, for example, in 1999 that six metal boxes containing 25,000 Afghan artefacts destined for London, Frankfurt, and Dubai were impounded by police at Peshawar airport. Documents seized during the investigation led police to state that the exporter, who fled to Dubai, could have made 'millions of pounds' from his operation (Levy and Scott-Clark, 1999).

The situation in Iraq is unlikely to be any better than that in Afghanistan. In 2005, Matthew Bogdanos, the New York District Attorney and US Marine Reserve Colonel who conducted the official US inquiry into the April 2003 looting of the Baghdad Museum, expressed his opinion that 'insurgents in Iraq have discovered a new source of income in antiquities', pointing to the June 2004 discovery by US marines of archaeological artefacts alongside weapons, ammunition, and other military equipment in an underground bunker used by insurgents (Bogdanos, 2005).

THE DEFICIENT ACADEMIC RESPONSE TO UNPROVENANCED MANUSCRIPTS

Despite these persistent reports in the media of criminal involvement with the artefacts and by extension the manuscripts trade, one searches in vain through scholarly publications of unprovenanced manuscripts for a decent account of provenance, or even for any indication that a scholar has attempted to research provenance or to take a broad view—in terms of criminality—of what provenance might mean. Academic concern over illegal trade only seems to arise when doubts over good title constitute a possible impediment to acquisition. In 1994, for example, the staff of the British Library debated the issue of good title before agreeing the acquisition of the Kharosthi manuscript fragments. In 2000, the Beinecke Library at Yale University declined the opportunity to acquire the Gospel of Judas because of doubts over title. Presumably, scholars who study this material are simply not interested in provenance because it has no bearing on their research, or are reluctant to investigate provenance too closely or to publicise what they know because of what it might reveal about the activities and associations of the private collectors who hold the material, and who in an academic sense might be considered to be their patrons. It might even be convenient for a scholar to remain ignorant of provenance as it makes for an easier judgement in favour of study and publication. This may be so, but unless the scholar is assiduous in researching and publishing provenance, he or she cannot claim to be acting in good conscience, and might even stand accused of passively colluding with the criminal trade.

Rigorous investigation of a manuscript's provenance might reveal it to have been exported illegally, at which point the police should be involved to ensure that it is returned to its rightful national owner, or, if the political situation does not permit an immediate return, held in trust until such time as a return is possible. Sometimes rigorous investigation is not necessary; illegal trade is openly admitted and justified through 'rescue'. Yet although it is clear that many scholars coming into contact with so-called unprovenanced manuscripts are aware of criminal involvement, they routinely fail to notify the appropriate law enforcement agencies. Bogdanos has gone further and argued that academics should become 'clandestine informants' (Bogdanos, 2005). When they are offered sight of material that they suspect might have passed through criminal hands, they should arrange a viewing but inform the police. Thus in the British Library example discussed above, the correct course of action would have been for the British Library staff to have arranged to meet the dealer who had brought the manuscripts to Britain, and to have informed the Metropolitan Police of the meeting, so that the police might then have taken appropriate action of their own. But at no point does it seem that the British Library made any attempt to go beyond what the intermediary offering the manuscripts (who was a British-based dealer) had to say about provenance, and to investigate the character or affiliations of the person who was in possession of the manuscripts and who had brought them to Britain from Pakistan. Nor do the staff of the Beinecke Library seem to have alerted the Egyptian authorities or US law enforcement agencies of the presence on the market of the Judas Gospel.

THE LIMITS AND EFFECTS OF ACADEMIC DISCOURSE

The criminal relations of the manuscripts trade are largely excluded from the academic debate over unprovenanced manuscripts. Sometimes criminality is touched upon, only to be dismissed. For example, the BAS statement against policies of non-publication contains 11 paragraphs, but the only paragraph mentioning criminal involvement is paragraph 10, which states that:

> The real objection to the antiquities market and unprovenanced material is that it somehow sullies our hands by participation in an illegal enterprise. But we believe

> a more refined judgment is called for. Yes, it would be nice if we always had professionally excavated materials to study and publish. But that is not the situation. Our choice is either to study unprovenanced material or ignore it. Given that choice, we prefer to study unprovenanced material. The sweeping exclusion of unprovenanced material from scholarly consideration results only in a loss to scholars, to scholarship and ultimately to the public.

The language chosen for this paragraph does nothing to reassure the sceptic that the potential consequences of 'participation in an illegal enterprise' are known, or have even been considered, and that hand-sullying is the least of them. John Boardman, too, of Oxford University, in an outspoken attack on the policy of non-publication, which he regards as censorship, wrote that 'I was brought up to believe that censorship is worse than theft, and especially so where scholarship is concerned' (Boardman, 2006: 40). In both cases, the issue of criminality is first trivialised and then summarily dismissed so that the argument can be brought back to the possible effects on scholarship of non-publication.

While it is not surprising that supporters of trade and publication are reluctant to talk about criminality, it is harder to understand why opponents also seem unwilling to discuss it. One reason might appear to be professional courtesy. While it is one thing to debate the consequences for scholarship of academic publication with a friend and colleague, it is quite another to accuse him or her of participating in an international money-laundering racket. But the prevailing norms of professional and personal etiquette that constrain conduct on both sides of the debate are simply the limiting effects of academic discourse, a discourse constructed around scholarship, narrowly defined as intellectual practice. Debate does not easily move against that discursive grain.

Consider, for example, the character assessments of people involved in the manuscripts trade. In a 2005 statement the British Library described the dealer who sold them the Kharosthi manuscript fragments, and who has in his possession more fragments, as 'reputable' (Brodie, 2005: 5). Yet this is a person the British Library knows full well to have handled and to be in possession of manuscripts that were taken illegally out of their country of origin. The British Library is only able to describe the dealer as reputable because, according to their own version of events, he helped save the material in 'the interests of scholarship'. It might be forced to consider him otherwise if the criminal articulations of the Kharosthi acquisition are opened to discussion. A more open discourse, one able to accommodate criminality alongside scholarship, or at least to conceive of scholarship more broadly as a social rather than a strictly intellectual practice, would reveal a different reality. The closed narrative of reputable dealers collaborating with scholars in the name of academic freedom and in the interests of scholarship would be replaced by a far less wholesome account of self-interested dealers and scholars pursuing their own ends in complete disregard of any social consequences, or of scholars condemned by political and economic circumstances beyond their control to engage in research of uncertain moral and intellectual quality.

Although academic discourse may appear at first glance to arise out of and correspond to a common-sense reality, it is clearly artificial. Attempts to broaden its reference beyond the immediate concerns of scholarship are routinely opposed by its beneficiaries. That much is clear from the failure of scholars to investigate provenance, and sometimes from their more active obstruction of attempts by others to investigate provenance. The British Library has still not answered allegations made in the *Skriftsamleren* programme concerning the possible illegal provenance of its acquisition. In fact, when challenged on *Skriftsamleren*, the responsible librarian affected outrage and walked out of the interview. This kind of response is not unusual. But beyond the passive and active obstructions of scholars, there are more powerful interests ready when necessary to ensure the purity of academic discourse by blocking unwelcome investigations. The most obvious example of outside coercion has been the aggressive response of the Schøyen Collection to an investigation conducted by University College London (UCL) into the Collection's Aramaic incantation bowls.

The NRK programme *Skriftsamleren* included a piece on the bowls, which at the time were in storage at UCL, alleging that they had been illegally excavated in Iraq in 1992 or 1993 (NRK, 2004; Lundén, 2005: 6–7). In view of the seriousness of the NRK allegations, UCL announced it was to convene a committee of inquiry with a remit to investigate the provenance of the bowls and to establish university policy towards the study of unprovenanced artefacts more generally (UCL, 2005). The committee submitted its report to UCL in July 2006, and a copy was sent to the Schøyen Collection.[2] Nothing was heard publicly, however, until March 2007 when the Schøyen Collection announced it was suing UCL for the recovery of the bowls (2007a). Finally, in June 2007 a joint press release was issued by UCL (2007) and the Schøyen Collection (2007b) stating:

> Following a searching investigation by an eminent panel of experts, and further enquiries of its own, UCL is pleased to announce that no claims adverse to the Schøyen Collection's right and title have been made or intimated. Having made all the enquiries that it reasonably could UCL has no basis for concluding that title is vested other than in the Schøyen Collection. UCL has now returned the Bowls to the Schøyen Collection and has agreed to pay a sum in respect of its possession of them.

UCL has refused to publish the report, although some of its findings have been leaked to the press. UCL's lawyers have tried to prevent publication

[2] Colin Renfrew, personal communication. Professor Colin Renfrew of Cambridge University was a member of the committee.

by writing to possible recipients, emphasising that copyright in the report is vested with UCL, and requesting recipients to return anything in their possession. They further requested that: 'Because of the confidential nature of the Report UCL is not able to enter into discussions … about the subject matter of the Report or the allegations it makes and we request that all communications about this subject are channelled between legal advisors'.[3] In August 2007, UCL refused an application made under the 2000 Freedom of Information Act to release the report into the public domain.[4]

The payment by UCL was made as part of an out-of-court settlement, and the suspicion can only be that non-publication of the report was part of the same settlement. No further explanation has been forthcoming from UCL. The report is thought to contain information supplied by, among others, NRK, Martin Schøyen, and Christopher Martin, the London-based dealer who sold Martin Schøyen most of the bowls. Thus it should provide a primary resource for research into the exchange chains that constitute the trade, and their possible criminal relations. Unfortunately, intervention by the Schøyen Collection has—for the time being at least—ensured its sequestration. In the absence of any evidence to the contrary (perhaps because the Collection has suppressed the report), the Schøyen Collection has since rejected 'any imputation of wrongdoing as wrong-headed and unwarranted' and has reaffirmed that it 'places a heavy duty on itself to publish as fast as possible, as well as conserve, all objects of international cultural interest and historical value in its possession' (Schøyen Collection, 2007c). The purity of academic discourse has been maintained, although it has taken court action to ensure that it is not tainted by talk of criminal involvement.

CONCLUSION

There is now a well-established literature on the illegal trade in archaeological artefacts, highlighting the damage it causes to archaeological sites and monuments, and the threat it poses to historical knowledge and cultural traditions (see generally, Gill and Chippindale, 1983; Brodie, Doole and Renfrew, 2001; Brodie et al, 2006; Watson and Todeschini, 2006). A parallel literature concerns legal countermeasures (see generally Gerstenblith, 2004; Hoffman, 2006). It is notable, however, that although criminologists have begun to study the trade as a criminal phenomenon (Mackenzie, 2005; Tijhuis, 2006), there has been hardly any consideration of the social harm

[3] Letter from Hunters solicitors to author, 28 June 2007.

[4] Application made by author. Despite the best efforts of UCL to suffocate public discussion and academic research by withholding the report's findings, it has been alleged that the report considered on 'the balance of probabilities' that the bowls had been illegally removed from Iraq sometime after August 1990, although there is no evidence to show that Schøyen was necessarily aware of that fact (Balter, 2007: 554).

that it might cause, or of how academic involvement with the trade might in itself contribute to that harm.

There is a broad measure of agreement within the academic community that artefacts shorn of their original archaeological context through unrecorded and usually illegal digging have in the process been deprived of valuable historical information, and that research based on such material is badly compromised. Ancient manuscripts are often seen to be a special case, however, because the information they contain is to some extent independent of find context. The perception that the scholarly importance of ancient manuscripts is not significantly lessened by loss of context disposes scholars to study them, but because most recently discovered manuscripts are thought to have been illegally traded, these scholars must be considered complicit to a greater or lesser extent in the commercial and thus criminal process, and thus bear some responsibility for any harm that is caused. Nevertheless, the nature and magnitude of the consequences of academic involvement are far from clear. There is an urgent need for primary research in this area to investigate the socio-economic and cultural contexts of the manuscripts trade, and a corresponding need for the academic community to reflect upon the broader social context of its research.

REFERENCES

ABC (2002) '"Mafia" gangs threaten Afghanistan's archaeological treasures', *ABC News Online*, 3 November.

ASOR (2006) 'American Schools of Oriental Research Publications. Publishing with ASOR', www.asor.org/pubs/howtopub.html, accessed 10 July 2008.

Astill, J (2003) 'Plunder goes on across Afghanistan as looters grow ever bolder', *Guardian*, 13 December.

Balter, M (2007) 'University suppresses report on provenance of Iraqi antiquities', 318 *Science* 554–55.

BAS (2006) 'Publication of Unprovenanced Artifacts. Statement of Concern', www.biblicalarchaeology.org/bswbOOunprovenancedstatement.html, accessed 24 October 2007.

Boardman, J (2006) 'Archaeologists, collectors and museums' in E Robson, L Treadwell and C Gosden (eds), *Who Owns Objects? The Ethics and Politics of Collecting Cultural Artefacts* (Oxford, Oxbow), pp 33–46.

Bogdanos, M (2005) 'The terrorist in the art gallery', *New York Times*, 10 December.

Bohlen, C (2001) 'Afghan art dispersed by winds of war', *New York Times*, 1 November.

Braarvig, J (ed) (2000) *Buddhist Manuscripts in the Schøyen Collection, Volume 1*, Manuscripts in the Schøyen Collection 1 (Oslo, Hermes).

—— (2002) *Buddhist Manuscripts in the Schøyen Collection, Volume 2*. (Manuscripts in the Schøyen Collection 3) (Oslo, Hermes).

—— (2004) 'The case of ancient Buddhist manuscripts from Afghanistan' in M Kimmich (ed), *Not For Sale. A Swiss–British Conference on the Traffic in Artefacts from Iraq, Afghanistan and Beyond* (Berne, British Council), pp 35–8.

Brodie, NJ (2005) 'The circumstances and consequences of the British Library's 1994 acquisition of some Kharosthi manuscript fragments' 17 *Culture Without Context* 5–11.

—— (2007) 'The lost, found, lost again and found again Gospel of Judas', 19 *Culture Without Context*, 17–27.

—— (2008) 'The market background to the April 2003 plunder of the Iraq National Museum' in P Stone and J Farchakh Bajjaly (eds), *The Destruction of Cultural Heritage in Iraq* (Woodbridge, Boydell Press), pp 41–54.

Brodie, NJ, Doole, J and Renfrew, C (eds) (2001) *Trade in Illicit Antiquities: the Destruction of the World's Archaeological Heritage* (Cambridge, McDonald Institute).

Brodie, NJ, Kersel, MM, Luke, C and Tubb KW (eds) (2006) *Archaeology, Cultural Heritage and the Antiquities Trade* (Gainesville, FL: University Press of Florida).

Byle, A (2004) 'A third of Israel Museum's inscriptions are forgeries', 30(5) *Biblical Archaeology Review* 52–53.

Cockburn, A (2006) 'The Judas Gospel', *National Geographic*, May, 78–95.

D'Arcy, D (2003) 'Collector gets tax break for donating cylinder seals to university', 139 *Art Newspaper* 5.

Dupree, N (1996) 'Museum under siege', *Archaeology*, March/April, 47.

—— (1998) 'The plunder continues', *Archaeology On-line*, www.archaeology.org/online/features/afghan/update.html, accessed 10 July 2008.

Eakin, H (2006) 'Must looted relics be ignored?' *New York Times*, 2 May.

Eskenazi, J (2002) 'My evening with Kalashnikovs and the Begram ivories', 121 *Art Newspaper*, 18 January.

Felch, J and R Frammolino (2006) 'Judas Gospel figure has tainted past', *Los Angeles Times*, 11 April.

Finkel, I (2004) 'Perspective of an academic' in M Kimmich (ed), *Not For Sale. A Swiss–British Conference on the Traffic in Artefacts from Iraq, Afghanistan and Beyond* (Berne, British Council), pp 41–42.

Foster, BR, Foster KP and Gerstenblith P (2005) *Iraq Beyond the Headlines. History, Archaeology, and War* (Singapore, World Scientific Publishing).

Friberg, J (2007) *A Remarkable Collection of Babylonian Mathematical Texts* (New York, Springer).

Gerstenblith, P (2004) *Art, Cultural Heritage, and the Law* (Durham, NC, Carolina Academic Press).

Gill, DWJ and Chippindale, C (1993) 'Material and intellectual consequences of esteem for Cycladic figurines', ? *American Journal of Archaeology* 601–59.

Gugliotta, G and Cooperman, A (2006) 'Newly translated Gospel offers more positive portrayal of Judas', *Washington Post*, 7 April.

Hoffman, BT (ed) (2006) *Art and Cultural Heritage* (Cambridge, Cambridge University Press).

Kluyver, R (2001) 'The drug trade in antiquities' 113 *Art Newspaper* 8.

Levene, D (2003) *A Corpus of Magic Bowls: Incantation Texts in Jewish Aramaic from Late Antiquity* (London, Kegan Paul).

Levy, A and Scott-Clark, C (1999) 'Looters take millions in Afghan treasures', *Sunday Times*, 11 July.

Lundén, S (2005) 'TV review: NRK (Norway) *Skriftsamleren* [The Manuscript Collector]', 16 *Culture Without Context* 3–11.

Mackenzie, SRM (2005) *Going, Going, Gone: Regulating the Market in Illicit Antiquities* (Leicester, Institute of Art and Law).

Naylor, RT (2005) *Wages of Crime: Black Markets, Illegal Finance and the Underworld Economy* (Ithaca, NY: Cornell University Press).

Norman, N (2005) 'Editorial policy on the publication of recently acquired antiquities', 109 *American Journal of Archaeology* 135–36.

NRK (2004) *Skriftsamleren* [TV programme].

Omland, A (2006) 'Claiming Gandhara: legitimizing ownership of Buddhist manuscripts in the Schøyen Collection, Norway' in J van Krieken-Pieters (ed) *Art and Archaeology of Afghanistan: Its Fall and Survival* (Leiden, Brill), pp 227–64.

Owen, DI (2005) 'An archaeological dilemma', 309 *Science* 1816.

Prott, LV (2006) 'The protection of cultural movables from Afghanistan: developments in international management' in J van Krieken-Pieters (ed) *Art and Archaeology of Afghanistan: Its Fall and Survival* (Leiden, Brill), pp 189–200.

Salomon, R (1999) *Ancient Buddhist Scrolls from Gandhara: The British Library Kharosthi Fragments* (Seattle, University of Washington Press).

—— (2003) 'The Senior manuscripts: another collection of Gandhāran Buddhist scrolls', 123 *Journal of the American Oriental Society* 73–92.

Schøyen Collection (2007a) 'Schøyen Collection sues University College London for recovery of incantation bowls', Press release, 9 March.

—— (2007b) 'The Schøyen Collection of Aramaic incantation bowls', Press release, 26 June.

—— (2007c) 'Correction of media innuendo concerning alleged "looted" provenance of incantation bowls', Press release, 14 October.

Sheptycki, J and Wardak, A (eds) (2005) *Transnational and Comparative Criminology* London: Glasshouse.

Sims-Williams, N (2000) *Bactrian Documents from Northern Afghanistan, I: Legal and Economic Documents* (Oxford, Oxford University Press).

—— (2002) 'New documents in ancient Bactrian reveal Afghanistan's past' *IIAS Newsletter* no 22, March, 12–13.

—— (2004) *Recent Discoveries in the Bactrian Language and their Historical Significance*, (Kabul, Society for the Preservation of Afghanistan's Cultural Heritage).

Stewart, R (2004) *The Places In Between* (London, Picador).

Tijhuis, AJG (2006) *Transnational Crime and the Interface between Legal and Illegal Actors* (place?, Wolf Legal Publishers).

UCL (2005) 'Incantation bowls: statement by UCL (University College London)', Press release, 10 October.

—— (2007) 'Aramaic incantation bowls – joint statement from UCL and the Schøyen Collection', Press release, 27 June.

Watson, P and Todeschini, C (2006) *The Medici Conspiracy* (New York, Public Affairs).

4

Border Controls in Market Countries as Disincentives to Antiquities Looting at Source?

The US–Italy Bilateral Agreement 2001

GORDON LOBAY

THE WORKSHOP FROM which this volume emerges was based on the idea that improving the current approach to countering the looting and trading of illegal antiquities should take place within an integrated, multi-disciplinary framework. This is reflected in the variety of contributions to this book, some tending towards theoretical development and analysis, such as Whyte's (chapter seven) and Ward's (chapter two), while others report hard data, such as Korsell and Källman's (chapter six), and Mackenzie and Green's (chapter eight). This chapter falls into the second category, providing an empirically based assessment of a bilateral agreement between the United States and Italy to restrict imports of certain Italian cultural property to America.[1]

To date, the majority of quantitative analyses of market activity have come from the archaeological community; for example, Gill and Chippindale (1993), Chippindale and Gill (2000), Elia (2001), and Nørskov (2002a). Although highly useful as sources of hard data, these studies often go unnoticed in the criminological and legal communities. Equally, many archaeologists are unaware of valuable socio-legal approaches to the problem, such as Prott and O'Keefe (1989), Palmer (1994), Polk (2000), and Mackenzie (2005a), (2005b). This lack of academic unification in tackling the problem hinders the creation of cohesive steps toward a solution.

This chapter focuses on the problem of archaeological looting in Central Italy and on how international methods to curb the trading of

[1] This contribution is based on a wider study completed by the author in 2007 as part of his PhD research at the University of Cambridge (Homerton College).

Figure 4.1. Map of the Regions of Italy
Note: The shaded areas show generally how the ancient cultures correspond to the modern regions of Italy.
Source: Map created by the author, based on Haynes, 2000: vi.

looted antiquities can affect the incentive to loot in the first place. The research area corresponds roughly to the modern Italian regions of Emilia-Romagna, La Marche, Lazio, Tuscany, and Umbria (Figure 4.1). The types of antiquities, or ancient artefacts, studied in this investigation are of pre-Roman origin from the Etruscan, Faliscan, Italic, Umbrian, and

Villanovan cultures.[2] Central Italy has endured a long history of illegitimate archaeological excavations, as described in Dennis (1883), Thoden van Velzen (1996), Pastore (2001), and George (2005).

Artefacts from the pre-Roman period are relatively distinguishable out of context, making them more identifiable when spotted on the antiquities market.[3] The term 'context' refers to the immediate matrix surrounding an archaeological find (or artefact) and usually consists of some form of sediment, as well as the provenience or stratigraphic (vertical and horizontal) position of the find within the matrix and its association to other finds (Renfrew and Bahn, 1996: 46). It is the context that archaeologists aim to protect from looting because only with the combination of an artefact and its context can a clear picture of the past begin to be reconstructed. If an artefact is removed from its context without proper recording it is impossible to replace that artefact in the context, which eliminates any available archaeological data. One can relate the situation to a modern crime scene where forensic specialists require the entire scene to be left undisturbed prior to investigation.

It is estimated that there are approximately half a million tombs in southern Etruria alone (Spivey, 1997: 194); most tombs contain, along with at least one human body, many artefacts. If one adds the vast quantity of other archaeological sites ranging from camps and huts to villas and temples and the multitude of other sites of ancient human habitation throughout Central Italy, the possible number of artefacts in circulation is staggering. Looting in the region is unfortunately ongoing and enhanced international cooperation in addressing the problem is necessary.

One mechanism intended to reduce looting in this region, and indeed throughout Italy, is a bilateral agreement between the US and Italy (hereinafter 'the Agreement') created on the basis that many of the antiquities looted in Italy are bound for the lucrative US antiquities market.

One of the key remits of the Agreement reads:

> Desiring to reduce the incentive for pillage of irreplaceable archaeological material representing the Pre-Classical, Classical and Imperial Roman periods of Italy's rich cultural heritage (US–Italy Bilateral Agreement, 2001: Introduction)

The Agreement restricts imports to the United States of groups of artefact types noted in a Designated List.[4] The list divides the types of restricted artefacts into five categories of artistic media: stone, metal, ceramic, glass, and wall paintings. In archaeological terms, the artefacts covered by the

[2] For histories of the region see Holloway (1994), Smith (1996), Spivey (1997), and Haynes (2000).

[3] Roman antiquities, for example, are not included because it is often difficult to determine, even in a basic sense, where a specific object originated in the vast Roman territory stretching from Europe to North Africa and beyond into the Middle East.

[4] See the Federal Register, http://exchanges.state.gov/culprop/it01fr01.html.

Agreement range from approximately the ninth century BC to the fourth century AD. These ancient artefacts are traded in several ways, for example, on the public international art market at dealers' shops, over the Internet at online dealers and auctions, as well as at traditional auction sales in prestigious auction houses such as Bonhams, Christie's, and Sotheby's. Antiquities are also traded invisibly through an underground network. Some observers have suggested that the public market presents two key problems. The first is that it comprises a mixture of legal and illegal antiquities (Brodie, Doole, and Watson, 2000; Renfrew, 2000). The second is that it represents a relatively small proportion of the overall trade with the majority of antiquities, and the most valuable, traded invisibly (Nørskov, 2002a, 2002b; Watson, 2006). The 'invisible trade', as it shall be referred to here, functions completely outside public view. While the public trade presents some research challenges, many public market venues such as auction houses and galleries publish widely available catalogues that allow a glimpse of the artefacts consigned for sale. Obtaining these types of observations from the invisible market is extremely difficult, due to its secretive nature. A key premise in the study of the illegal antiquities trade is that it is the high prices achieved on the market that drives the trade (Renfrew, 1993; Elia, 2001). This study aims to use data gathered from auction sales, a significant element of the public antiquities market in the United States, to explore how the Agreement aims to reduce the incentive to loot antiquities from Central Italy.

This investigation will explore auction market activity covering the time period immediately before and after the Agreement's implementation in 2001. The objective is to explore how, if at all, the Agreement has affected market activity. The particular approach applied here to analyse any apparent effects of the Agreement on the US market is to identify and chart trends in the auction market data of pre-Roman antiquities from Central Italy before and after implementation of the Agreement.

Defined as an interrupted time-series design (Neuman, 1997), this approach uses a series of cross-sections of data (in this case volume, price, and provenance data from auction sales) in order to chart trends in the data before and after a given 'intervention'—in this case the intervention is the Agreement. An unavoidable facet of studying the antiquities market is the relatively small amount of data available. Researchers find that statistics are less readily available than in many other international markets, largely because of the comparatively small size of the market, its submersion in the wider art market, and the lack of an independent overseeing body charged with the production of statistics and record-keeping. In addition, concerns about import controls in the United States displacing antiquities to markets in other nations made it particularly difficult to determine an effective control group. The above factors all formed limitations on the extent to which the analysis of the time-series data used here could achieve the full rigour of an experimental research design. This study is important because it tackles head on the difficulty of gathering market data, and for the first time uses auction data to investigate specifically the impact of a bilateral agreement.[5]

The dataset used in this assessment of the Agreement between the United States and Italy includes 48 auctions at Sotheby's and Christie's New York sales between 1997 and 2005. As part of the broader project on which this chapter is based, I also developed a UK dataset comprising 52 auctions at Bonhams, Christie's, and Sotheby's at their respective London locations. Where relevant I will draw upon this dataset to inform my analysis of the Agreement. In order to organise this information more effectively I shall designate the years 1997–2000 as Period A, prior to implementation, while 2001–05 shall be Period B, post-implementation. Data collection involved creating a basic toolkit of information about Central Italian antiquities available in auction catalogues centring on three key indicators. These were:

— the *volume* of antiquities reaching the US market;
— the provenance *details* included with the antiquities in auction catalogues; and
— the *realised prices* (if any) achieved at the auction sale.

An effective bilateral agreement measured against these indices would be expected to be evidenced in:

— a *reduction in volume* of antiquities reaching the US market;
— an *increase in provenance* details published with antiquities in auction catalogues; and
— an *increase in realised prices* achieved at auction (produced by the diminished supply of antiquities)

This constitutes a hypothesis that we can test against the data gathered, but before doing so some explanation of the 'provenance' and 'realised prices' indices used is required.

'Provenance' is defined as 'the history of ownership of an item' (HC 371-II Deb 25 July 2000; Sotheby's Memorandum, point 12).[6] 'Provenance' should be distinguished from the term 'provenience', which refers more specifically to the archaeological findspot or context of the artefact (Coggins,

[5] Auction data has been used by Chippindale and Gill (2000), Elia (2001), Nørskov (2002a), (2002b), and to an extent in Gill and Chippindale (1993), but these studies were not focused specifically on assessing policy issues, nor did they attempt to understand how all types of antiquities from a given region were affected; they focused on the looting and trading of specific artefact types only.

[6] Bonhams and Christie's use provenance descriptions in a similar manner.

1995: 71). Four provenance groupings of auction data have been constructed to reflect how provenance is provided in auction catalogues:

1. *Name*. Any consigned artefact that includes the publication of names of people, such as former owners or others associated with the artefact in the auction catalogue.
2. *No Provenance*. Artefacts that are published with no supporting provenance information whatsoever or information deemed utterly useless; for example, 'acquired by the present owner as a 21st birthday present in 1960' (Bonhams London, Antiquities, 21 April 2005, Sale ID 11597, lot 438).
3. *Previous Sale*. Artefacts published only with information about past sales in which the artefact is said to have appeared, such as in dealers' shops or auction houses. This type of provenance information is not ideal because it does not imply legitimacy or even ownership, merely that an artefact has previously appeared on the market.[7] However, since this information does provide a sale history, it should not be discounted because it does help to create a timeline for appearances on the public market.
4. *Vague*. Consigned artefacts described only with information such as the name of a region where the artefact might have originated archaeologically (for example Umbria), dates of acquisition (without the name of an owner), or other types of information that contribute to provenance only vaguely.[8]

Realised prices are included as a means of substantiating changes in demand for the various artefact types. If prices increase over time it is assumed that the demand for that particular artefact type is also increasing, whilst the opposite would describe a reduction in demand.[9] All prices used in this study were adjusted for inflation to December 2005 prices in order to compare more effectively the market value of similar artefacts over the time period.[10]

[7] Dealers and auction houses do in certain cases hold ownership or a stake in some consignments, although this is relatively rare and often explicitly stated.

[8] If the all-too-common provenance 'property of a private collector' (or similar) is given with a consignment the example is placed in the 'no provenance' category.

[9] Demand can also be gauged by the volume of objects reaching the market; the more a specific artefact type is consigned for sale, the greater the demand for those artefacts. The two means of establishing demand as changes in price or volume of objects are outlined in Smith (1989).

[10] Calculating accurate realised prices at auction sales is only possible if one artefact is included in a single lot; if multiple artefacts appear in one lot it is not possible to determine the price of each specific object. Although trends in prices over time can be determined from the overall values of lots, rather than single objects, we must bear in mind that these price trends are less reliable than single object trends, given that they mask the possibility of varying lot sizes over time.

Before examining the data generated in this study we can briefly consider the context from which the bilateral agreement in question emerged.

HISTORY AND FUNCTION OF THE CULTURAL PROPERTY IMPLEMENTATION ACT

The US system of bilateral agreements is possible because of the Cultural Property Implementation Act (CPIA) of 1983, which forms the basis of cultural property legislation in the United States. Prior to 1983 the United States did not have a comprehensive policy regarding the international movement of cultural property (Herscher, 1983: 117). The CPIA endured a very long development period that in effect began 'after World War II, [when] many states recognised the need for a global approach to the protection of cultural and natural heritage. The context of their concern was rapid post-war development that endangered the very resources that were proving valuable for economic expansion' (Magness-Gardiner, 2004: 27). Papa Sokal (2006) explains that during the post-war period it became clear that it was necessary to address the problem of illegally traded art and archaeology, which was then raised at the 1960 UNESCO[11] General Conference, and a resolution was passed that asked the Director-General for a report about illicit imports, exports, and sales of cultural property.

In 1969 a UNESCO committee proposed a preliminary draft of a convention, which was passed to member states for comment. Finally, in 1970 the UNESCO Convention on the Means of Prohibiting and Preventing the Illicit Import, Export and Transfer of Ownership of Cultural Property (hereinafter 'the 1970 Convention') was created, which provides guidelines that manage theft and illegal exports on a general level (Prott, 1998: 205). The 1970 Convention operates by imposing duties on states party to the Convention by providing a basic framework for the recovery of unlawfully removed cultural property, as well as helping to prevent the acquisition and import of illicitly acquired cultural objects (DCMS, 2000 ('the ITAP Report'): 20–21). The Convention has been, at the time of writing, adopted by 117 states.[12] Such widespread adoption makes it extremely valuable as a means of recovering unlawfully removed cultural objects.

The 1970 Convention is comprised of 26 Articles; those directly relevant to this discussion include Articles 6 to 9, which pertain to the movement of cultural property between member states. Articles 7b and 9 are the key provisions with regards to the Agreement and require member states to

[11] UNESCO; the United Nations Education, Science and Culture Organization.

[12] These 117 states parties have either ratified, accepted, or are in the process of providing notification of succession, see http://portal.unesco.org/la/convention.asp?KO=13039&language=E.

introduce a system of export licences to prohibit the export of cultural property unless it is accompanied by an export licence. The 1970 Convention allows emergency export bans to be adopted when the cultural heritage of a state party is seriously endangered due to intense looting (DCMS, 2000: 20 fn 19). Article 7 specifically contains provisions governing the return of cultural property at the request of another state party through diplomatic channels (DCMS, 2000: 20 fn 19).

The 1970 Convention created a framework enabling member states to protect cultural heritage, including antiquities, in times of peace.[13] Previously, it was up to individual states to care for their cultural property, which meant formally constructing unilateral, bilateral, and multilateral agreements to protect antiquities and cultural objects on an international scale. Papa Sokal (2006) explains that the draft of the Convention contained some very stringent obligations that many market nations would not accept, such as a commitment from art-importing nations to enforce the export control laws of other nations. The US delegation to UNESCO proposed limited procedures that centred on only two of the 26 Articles of the 1970 Convention; in this manner, the Convention was submitted to the US Senate for ratification in 1972. Unfortunately, after ratification the United States did not formally accede to the 1970 Convention until 1983 (Guthrie-Hingston, 1989; Papa Sokal, 2006). The 1970 Convention is not self-executing; therefore, signatory nations are obliged to create or adjust legislation in order to allow the 1970 Convention to take effect. The CPIA was created as a vehicle for the US government to implement the 1970 Convention; however, 'the Cultural Property Implementation [*sic*] Act is a compromise measure' (Guthrie-Hingston, 1989: 131) as it only implements Articles 7b and 9 of the 1970 Convention.

Article 7b authorises the government to enforce import restrictions on cultural property stolen from inventoried collections, such as those in museums in states party to the 1970 Convention (Magness-Gardiner, 2004: 33; Luke and Kersel, 2005: 195; Papa Sokal, 2006: 70–71). In addition, Article 7b allows the US government to take steps to recover and return property in response to a request from such states (Papa Sokal, 2006: 70). Article 9, as the US government implemented it, provides the mechanism with which the United States can create and enter into bilateral and multilateral agreements that involve import controls (Magness-Gardiner, 2004: 33; Papa Sokal, 2006: 72).

Article 9

Any State Party to this Convention whose cultural patrimony is in jeopardy from pillage of archaeological or ethnological materials may call upon other States

[13] The Hague Convention for the Protection of Cultural Property in the Event of Armed Conflict (1954) protects ancient and cultural property during times of conflict (Toman, 1996; O'Keefe, 1999).

> Parties who are affected. The States Parties to this Convention undertake, in these circumstances, to participate in a concerted international effort to determine and to carry out the necessary concrete measures, including the control of exports and imports and international commerce in the specific materials concerned. Pending agreement each State concerned shall take provisional measures to the extent feasible to prevent irremediable injury to the cultural heritage of the requesting State. (UNESCO Convention 1970: Article 9)

Implementation of Article 9 gives member states a tool to restrict imports and exports of artefacts, which is the mechanism that enables other countries to make requests to the United States for import restrictions on certain types of artefacts. The CPIA allows the US government to act upon requests by nations that have reason to believe that all or part of their cultural heritage is under threat from looting and that import restrictions in the United States would help to reduce the incentive to further pillage. Such requests are received and investigated on an individual basis by the Cultural Property Advisory Committee (CPAC) at the Department of State (Kouroupas, 1995: 86; Luke and Kersel, 2005: 195).

If the CPAC finds that import restrictions would indeed help reduce the threat of looting then a Memorandum of Understanding (MoU) may be entered into with the requesting nation. A designated list of artefact types under threat is drawn up and included in a federal register. These artefacts may not enter the United States unless they are accompanied by an official export licence from the country of origin or they can be proved to have left the country of origin before the import restriction took effect (Magness-Gardiner, 2003: 477). In the case of Italy, the bilateral agreement came into effect on 19 January 2001.[14] The CPIA compels requesting nations to demonstrate the following four determinations to the CPAC in order to be eligible to enter into a bilateral agreement with the United States:

> A) That the cultural patrimony of the State Party is in jeopardy from the pillage of archaeological or ethnological materials of the State Party;
> B) That the State Party has taken measures consistent with the Convention to protect its cultural patrimony;
> C) That i) the application of the import restrictions set forth in section 307 with respect to archaeological or ethnological material of the State Party, if applied in concert with similar restrictions implemented, or to be implemented within a reasonable period of time, by those nations (whether or not State Parties) individually having a significant import trade in such material, would be of substantial benefit in deterring a serious situation of pillage, and ii) remedies less drastic than the application of the restrictions set forth in such section are not available; and
> D) That the application of the import restrictions set forth in section 307 in the particular circumstances is consistent with the general interest of the

[14] See the Agreement, http://exchanges.state.gov/culprop/it01agr.html.

> international community in the interchange of cultural property among nations for scientific, cultural, and educational purposes. (CPIA, 1983, section 303.a.1)[15]

The onus to reduce the incentive to loot archaeological sites is clearly on Italy, as it must comply with, and attempt to satisfy, additional provisions specific to how it manages and protects cultural objects within its territory. The Italian Government must provide for:

1. Instituting more severe penalties and prompt prosecution of looters,
2. Regulating the use of metal detectors,
3. Providing additional training for the Carabinieri Special Unit for the Protection of Artistic Patrimony,
4. Intensifying the investigations of the Carabinieri Special Unit for the Protection of Artistic Patrimony on the looting of archaeological sites and on the routes of the smugglers of these artefacts. (The Agreement, 2001: Article II.C)

THE DESIGNATED LIST: INCONSISTENCIES AND OMISSIONS

Figure 4.2 displays the Central Italian artefact types documented in the Designated List. The list is accompanied by an image database giving generic photos of artefact types.[16] By compiling information from auction sales of these artefact types we can begin to understand the effect that the Agreement has had on the auction market and on a real or perceived reduction of the incentive to loot antiquities in the region.

The Federal Register and Image Database are representational tools that describe artefact types covered by the Agreement, not specific artefacts. They are not meant to be ethical tools for dealers to use as a way of personally monitoring the legitimacy of antiquities from Italy that they wish to import to the United States. Although the Designated List presents a large body of artefact types covered under the Agreement, two key problems remain; the first relates to inconsistencies in documenting certain types of artefacts, while the second relates to artefact types that are not included.

Regarding the inconsistencies, it is apparent that the protection of certain artefact types are only implied rather than explicitly stated. An example of implied inclusion is when one cannot find a reference to an artefact type in the text of the Designated List, but when the Image Database is consulted and often after a great deal of digging the artefact type is found in the image database. If an artefact type is not explicitly included in the text of the Designated List, but does appear in the image database then there can be some uncertainty in determining if the Agreement protects that

[15] For further explanation of US cultural property legislation see Bator (1983) and Papa Sokal (2006).

[16] See the Italy Image Collection, http://exchanges.state.gov/culprop/itimage.html.

	Stone		**Metal**
1	*Sculpture*	1	*Sculpture*
a	Architectural Elements	a	Large Statuary
b	Architectural and Non-Architectural Relief Sculpture	b	Small Statuary
c	Monuments	2	*Vessels*
d	Sepulchres	3	*Personal Ornaments*
e	Large Statuary	4	*Weapons and Armour*
		5	*Inscribed or Decorated Sheet Metal*
	Ceramics		**Glass**
1	*Sculpture*	1	*Architectual Elements*
a	Architectural Elements	2	*Sculpture*
b	Monuments	a	Intarsia
c	Large Statuary	b	Small Statuary
d	Objects with Relief Decoration		
2	*Vessels*		
a	Etruscan		
b	South Italian and Italic		**Painting**
c	Imported Vessels	1	*Wall Painting*
i	Attic Black-Figure, Red-Figure and White Ground Pottery	a	Domestic and Public Wall Painting
ii	Corinthian Pottery	b	Tomb Painting

Figure 4.2. The Designated List of the US–Italy Bilateral Agreement 2001
Note: See the Federal Register, http://exchanges.state.gov/culprop/it01fr01.html.

particular artefact type. This problem is particularly apparent with impasto artefacts, which do not appear in the Designated List, but are perhaps implied because they do appear in the Image Database; nevertheless these inconsistencies should be rectified considering the large volume of impasto antiquities on the market (Lobay, 2007).[17]

Another example relates to Faliscan ceramics, which are noted once in the Designated List, but specifically only those artefacts of 'Faliscan pottery in imitation of Attic red-figure, often in oversize vessels' (Designated List, 2001: Section III.B.1.B). Unfortunately, other Faliscan ceramics, such as buff-ware pottery, black glazed vessels, as well as various Etruscan red-ware ceramics from the heavily looted area north of Rome are excluded from the Agreement, suggesting that these artefact types are not protected.[18] For the purpose of clarity it would help to specify more clearly which Faliscan

[17] Section III B.1.A of the Designated List implies the inclusion of impasto artefacts; but considering the many different pottery shapes, from amphorae to utilitarian wares to biconical urns, observed on the market, clarity in distinguishing artefact types covered by the Designated List is desirable.

[18] Nørskov has recorded similar red- and black-figure artefacts; she states, 'the best objects of Attic red-figure were very seldom offered in catalogues of the kind used in the statistics, but were instead traded on the "invisible" market. The same argument applies to Etruscan art' (Nørskov, 2002a: 291).

types are included, and the Federal Register, Designated List Sections III.B.1 and III.B.2 should be amended accordingly.[19]

This lack of clarity is unacceptable when the purpose of the Agreement is to restrict specific categories of artefacts from entering the United States. The problem can be addressed by correcting the inconsistencies in the Designated List and Image Database. Creating a more coherent Agreement unfortunately does not completely create a disincentive to loot antiquities in Central Italy, but clearer definitions, as noted here, would make it easier to protect antiquities on the Designated List from illegal import to the United States.

The second key problem relates to artefact types that do not appear in either the Designated List or Image Database. The following list of artefact types require inclusion, which could take place when the Agreement is next reviewed:

- Bronze horse bits: these types are quite prevalent at auction.
- Agate, carnelian, and amber artefacts (generally figurines, amulets, and other jewellery types).
- Nenfro artefacts: appear at auction in similar quantities to other stone artefact types that are included on the list.
- Faliscan artefact types require more accurate consideration. As mentioned above, the term 'Faliscan' does appear in the Designated List, but strangely only in relation to one artefact type; oversize pottery vessels in imitation of Attic red-ware. All Faliscan pottery types should be included due to their frequent appearances on the market.
- There is no mention of Umbrian artefact types specifically; general terms perhaps cover this, but a more specific representation would be desirable.
- Terracotta figurines: consistently appear on the market (Lobay, 2007); while large statuary are included on the list there is no mention of small figurines.

FINDINGS IN RELATION TO PRE-ROMAN ANTIQUITIES FROM CENTRAL ITALY AT US ANTIQUITIES AUCTIONS 1997–2005

We can now examine the data gathered in relation to the three key indicators: volume, provenance, and auction sale prices. As noted above, the hypothesis is that an effectively functioning agreement would be evidenced by a reduction in market volume, increased frequency of provenance details included with artefact consignments, and an increase in sale price, due to

[19] It is, of course, not the point of the Agreement to cover 'all' artefact types or there would be no need for the Designated List; the point is that a high degree of clarity is in fact necessary in order to accurately protect antiquities.

the diminished supply. The quantitative data gathered from US auctions in this study constituted a total of 642 artefacts categorised into ceramics, metals, terracottas, and others during Period A (1997–2000) and Period B (2001–05). For the purposes of the broader study on which this chapter is based, artefacts were classified into a range of specific sub-categories (Lobay, 2007). Here, however, I report on some of the more general trends suggested by the data. We can examine our three indices in more detail here.

Volume

The data presented in Table 4.1 reveal that a reduction in the volume of Central Italian antiquities at auction did not occur.[20] In terms of the overall consignment volume per period, there was an increase of 39% in Period B over Period A. While a reduction in the overall volume of antiquities at US auctions is not apparent, certain isolated artefact types display notable declines in volume after 2001. The category of 'other' artefact types, including glass, agate, and carnelian objects, grouped together because they often appear in jewellery consignments, demonstrates a decline over time.

Table 4.1. Overall Aggregate Volume of Consignments (per provenance type) in the US during Periods A and B

Period A	Total Consignments	No Provenance	Name	Previous Sale	Vague
1997	24	13	11	0	0
1998	54	32	18	3	1
1999	73	26	42	5	0
2000	118	29	84	5	0
Total	269	100	155	13	1
Period B	**Total Consignments**	**No Provenance**	**Name**	**Previous Sale**	**Vague**
2001	113	33	26	54	0
2002	100	45	50	4	1
2003	31	13	14	4	0
2004	102	10	84	6	2
2005	27	7	12	8	0
Total	373	108	186	76	3

[20] I do not suggest that the antiquities referred to in Table 4.1 are illegally present on the market. I am proposing that a greater volume of objects appearing on the auction market suggests a sustained demand for antiquities. The significance of a sustained demand provides a continued incentive to loot archaeological sites.

Whether the decline in these particular artefact types can be attributed to the Agreement remains unclear. The general trend of an increasing consignment volume over time appeared in the United Kingdom as well, with a 20% increase over the same time period, with particularly large volumes apparent in 2001 and 2002.

Provenance

It is important to note that the inclusion of a published provenance is becoming more common and provenance descriptions in general are presented in a more consistent manner in US auctions (see Table 4.1 above). This assertion is further substantiated in Lobay (2007); the use of provenance descriptions at auction sales is higher now than at any time since 1970, which is extremely positive.

Consigned antiquities published with the name of a specific person increased by 20% from Period A to Period B, which is certainly positive. Unfortunately, the use of previous sales as provenance increased considerably over time. Previous sales provide adequate provenance under the terms of the Agreement because it is not retrospective, meaning all antiquities demonstrated to have been located in the United States prior to implementation of the Agreement in January 2001 do not fall under its remit. Even though provenance is being used with greater frequency, it is misleading to call this a complete success. The problem is that previous sale information, even if it is verifiable, only reveals the location of an artefact prior to a specific date; it does not contribute to a better understanding of the legitimacy of an artefact.[21]

In the United Kingdom the use of names provided with provenance details increased dramatically, but the rise in previous sale use was not as dramatic as in the United States. Vague provenance also increased, although the number of observable examples were few.

Realised Prices

Table 4.2 reveals the changes in realised prices of artefact types during the two periods. Although average realised prices in the metals and other artefacts categories reduced, those in the ceramics and terracotta categories increased. This demonstrates that the realised price data is inconclusive

[21] The inclusion of previous sale information does help to provide the sale history of an object, and if it has appeared at auction, verifying the claim is often straightforward. However, if the object is described as having been sold in an obscure or now out-of-business dealer's shop, then it is very difficult to verify the claim. Previous sale information lacks potential for substantiating the legitimacy of objects because of its unreliable nature.

Table 4.2. Average Realised Prices at US Auctions per Artefact Type, 1997–2005

Metals

Period	Arms/Armour	Implements	Vessels	Sculpture	Gold	Others	Average Price
A	27,882.21*	9,964.56	36,683.73	18,083.73	22,877.20	<>	19,248.57
B	5,775.50*	9,105.00	20,698.00	20,199.00	1,967.10*	1,018.56*	9,793.86

Ceramics

Period	Pottery	Impasto	Black Figure	Red Figure	Bucchero	Others	Non-vessels	Average Price
A	15,034.50	6,294.94	11,173.90	11,789.91	7,264.20	12,547.00*	<>	9,157.78
B	8,498.00	15,224.00	14,187.00	9,120.00	5,073.40	15,063.21*	<>	9,595.09

Terracotta

Period	Architectural	Sculptural	Vessels	Sepulchres	Average Price
A	4,647.40	23,283.70	<>	5,797.53*	8,432.16
B	5,304.00	28,328.54	<>	10,908.81*	11,135.34

Other

Period	Glass/Gems	Various	Stone Architectural	Stone Sculpture	Stone Sepulchre	Average Price
A	1,626.34	1,592.74	54,559.42*	<>	23,187.76*	16,193.25
B	3,120.00*	590.23	<>	12,000.00*	<>	3,142.05

Notes: All prices are in US dollars and adjusted to December 2005 prices.
* indicates that only one artefact was observed; <> indicates that none were observed.

in demonstrating a reduction in demand and by extension a reduction in the incentive to loot antiquities. As noted, data on realised prices suffer the most from the paltry amount of information available because only single artefacts in single lots can be used, but it is hoped that the inclusion of this information at least gives the reader a sense of the prices realised for Central Italian antiquities, which are attractive to both the open and invisible markets. In the United Kingdom realised prices for all four artefact categories increased over time.

THE AGREEMENT IN A GLOBAL MARKET CONTEXT

Whatever impact the Agreement might have on the US market for Central Italian antiquities, the United States represents only one, albeit large, part of a global trade in antiquities. There are other markets available which may take up the slack caused by displacement from the United States; in particular, the large UK market. US policy changes can be subsequently undermined because of the consistently high volume of consignments in the United Kingdom and the international nature of the antiquities trade and collectors. Consistency in policy changes would provide the greatest protection to cultural property if implemented by multiple market nations.[22]

While export controls can inadvertently control supply and demand they generally do not take economic principles into consideration, thus demand cannot be satisfied and is driven underground (Park, 2002: 941). Prohibitive regulations have also been demonstrated to be ineffective (Mackenzie, 2002). The Agreement recognises these problems; it is not a blanket ban on all Italian artefacts. Legitimate trading conduits—the auction sales discussed here being only one kind—are retained, making it a very useful framework and one that is quite straightforward in its application. In terms of supply and prices, an interesting paradox arises; namely, that a reduced supply of artefacts should increase prices, but higher prices would increase the incentive to loot antiquities. This suggests that any regulation that has a negative impact on the supply of antiquities available to the market would inadvertently increase the incentive to loot since a reduced supply should increase prices.

If the premise holds that the market drives the incentive to loot artefacts (Renfrew, 1993; Elia, 2001) then a better understanding of the relative demand for specific artefact types on the auction market can help us

[22] In the United Kingdom, the Dealing in Cultural Objects (Offences) Act 2003 must be mentioned, but it does not protect antiquities at source in the same way as the Agreement. Also, important new legislation in Switzerland has been passed that strengthens previously relaxed regulations on the trading of cultural objects (Gerstenblith, 2006; Weber, 2006).

better protect antiquities. Recording the types of artefacts seized from apprehended looters is also a good way of establishing demand and, by extension, establishing which regulatory mechanisms should be applied to protect artefacts from specific regions. Market monitoring can help to verify links between artefact types found in the possession of looters and those on the market. These links can help build a better understanding of the relationship between artefacts, looters, the public and invisible markets and of the impact of new regulations applied to antiquities trading. Recent reports suggest that the number of looters in Italy is reducing (David, 2007). But, since a demand for artefacts clearly remains in market nations such as the United States and the United Kingdom, if there is such a reduction it would appear to be the result of other factors deterring looters in Central Italy; it seems, for example, that the augmented Carabinieri art squad is making a significant impact.[23]

There is also of course, the invisible market to consider, which operates completely outside the public eye. Due to the inherent secrecy in this market, information is not readily available and it is only recently that reliable data have begun to emerge—specifically from contact with looters (Thoden van Velzen, 1996; Watson, 1997; Watson and Todeschini, 2006). For this reason, auction sales are a positive trading venue because they occur publicly and can be monitored, while the invisible market is secretive and cannot be easily monitored. The invisible market must be addressed more effectively and the Carabinieri must continue to function in their increased capacity.

As illustrated in Table 4.1, the volume of antiquities in circulation on the US auction market increased after implementation during the 2001–05 period; this increase represents the largest increase in Central Italian antiquities consignments than at any time since 1970 (Lobay, 2007). Prices of artefact types remain inconclusive in their ability to inform the incentive reduction debate due to the small number of observable single-object auction lots appropriate for this measure. The increased use of provenance descriptions is a very positive development, which demonstrates the worth of the Agreement. Although a substantial number of those provenance descriptions are of previous sales or provide only vague descriptions, the overall trend to include more details is useful for increasing monitoring capabilities within the market.

Within the Federal Register, the Designated List and Image Database could be redesigned to address the inconsistencies and omissions mentioned; this would provide the Agreement with a greater degree of clarity enhancing the accuracy and efficiency of its import control functions.

[23] In 1995 the Carabinieri increased their resources and personnel dedicated to addressing cultural property protection (Benedetti-Aloisi, 1997; Isman, 2002; Watson and Todeschini, 2006).

In 2006 the Agreement was renewed for another five years.[24] An assessment focusing specifically on how well the Agreement is reducing the incentive to loot antiquities should occur during the next renewal process in 2011. This assessment should explore volume, provenance, and price changes in market activity, looting in Central Italy, and the regulatory climate in market nations. Determining links between the market, looters, and the regulatory framework would allow the Agreement to be adjusted to maximise its protective capacity. In addition to import controls, the Agreement is initiating cultural exchanges and scientific programmes, and has the potential to double its utility as a due diligence mechanism. The Agreement creates an effective venue for diplomatic contact and heightened governmental obligations; such relations between the United States and Italy can help negotiate an effective interface between archaeologists, governmental policy leaders, and antiquities dealers that, in time, might have an effect on reducing the incentive to loot antiquities in Central Italy. However, inroads into the operation and scale of the invisible market must also be understood to better protect antiquities and to better equip regulatory mechanisms such as the Agreement.

CONCLUSION

The present study used three indicators—volume, provenance, and realised prices—to investigate the hypothesis that the Agreement should reduce the incentive to loot antiquities in Central Italy by reducing the volume of antiquities on the market, increasing provenance usage, and increasing prices. Two of the three indicators have not achieved their goals; volume has increased over time, and realised prices, albeit with a very poor set of observable examples, returned an inconclusive result. On the basis of this investigation, the Agreement does not seem to have achieved an incentive reduction effect. What it has achieved is meeting the goal of the third indicator and encouraging auction houses to pay more attention to provenance. Unfortunately, the type of provenance information which is becoming common is references to previous sales. For the reasons stated above, previous sales do not provide sufficient protection against the purchase of looted artefacts, although the increased use of provenance descriptions in general is indeed positive.

The fact that regulations such as the Agreement have not been invoked in other major market nations, such as in the United Kingdom, undermines incentive reduction initiatives implemented by US policy makers. This

[24] See Extension and Amendment to the Agreement, http://exchanges.state.gov/culprop/it06agr.html.

signals the need for increased international integration of approaches to this global problem. An international, inter-disciplinary community of scholars has grown up around the antiquities market and the potential these scholars bring for creating new antiquities monitoring mechanisms must be developed.

REFERENCES

Legislation, Policy Documents and International Conventions

Cultural Property Implementation Act (CPIA), (1983) Law 97–446 [HR 4566], 96 Stat. 2329, approved 12 January 1983. http://exchanges.state.gov/culprop/97–446.html, accessed 9 July 2005.

DCMS (Department for Culture, Media and Sport) (2000) *Ministerial Advisory Panel on Illicit Trade Report* ['the ITAP Report'] (London: DCMS).

Dealing in Cultural Objects (Offences) Act 2003.

Extension and Amendment to the Agreement between the Government of the United States of America and the Government of the Republic of Italy (2001) Concerning the Imposition of Import Restrictions on Categories of Archaeological Material Representing the Pre-Classical, Classical and Imperial Roman Periods of Italy, 19 January 2006, http://exchanges.state.gov/culprop/it06agr.html, accessed 7 June 2006.

Federal Register Notice, 23 January (2001) 66(15): 7399–7402, *Import Restrictions* Imposed on Archaeological Material originating in Italy and Representing the Pre-Classical, Classical, and Imperial Roman Periods, http://exchanges.state.gov/culprop/it01fr01.html, accessed 9 July 2001.

HC 371-II Deb, 25 July 2000, *Cultural Property: Return and Illicit Trade, Evidence, Vol 2*, www.publications.parliament.uk/pa/cm199900/cmselect/cmcumeds/371/37102.htm#evidence, accessed 17 February 2005.

Italy Image Collection, (2001) *Illustrations of Artifact Categories Subject to U.S. Import Restriction*. http://exchanges.state.gov/culprop/itimage.html, accessed 9 July 2001.

UNESCO, Hague Convention for the Protection of Cultural Property In the Event of Armed Conflict (1954), http://portal.unesco.org/en/ev.phpURL_ID=15391&URLDO=DO TOPIC&URLSECTION=201.html, accessed 11 June 2006.

UNESCO Convention on the Means of Prohibiting and Preventing the Illicit Import, Export and Transfer of Ownership of Cultural Property (1970), http://portal.unescoorg/en/ev.phpURL_ID=13039&URL_DO=DO_TOPIC&URL_SECTION=201.html, accessed 11 June 2006.

US–Italy Bilateral Agreement (2001) Concerning the Imposition of Import Restrictions on Categories of Archaeological Material Representing the Pre-Classical, Classical, and Imperial Roman Periods of Italy, 23 January 2001, http://exchanges.state.gov/culprop/it01agr.html, accessed 9 July 2005.

USA Department of State, Chart of Emergency Actions and Bilateral Agreements (2007), http://exchanges.state.gov/culprop/chart.html, accessed 2 August 2007.

Secondary Sources

Bator, P (1983) *The International Trade in Art* (Chicago, University of Chicago Press).

Benedetti-Aloisi, FM (1997) 'Sistemi di Beni Culturali e Tutela: Aspetti Della Lotta alle Reti Criminali', *La Gestione del Patrimonio Culturale, Sistemi di Beni Culturali e Ambienale, Atti del II Colloquio Internazionale*, Viterbo, 5–8 December.

Brodie, N, Doole, J, and Watson, P (2000) *Stealing History: The Illicit Trade in Cultural Material: Report for the Museums Association* (Cambridge, McDonald Institute).

Chippindale, C and Gill, D (2000) 'Material Consequences of Contemporary Classical Collecting' 104 *American Journal of Archaeology* 463–511.

Coggins, C (1995) 'A Licit International Traffic in Ancient Art: Let there be Light!', 4 *International Journal of Cultural Property* 61–80.

David, A (2007) 'Modern-day 'Tomb Raiders' Feel the Heat', www.msnbc.msncom/id/19585643/.from/ET/, accessed 6 July 2007.

Dennis, G (1883) *The Cities and Cemeteries of Etruria* (London, John Murray).

Elia, RJ (2001) 'Analysis of the Looting, Selling, and Collecting of Apulian Red-Figure Vases: a Quantitative Approach' in N Brodie, J Doole, and C Renfrew (eds), *Trade in Illicit Antiquities: the Destruction of the World's Archaeological Heritage* (Cambridge, McDonald Institute), pp 145–53.

George, R (2005) 'The Great Smash and Grab' *The Independent on Sunday*, 1 May, 27–30.

Gerstenblith, P (2006) 'Recent United States Legal Developments in the Protection of the Archaeological Heritage' in N Brodie, M Kersel, C Luke, and K Walker-Tubb (eds), *Archaeology, Cultural Heritage, and the Trade in Antiquities* (Gainesville, University of Florida Press), pp 134–87.

Gill, D and Chippindale, C (1993) 'Material and Intellectual Consequences of Esteem for Cycladic Figures' 97 *American Journal of Archaeology* 601–59.

Guthrie-Hingston, A (1989) 'US Implementation of the UNESCO Cultural Property Convention' in P Mauch-Messenger (ed), *The Ethics of Collecting Cultural Property: Whose Culture? Whose Property?* (Albuquerque, University of New Mexico Press), pp 129–48.

Haynes, S (2000) *Etruscan Civilization: A Culture History* (London, British Museum Press).

Herscher, E (1989) 'International Control Efforts: are There Any Good Solutions?' in P Mauch-Messenger (ed), *The Ethics of Collecting Cultural Property: Whose Culture? Whose Property?* (Albuquerque, University of New Mexico Press), pp 117–28.

Holloway, RR (1994) *The Archaeology of Early Rome and Latium* (London, Routledge).

Isman, F (2001) 'Sleuthing with Italy's Art Squad', *The Courier UNESCO*, April, www.unesco.org/courier/2001_04/uk/doss24.htm, accessed 10 April 2006.

Kouroupas, M (1995) 'United States Efforts to Protect Cultural Property: Implementation of the 1970 UNESCO Convention' in K Walker-Tubb (ed), *Antiquities Trade or Betrayed: Legal, Ethical and Conservation Issues* (London, Archetype), pp 83–93.

Lobay, G (2007) *Objects and Objectivity: An Archaeology of Auctions. Central Italian Antiquities at Bonhams, Christie's and Sotheby's 1970–2005* (Unpublished PhD Thesis, University of Cambridge, Homerton College).

Luke, C and Kersel, M (2005) 'A Retrospective and a Look Forward', 30 *Journal of Field Archaeology* 191–200.

Mackenzie, S (2002) 'Illicit Antiquities, Criminological Theory and the Deterrent Power of Criminal Sanctions for Targeted Populations', 7 *Art, Antiquity and Law* 125–62.

—— (2005a) 'Dig a Bit Deeper: Law, Regulation and the Illicit Antiquities Market', 45 *British Journal of Criminology* 249–68.

—— (2005b) *Going, Going, Gone: Regulating the Market in Illicit Antiquities* (Leicester, Institute of Art and Law).

Magness-Gardiner, B (2003) 'Long-term Archaeological Loans from Italy: Summary of Roundtable Discussions', 107 *American Journal of Archaeology* 477–81.

—— (2004) 'International Conventions and Cultural Heritage Protection' in Y Rowan and V Baram (eds), *Marketing Heritage: Archaeology and the Consumption of the Past* (Walnut Creek, Altamira), pp 27–39.

Neuman, WL (1997) *Social Research Methods: Qualitative and Quantitative Approaches* (Boston, Allyn and Bacon).

Nørskov, V (2002a) *Greek Vases in New Contexts: The Collecting and Trading of Greek Vases—An Aspect of the Modern Reception of Antiquity* (Aarhus, Aarhus University Press).

—— (2002b) 'Greek Vases for Sale: Some Statistical Evidence' in N Brodie and K Walker-Tubb (eds), *Illicit Antiquities The Theft of Culture and the Extinction of Archaeology* (London, Routledge), pp 23–37.

O'Keefe, R (1999) 'The Meaning of "Cultural Property" under the 1954 Hague Convention', 46 *Netherlands International Law Review* 26–56.

Palmer, N (1994) 'Recovering Stolen Art', 47 *Current Legal Problems* 215–54.

Papa Sokal, M (2006) 'The US Response to the Protection of World Cultural Heritage' in N Brodie, M Kersel, C Luke, and K Walker-Tubb (eds), *Archaeology, Cultural Heritage, and the Trade in Antiquities* (Gainesville, University of Florida Press), pp 69–133.

Park, S (2002) 'The Cultural Property Regime in Italy: an Industrialized Source Nation's Difficulties in Retaining and Recovering its Antiquities', 23 *University of Pennsylvania Journal of International Economic Law* 931–54.

Pastore, G (2001) 'The Looting of Archaeological Sites in Italy' in N Brodie, J Doole, and C Renfrew (eds), *Trade in Illicit Antiquities: the Destruction of the World's Archaeological Heritage* (Cambridge, McDonald Institute), pp 155–60.

Polk, K (2000) 'The Antiquities Trade Viewed as a Criminal Market', September *Hong Kong Lawyer* 82.

Prott, LV and O'Keefe, P (1989) *Law and the Cultural Heritage, Volume 3: Movement* (London, Butterworths).

Prott, LV (1998) 'UNESCO and UNIDROIT: A Partnership Against Trafficking in Cultural Objects' in N Palmer (ed), *The Recovery of Stolen Art: A Collection of Essays* (London, Kluwer Law International), pp 205–15.

Renfrew, C (1993) 'Viewpoint: Collectors are the Real Looters', 46 *Archaeology* 16–17.

—— (2000) *Loot, Legitimacy and Ownership* (London, Duckworth).

Renfrew, C and Bahn, P (1996) *Archaeology Theories, Methods, and Practice* (London, Thames & Hudson).

Smith, CJ (1996) *Early Rome and Latium Economy and Society c.1000–500BC* (Oxford, Clarendon).

Smith, CW (1989) *Auctions: the Social Construction of Value* (London, Harvester).

Spivey, N (1997) *Etruscan Art* (London, Thames and Hudson).

Thoden van Velzen, D (1996) 'The World of Tuscan Tomb Robbers: Living with the Local Community and the Ancestors', 5 *International Journal of Cultural Property* 111–26.

Toman, J (1996) *The Protection of Cultural Property in the Event of Armed Conflict* (Paris, UNESCO).

Watson, P (1997) *Sotheby's: Inside Story* (London, Bloomsbury).

—— (2006) 'Convicted Dealers: What it Tells Us' in N Brodie, M Kersel, C Luke, and K Walker-Tubb (eds), *Archaeology, Cultural Heritage and the Antiquities Trade* (Gainesville, University of Florida Press), pp 188–97.

Watson, P, and Todeschini, C (2006) *The Medici Conspiracy* (New York, Public Affairs Books).

Weber, M (2006) 'New Swiss Legislation on Cultural Property' 13 *International Journal of Cultural Property* 99–113.

Part III

Supply of Looted Antiquities

5

The United Kingdom as a Source Country

Some Problems in Regulating the Market in UK Antiquities and the Challenge of the Internet

ROGER BLAND

INTRODUCTION

IN DISCUSSIONS OF cultural property issues, and the trade in antiquities in particular, it has become conventional to regard the world as being divided into source countries and market countries. On this view, source countries are rich in antiquities but generally have only a restricted market in them. Market countries are those into which the antiquities that are discovered in the source countries are attracted, as if by a magnetic force. Under this model the wealthiest collectors reside in the market countries such as the United States, Europe, and Japan, and the market flourishes in those countries because it is there that the objects will sell for the highest prices (Merryman, 1994).

This is a useful model which has served well for over 10 years but, like all such models, it is an over-simplification, as the market countries themselves can be the source of important antiquities. That is certainly the case with the United Kingdom, which, according to a market survey carried out in 2002, had the second biggest art market in the world, with 25 per cent of the world market—second only to the United States, with 47 per cent (Kusin and Company, 2002)—although the market in antiquities only forms a small part of this.[1] On the other hand, the United Kingdom

[1] The ITAP Report (DCMS, 2000: 46) suggested that the market in antiquities and coins may only account for about 2% of the total art market, but hard figures in this area are very difficult to establish as the data necessarily come from the market players themselves, who may wish to downplay the size of the antiquities market.

is undoubtedly very rich in antiquities, as can be shown by the results of the Treasure Act 1996 and the Portable Antiquities Scheme: in 2007, 744 finds were reported as treasure (compared with an average of 25 finds a year that were being declared treasure trove before the law changed in 1996), and 77,606 objects were recorded by the Portable Antiquities Scheme.

This chapter looks at some of the tensions posed by the fact that there is a large and flourishing art market in the United Kingdom while it is also a country rich in archaeology. It is an area in which the government has made great progress during the last 10 years, starting with introduction of the Treasure Act 1996 and first Portable Antiquities pilot schemes in 1997, both of which provide protection to objects found in England and Wales.

In 2000 the Culture, Media and Sport Select Committee undertook an inquiry into cultural property (House of Commons CMS Committee, 2000) which led directly to the establishment by the Department for Culture, Media and Sport (DCMS) of the Illicit Trade Advisory Panel (ITAP) under the chairmanship of Professor Norman Palmer. The publication that year by the Museums Association and the International Council of Museums of the report *Stealing History* (Brodie, Doole, and Watson, 2000) was also influential in raising the issue of the illicit trade in antiquities higher up the agenda. In December 2000 the DCMS published the ITAP Report (DCMS, 2000), which in turn led in 2002 to the United Kingdom's accession to the 1970 UNESCO Convention; in the following year to the passage by Parliament of the Dealing in Cultural Objects (Offences) Act 2003; in 2005 to the publication of acquisition guidelines for museums, libraries, and archives (DCMS, 2005); and in February 2007 to the establishment by the Museums, Libraries and Archives Council of a website giving advice on issues relating to the buying and selling of cultural objects.[2] The government also announced its intention to publish a draft Bill to implement the Hague Convention in 2007, and the clauses that gave effect to that were included in the Heritage Protection Bill that was published in draft in April 2008. However, that Bill was not included in the government's legislative programme for 2008/09 and at the time of writing its future is still uncertain.

At the same time, the art market itself has changed rapidly in the last 10 years, in particular with the great growth in the use of the Internet as a medium for sales. While many dealers and auction houses sell objects from their own websites, one site in particular, eBay, has risen to prominence, becoming what is probably the largest single outlet worldwide for cultural goods in general and antiquities in particular.

2 www.culturalpropertyadvice.gov.uk.

THE CURRENT LEGAL FRAMEWORK IN ENGLAND AND WALES

The Treasure Act 1996

Until 1997, effectively the only legal protection afforded to antiquities found in England and Wales was provided by the common law of treasure trove. Only objects of gold or silver that had been deliberately hidden, with the intention of recovery, qualified as treasure trove and became the property of the Crown (Hill, 1936). Treasure trove was historically one of the feudal rights of the Crown and was never intended as an antiquities law, although from 1886, when the Treasury began to pay ex gratia rewards to finders, it operated as that. It was extremely restricted in scope, riddled with anomalies, and was legally unenforceable.

The Treasure Act was the culmination of a long series of unsuccessful attempts to reform the common law of treasure trove. The final, and successful, attempt to reform the law was started by the Surrey Archaeological Society at the end of the 1980s, a response to the looting by metal detector-users of the site at Wanborough (O'Connell and Bird, 1994) where a very large hoard of Iron Age coins had been systematically stolen by detectorists, and great damage was done to the Romano-Celtic temple there; subsequent prosecutions failed because of the deficiencies of the common law of treasure trove (Palmer, 1993; Bland, 1996).

The Treasure Act passed through Parliament in 1996 and came into effect on 24 September 1997 (Bland, 2005).[3] It has effect in England, Wales, and Northern Ireland (DCMS, 2002), but not Scotland.[4] Under the Treasure Act 1996 the following finds are treasure, provided they were found after 24 September 1997:

(a) objects other than coins, at least 300 years old, with a minimum precious metal content of 10 per cent;
(b) all groups of coins from the same find at least 300 years old (if the coins have a precious metal content of less than 10 per cent then the hoard must consist of at least 10 coins); and
(c) objects found in association with treasure.
From 1 January 2003 the Act was extended by Order to include:
(d) groups of prehistoric base-metal objects from the same find.

Objects belonging to their original owner or his or her heirs are excluded, as are unworked natural objects (such as fossils) and wreck.

[3] However, even after the implementation of the Treasure Act 1996, the great majority of objects found by members of the public (principally metal detector-users, who find 95% of treasure cases) are not treasure.

[4] Scotland has a completely separate legal framework governing finds: there is, in effect, a legal requirement to report all finds (Saville, 2002; Normand, 2003).

Finders have a legal obligation to report finds which they believe to be treasure within 14 days, and there is a maximum penalty of three months' imprisonment or a £5,000 fine for failure to report without a reasonable excuse. Any object that a museum wishes to acquire is valued by a committee of independent experts, the Treasure Valuation Committee, whose remit is to determine the full market value of the object in question. The reward is normally divided equally between the finder and landowner. The Committee is advised by a panel of valuers drawn from the trade, and interested parties can commission their own valuations which the Committee will consider. The Committee can recommend that the reward be reduced or not paid at all if there is evidence of wrongdoing, and once a valuation has been agreed museums have up to four months to raise money. Archaeologists are not eligible for rewards (DCMS, 2002).

In 2001 there was a review of the Act (DCMS, 2001) which recommended, among other things, that the definition of treasure be extended to include prehistoric base-metal hoards, and an Order implementing this, together with a revision of the Code of Practice, came into effect in January 2003 (DCMS, 2002). A further review of the Act was due in 2007 but is now awaiting the final outcome of the Coroners and Justice Bill being debated in Parliament in 2009, as this Bill is expected to make amendments to the Treasure Act.

Non-Treasure Finds

In the case of all archaeological finds which fall outside the definition of treasure, the owner of the land where the find was made generally has a superior claim to the find than the finder if the object was buried in the ground (*Waverley Borough Council v Fletcher* [1996] QB 334). The finder may have a better claim to objects found lying on the surface in public places, such as airports (*Parker v British Airways* [1982] QB 1004), but of course archaeological finds are unlikely to be made in such circumstances.

Metal Detecting

Metal detecting is legal in England and Wales, provided the detector-user has the permission of the landowner and avoids scheduled monuments, which are protected by the Ancient Monuments and Archaeological Areas Act 1979. Under section 42 of this Act it is an offence to use a metal detector on protected sites without the consent of English Heritage. There are some 19,500 scheduled monuments in England, although this only represents a small proportion of the total number of archaeological sites known.

It is impossible to obtain a precise figure on the number of active metal detector-users in England and Wales: figures of 30,000 from 1995 and 180,000 from 1980 (Dobinson and Denison, 1995) are frequently quoted but may well have been over-estimates. A survey carried out by the Portable Antiquities Scheme (PAS) in 2007 (unpublished) showed that there were at least 6,227 members of 171 metal detecting clubs in England and Wales, and that PAS staff are also in touch with some 1,365 independent detector-users who are not members of any club, and it is possible that there are as many independent detector-users again who do not report finds to PAS. On this basis the total number of active detector-users might be around 9,000 in all (Bland, 2006 suggested 8,000); a figure of 10,000 has also been suggested (Barford, 2006). In 2007 some 4,308 metal detector-users offered finds for recording under the Portable Antiquities Scheme. It does seem, therefore, that there are fewer active detector-users now than there were 10 or 20 years ago.

Illegal Metal Detecting

Illegal metal detecting, sometimes known as 'nighthawking' (that is metal detecting on land without the permission of the landowner, metal detecting on scheduled monuments, or failing to report treasure finds), is a significant problem in parts of England and Wales. In 1995 the Council of British Archaeology carried out a survey (Dobinson and Denison, 1995) which found that over a five-year period there was evidence that 188 Scheduled Ancient Monuments had been attacked by unauthorised metal detector-users, and that 37 out of 50 (74%) professional archaeological units reported raids on their excavation sites during the same period. Some well-known sites seem to act as a honey-pot for illicit detectorists: one such, the Roman site at Corbridge in Northumberland, had suffered 23 raids over four years. In 2007–08 Wessex Archaeology carried out a survey of nighthawks and nighthawking across the United Kingdom, which has been funded by a consortium of national heritage bodies and museums, and this was published in February 2009 (Oxford Archaeology 2009). Significantly, the results seem to show that nighthawking was less of a problem in 2008 than in 1995: only 15 out of 54 archaeological units reported that their excavations had been affected by nighthawking (28%), while only 70 scheduled sites were reported as having been attacked.

THE PORTABLE ANTIQUITIES SCHEME

Only a very small proportion of all archaeological objects that are found fall under the scope of the Treasure Act 1996, and archaeologists have rightly pointed out that the definition of treasure is still heavily rooted in the old treasure trove concept that precious-metal artefacts were the only objects worth saving. For this reason the government also funds the Portable Antiquities Scheme, first established as a number of pilot schemes in 1997 and extended across the whole of England and Wales from the end of 2003. The Scheme encourages all members of the public who find archaeological objects (those more than 300 years old) to report them voluntarily to a network of locally based Finds Liaison Officers (FLOs).

The Portable Antiquities Scheme, which has a total of 47 staff and is run from the British Museum, is now having a major impact on our understanding of the history and archaeology of England and Wales. In 2007, 77,606 finds were recorded and the online database[5] now contains records of over 360,000 objects: it is believed to be the largest database of its kind in the world. The FLOs also provide an essential resource to help finders to report treasure finds and, since the Scheme was extended nationally in 2003, the number of finds of treasure reported has risen from 201 in 1998 to 744 in 2007.

The Scheme has done a great deal to raise standards of metal detecting, and in May 2006 it published a Code of Practice on Responsible Metal Detecting in England and Wales,[6] endorsed by all the leading metal detecting, archaeological, and museum bodies, which for the first time provides an agreed definition of what constitutes 'responsible' metal detecting. The two key elements in it are to avoid damaging archaeological sites, whether scheduled or not, and to report all finds.

No other country has anything quite like the Portable Antiquities Scheme with its national network of archaeologists whose role is proactively to make contact with the detector-users and others who make finds, to record what they find, and to educate them in good practice. The Scheme is in fact a product of the unusually liberal framework governing discovered antiquities that exists in England and Wales and it would be difficult to establish a similar operation in the great majority of countries, which have laws requiring most finds to be reported and which also exercise strict controls over metal detecting.

INTERNET SALES: eBay

A key element of public policy in this area should be to make it harder for thieves to sell their finds. It is still too easy for illicit detector-users to sell their finds to dealers who are happy to purchase such objects without checking that the vendors are acting legally, with the agreement of the landowners. Many items of potential treasure are openly offered for sale on

[5] www.finds.org.uk.
[6] www.finds.org.uk/documents/CofP1.pdf.

the Internet, especially on eBay.[7] eBay, according to its own press release, was founded in 1995 and by May 2006 had 15 million users worldwide.[8] By June 2006 it had 10 million items for sale on its website at any one time, and 41.59 per cent of all active users of the Internet in the UK had visited eBay during the past month. Objects may be posted on eBay for between two and seven days, so, in order to be certain of missing nothing, it is necessary to visit the site every day, including weekends.

In August 2006 two volunteers at the British Museum, Maha Munir and Afra Morris, monitored antiquities offered for sale on www.eBay.co.uk (that is, the UK version of eBay) each week day (Lewis, 2007). They focused on potential treasure finds offered for sale on eBay because, although these only represent a small proportion of all British antiquities on eBay, they were the ones that seemed to offer the best possibility of further action. The British Museum had been aware for some time that a significant number of potential treasure finds were being sold on eBay and felt that the very open nature of the trade in these objects sent a poor signal to those detector-users who reported their treasure finds correctly.

Munir and Morris found that there were about 3,500 listings that were classified as 'antiquities' on eBay each day and of these some 600 'British antiquities' were offered for sale each day, 17 per cent of the total. Fifty-four of these 'British antiquities' were initially considered to be potential treasure finds. Twenty-four of the 54 finds were followed up through further enquiries and, as a result, eight (a third of the total) were subsequently considered not to be treasure. On this basis, it was estimated that perhaps two-thirds, or 36, of the 54 finds initially identified as potential treasure were indeed likely to be treasure.

Subsequent monitoring of eBay suggests that there may be a decline in the number of antiquities being sold on its website. In March 2007 the British Museum recorded the number of antiquities listed each day and found that on average there were 2,838 listings classified as 'antiquities', of which 541 were said to be 'British'. Since October 2007 the British Museum has been repeating this exercise and has found that the number of antiquities listed each day is slightly lower again, at 2,464 listings each day, of which an average of 418 items are classified as 'British'. Considerable caution is needed in interpreting these data, since the classification is selected by the vendor, and books on antiquities will be included among the 'antiquity' classification.

[7] The problem is not limited to eBay, although that is the largest internet site; many other dealers have their own websites offering antiquities for sale, and some of these too have potential treasure finds.

[8] These figures, and the following ones, come from the press release issued by the British Museum on 3 October 2006 announcing the Memorandum of Understanding between the British Museum and MLA and eBay (www.thebritishmuseum.ac.uk/newsroom/current2006/eBay%20Mou%20release.doc).

Likewise many of the items listed as British are clearly not from the United Kingdom.

In the 20 months between October 2006 and May 2008, the British Museum noted 290 cases of potential treasure listed on eBay, 144 for the calendar year 2007. The chart in Figure 5.1 below shows the monthly distribution of finds noted.

To put this number into context, 673 finds were reported as treasure in 2006 and 744 in 2007, so eBay would appear to be a significant outlet for unreported treasure finds. It can also be assumed that at least some of the UK antiquities sold on eBay that fall outside the scope of the Treasure Act 1996 will have been illegally recovered, but it is impossible to tell how big a proportion this might be. Since at no point does eBay ever actually physically handle the objects that are offered for sale on its website, it falls outside the scope of the new offence of dealing in tainted cultural objects created by the Dealing in Cultural Objects (Offences) Act 2003.

The British Museum first approached eBay in early 2004, and in September 2006, after discussions that took more than two and a half years, the British Museum and Museums, Libraries and Archives Council jointly agreed a memorandum of understanding with eBay whereby the museum will monitor eBay and notify the Art and Antiques Unit at Scotland Yard when it sees a find which it believes to be potential treasure. eBay will then take the find down from its website when it receives formal notification from the police, and the police may make further enquiries.[9]

Since the memorandum came into effect in October 2006, the British Museum has been monitoring eBay on a regular basis, generally once a week, but after 18 months the procedure of reporting finds believed to be treasure to the police has been invoked only once, although about 6 per cent

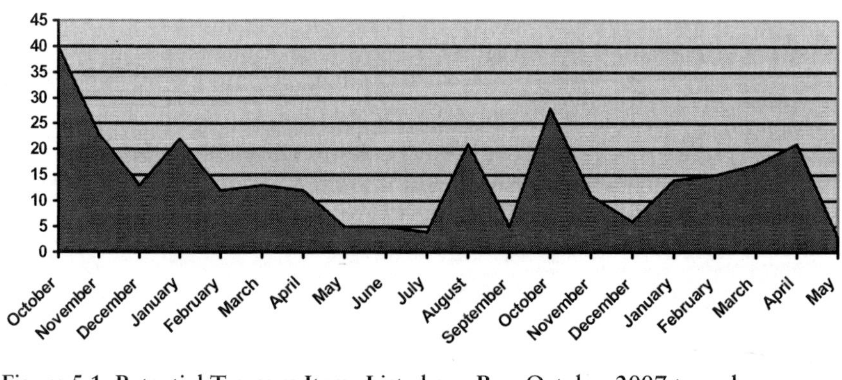

Figure 5.1. Potential Treasure Items Listed on eBay, October 2007 to end May 2008

[9] See www.finds.org.uk/treasure/ebay.php.

of vendors contacted have promised to report their finds. On the face of it, therefore, the memorandum would seem not to be worth the paper it is written on and it is certainly weaker than the British Museum would have liked: not only is the bar set very high by eBay before it will take finds down from the website—the British Museum more or less has to prove that a find will be treasure before eBay will act, whereas the Museum feels that eBay should take down finds if there is suspicion about them—but also eBay itself puts no resources into this checking, which is very time-consuming. However, there have been some benefits. The announcement of the agreement received very significant publicity in the media, which itself helped to raise awareness of the issues surrounding the laws concerning antiquities. In addition, eBay has developed its own guidance, 'Buying and Selling Antiquities Safely on eBay',[10] which is prominently available next to the antiquities listings.

In fact, monitoring eBay for treasure finds has clearly shown how difficult it is to prove that an object offered for sale should be reported under the Treasure Act 1996. Some of the responses given by vendors of potential treasure finds who were contacted by the British Museum are set out in Table 5.1, and these are extremely revealing. Some of the vendors when contacted appeared to be private individuals who were genuinely ignorant of their legal obligations and who voluntarily offered to report their finds as treasure. There have been about half a dozen cases of this in the five months since the British Museum has been monitoring eBay. These are encouraging and demonstrate the value of this exercise.

However, many more vendors are dealers who seem to be well aware of their obligations but who choose to evade them. The greatest difficulty as regards enforcing the Act lies in the fact that it is not retrospective and only applies to objects discovered after 24 September 1997. All a vendor has to say is that the object came from an old collection, or at least was found before September 1997, and it is difficult in practice to pursue the matter any further unless the item would have qualified as treasure trove under the old criteria. Another excuse frequently offered by vendors is to say that the object was purchased abroad. For some types of objects, such as Roman artefacts, most of which could have been found anywhere within the Roman Empire, this is more plausible than for other types of objects, such as Anglo-Saxon finds, which are likely only to have been found within England.

Most revealingly of all, many of those who sell potential treasure finds on eBay say that, because they did not find the objects, but purchased them from a third party (whether that third party was the finder or not), they have no obligation themselves to report them (see table). This is indeed technically correct: under section 8 of the Treasure Act 1996 the obligation to report rests solely with the finder. Of course, this response ignores the

[10] http://pages.ebay.co.uk/buy/guides/antiquities.

fact that, even if the person into whose hands an unreported treasure find has come does not himself have an obligation to report it under the Treasure Act 1996, he is dealing in stolen property, if the object can be shown to be treasure. However, for the reasons already noted, it is in fact still very difficult to prove that an object is treasure once it has left the ground and lost its provenance, so it will always be very difficult to prove that a vendor of a potential treasure find is dealing in stolen property. In June 2006 a draft Bill to reform coroners was published by the government (DCA, 2006: 90–96) and this provided the first opportunity to amend the Treasure Act 1996.[11] It included a proposal to extend the obligation to report treasure to anyone who came into possession of it, which would have provided a very useful way of making the obligation to report treasure much more enforceable. The Coroners and Justice Bill is, at the time of writing (August 2009), currently being debated in Parliament. Although the Bill contains a number of measures that relate to Treasure including, most importantly, a specialist Coroner for Treasure, the Government has omitted the clause in the 2006 draft Bill extending the obligation to report Treasure. This has been tabled as an amendment to the Bill by peers from the All-Party Parliamentary Archaeology Group and the final outcome is awaited.

Table 5.1. Some Responses from eBay Vendors Dealing in Potential Treasure Finds

A. Pre-Treasure Act 2006 finds	
Object	*Vendor's Response*
Medieval silver(?)—various finds	'All items here I found way back 1982–84, the only silver items are the coins—these are worn, and of not much interest, our local Finds Liaison Officer records our finds now at Reading Museum, I haven't found any treasure yet, but I shall keep trying.'
Post-Medieval silver button	'Old detecting finds from Yorkshire (Treasure Trove).'
Medieval gold brooch	'Yes, the gold brooch has been booked and numbered at Birmingham University. I do not have a date at present; it is extremely rare. I was given permission to do a dig just outside the grounds of Warwick Castle; I found it with a number of various coins from the same period. The brooch is one of two ever to have been found—the other is in the Musée de Cluny in Paris. Warwick Castle has a lot of French connections so that is thought why it was found there.'

(continued)

[11] Coroners have always had a role of inquiring into treasure since at least the twelfth century, and under the Treasure Act 1996 they retained this responsibility. The Coroners and Justice Bill will establish a single coroner for treasure.

Table 5.1. (Continued)

Post-Medieval silver fastener	'I have just in the past two weeks recorded all my finds which I have found in the past six months. This is not my find; a man found this in the 1980s, I told him that he should have reported it as treasure, but he didn't know of this at the time. I know all about the treasure trove and items being sold on eBay that are not recorded. In my eyes I'm a detectorist, not a dealer. And I do not think I'm breaking any law. I think, and told my local FLO that I think, a lot more finds as treasure would come to surface, if the British Museum did not hang on to the finds for one and a half years, which is far too long, and I know this as friends have put finds in as treasure to the British Museum. Thank you.'
B. Purchased from third parties	
Post-Medieval silver seal matrix	'This item was purchased by me from a coin fair that is held once a year in London (one of the UK's largest) many years ago. The information I have given in the listing is what I was told at the time. This fair had approximately a hundred reputable dealers all selling coins of all ages and thousands of artefacts and antiquities. I would assume all legal obligations that were required will have been taken into account by those dealers.'
Medieval silver finger ring	'I do not know where these items were found, I purchased them off eBay, I'm not the finder, I'm not a metal detector person, I'm 55 years old and registered disabled. I'm sure eBay will assist you with contacting the person who sold them to me. I love history and buy off eBay and sell to try and make a profit, as I'm disabled. I have very little money, my daughter bought my computer for me, thank you for talking to me … I have responded and answered all your questions, I have been polite and curious, I would now appreciate you cease this harassment, and deal with eBay and they will give you the details that is on eBay files of the finders who sold their property to me, as previously stated it is the finder that should declare their finds, I'm unable to provide any information you require, as only the finder has that information you require, I also wish to add by using my messages to harass me is against eBay rules as you are not involved in a open transaction with me, I will be informing eBay in relation to this harassment and infringement of eBay's rules and regulations.'

(continued)

Table 5.1. (Continued)

Medieval silver brooch	'Bought at an antiques fair in Newark 15 years ago.'
(?)Medieval gold finger ring	'Purchased in group of detector finds—it's the finder's responsibility to report.'
Medieval silver clasp	'Thank you for your message and the information contained. Unfortunately, I am unable to offer any information about this item as it was passed to me many years ago along with various other small antiquities in exchange for some coins I had at the time. I am aware of the Portable Antiquities Scheme and have presented all my personal finds to Ipswich Archaeology Unit. If I can help further please contact me.'
Post-Medieval silver clasp	'Bought from a chap at a fair last week.'
Medieval gilt silver finger ring	'Bought as part of house clearance.'
Post-Medieval silver seal matrix	'I am a keen metal detectorist and I am aware of having to report any gold or silver artefacts I may find as they could be treasure, as the gold ring I found last year at Connington and reported to the finds officer for the Cambridge area (was returned to me as it was not over 300 years old), however I am also a keen car boot enthusiast and this seal matrix was purchased from a stall at the last car boot sale I went to at Crystal Lakes car boot near Godmanchester. I always browse the stalls looking for coins, silver buttons, etc, and I came across this item.'
Medieval silver buckle	'I didn't find any of the coins or artefacts that I am currently selling or sold on eBay, the silver buckle was bought from a reputable dealer in coins and antiquities. I bought this buckle from his Christmas list 2004 in which as I recall he described it as a Byzantine silver buckle. The other artefact, Viking hack silver(?), I bought in May this year on eBay, the Roman(?) eagle mount I have on at the moment was also bought on eBay from a dealer (I bought two artefacts from him), the Stephen cut half was bought in September '05, the rest of coins were also bought recently off eBay.'
C. Purchased abroad	
Roman silver phallic pendant	'Object bought overseas.' Vendor said he was going to report the British Museum to eBay.

(continued)

Table 5.1. (Continued)

Early Medieval gold pendant	'Purchased at a German Antiquities Fair in the 1980s.'
Early Medieval silver pin	'Purchased from a Munich dealer in 2004.'
Roman gold finger ring	'Found in Anglo-France and inspected at the British Museum.'
Roman silver bracelet	'I am aware of the UK antiquities law and I consider it when selling my items. Thank you for contacting me, but there is none of my items that have been found on the territory of the UK. This bracelet origins from Italy. All of my items are bought from private collections of Central Europeans. Thank you again for the information.'
Early Medieval silver strap end	'This item is not found in the UK, and not in any way more than 10% silver. As far as I know there is no obligation to report this. Any further questions or queries on this or any other items feel free to ask.'
Medieval silver finger ring	'This ring is not British—most of my antiquities are not British. I am aware of your schemes and so no longer sell British gold and silver antiquities on eBay.'
D. Other reasons	
Early Medieval silver(?) rings	'I appreciate your concern but am quite confident these items have met the expectations required as per the Treasure Act. I will contact you shortly by private email to clarify this lot can remain for sale on eBay. I don't believe any of these rings are both silver or gold and date over 300 years old. The gold appear to be plated, and the silver are modern. The oldest appear to be brass/bronze, or whatever was the common base metal of the period. I collect Georgian items and most of these were actually dug in France and if absolutely necessary I can produce the item number of the auction to prove this. Having no interest in ancient finds the British Museum would certainly be welcome to anything I am selling off. All that being said, I am guessing the interest in this lot has gone? Please get back to me if you have any questions and trust me I'd fill your inbox with pictures if I actually thought I had something worthy of treasure. Take care.'

(continued)

Table 5.1. (Continued)

Medieval silver(?) dagger decoration	'We are established dealers and are fully aware of the requirements of the Treasure Act. We can confirm that this item was not treasure.'
Roman silver coins	'Nowhere in the description did I say this was a hoard. I am well aware of the treasure trove laws. These are a collection of single coin finds, from different sites, put together to sell as a job lot. Single finds of silver coins don't count as treasure under the new Act.'
Roman silver finger ring	'Whatever.'
E. Promised to report	
Post-Medieval gilt silver pinhead	'Didn't know what object was.' Seller said he would report it.
Medieval gold posy ring	'Bought from dealer.' Seller was unaware that he may have been breaking any laws, but has removed the ring from eBay and has taken it to his local Finds Liaison Officer to be reported.
Medieval silver button	Item taken off eBay, and seller will take the item to local Finds Liaison Officer to be recorded.
Medieval silver spur	'Happy to record.'

The systematic monitoring of eBay for finds of potential treasure has now been going on for 18 months, but it is still rather early to judge its effectiveness. The aim is that, in time, it will become known that offering potential treasure finds for sale on eBay and other websites is not risk-free, and that the number of such finds being offered for sale will decrease. But in order to monitor the trade properly, eBay and the other sites need to be checked daily and each positive result needs to be followed up, either by asking questions of the vendor or, sometimes, by passing information to the police. More resources are needed in order to pursue this work. eBay profits from the sale of objects on its website but it does not have any responsibility to check the provenance of objects sold on its website, as dealers have, since it does not actually handle the finds and is protected from liability by The Electronic Commerce (EC Directive) Regulations 2002.

CASE STUDIES

The British Museum and Portable Antiquities Scheme have become involved in a number of other cases involving illicit metal detecting which also demonstrate the difficulties of successfully combating this activity.

The East Leicestershire Hoard

A major hoard of about 5,000 Iron Age coins and other artefacts, including a fragmentary Roman helmet, was excavated by archaeologists in 2001–03 following an initial discovery by an amateur archaeologist, Ken Wallace. Following a programme on the find screened on BBC 2 in the series Hidden Treasure in autumn 2003, the site was attacked by illicit detector-users (Faulkner, 2003: 49–55; Priest, Hill, and Leins, 2006). Despite the attempts of the archaeologists concerned to keep the findspot secret, there were enough clues in the programme to enable the findspot to be identified and shortly after the programme was aired the site began to be raided by illegal metal detector-users. The initial police response was ineffective but, following pressure from the local MP, Leicestershire Police gave the issue higher priority and, after deploying a police helicopter, arrested detector-user Raymond Tebble, from South Shields, at the site. Tebble was subsequently convicted of going equipped to steal and was sentenced to a month in prison and the confiscation of his metal detector (Punter, 2004a). However, on appeal, his prison sentence was quashed and replaced with a £250 fine (Punter, 2004b). Although the press report does not give any reason for the reduction of the sentence, it is all too typical that the courts treat this sort of crime as a minor matter. However, the damage to archaeology is potentially very great. Following the publicity from this case, an unnamed individual placed a map of the site on eBay, presumably to encourage more people to detect on the site. eBay took this down following pressure from the British Museum, but the damage had already been done. The site was subsequently protected by electronic surveillance equipment paid for by the Leicestershire Police and the Portable Antiquities Scheme, and this was successful in preventing further attacks.

Ramsgate Bronze Age Hoard

In July 2005 a metal detector-user reported a find of 78 Bronze Age metal artefacts and associated pot sherds from Ramsgate to the Finds Liaison Officer for Kent. By his own admission, he had recovered these from the site of an archaeological excavation without permission. A subsequent visit by the police to his home revealed more objects likely to be from the same find, which he had concealed. Unfortunately, however, by the time a coroner's inquest had been held on the find, under the Statute of Limitations it was too late to bring a prosecution under the Treasure Act 1996 because it was more than a year since the alleged offence had been committed. In such circumstances, however, the Treasure Valuation Committee has the power to recommend that a reduced reward or no reward at all be paid to the finder, and in this case, for the first time, the Committee recommended that the finder should completely forfeit any reward. The hoard is now in the local museum.

Buckinghamshire Bronze Age Hoard

In October 2004 the British Museum was contacted by a Dutch collector and experimental metallurgist, Jeroen Zuiderwijck, who had purchased on eBay for £205 a small hoard of Bronze Age objects said to have been found in Buckinghamshire. Mr Zuiderwijck was extremely public-spirited as he wanted to make sure the find was properly recorded and housed in a museum, and he very generously sent it back to the British Museum without charge. The case would seem to have entailed two clear breaches of the law: a failure to report under the Treasure Act 1996 and a failure to obtain an export licence. Mr Zuiderwijck passed on details of the person from whom he bought the find, and this was passed to the police, who investigated the case. However, it emerged that the individual who sold the objects was not the finder and, indeed, was not a dealer but someone who had an eBay account and sold them as a favour for the finder. The police took no further action, but Mr Zuiderwijck has presented the find to Buckinghamshire County Museum.

Dutch Metal Detector-Users in England

In August 2005 the Finds Liaison Officer in Norfolk was contacted by a Dutch national, who was organising a metal detecting holiday in Norfolk for a group from the Netherlands. Despite repeatedly warning him that he needed to obtain export licences for anything that he found before he took it back to Holland and that there was a legal requirement to report potential treasure finds, he failed to do so and, acting on information supplied by the FLO, HM Revenue and Customs intercepted the party as they were leaving the United Kingdom at Harwich and confiscated several bags of metal detected finds. In all, 1,857 objects were recovered, all but 224 of which were more than 50 years old and thus required export licences. Amongst the finds were no fewer than 11 potential treasure cases. They have all been seized by HM Revenue and Customs, and Norfolk Museums and Archaeology Service has selected those objects that it wishes to retain for its collection. This case reveals another aspect of metal detecting that takes place in this country: organised tours for foreign nationals, who detect in this country and take home what they find. It is important to ensure that such people are aware of the need to obtain export licences for any objects that they find that are more than

50 years old. It is, of course, difficult for them to do this, as it takes at least a month to obtain a licence unless they can find an agent in this country who is prepared to arrange a licence for them more quickly. One organiser, Discovery Tours, is scrupulous in recording all the finds made and securing export licences for them, but many other organisers do not record their finds or obtain licences.

CONCLUSIONS

The Dealing in Cultural Objects (Offences) Act, which came into force on 30 December 2003, created an new offence of dealing in 'tainted' cultural objects (defined as those which have been removed from sites contrary to local law), with a maximum penalty of seven years' imprisonment (see also Polk, chapter one, and Mackenzie and Green, chapter eight, this volume). One of its aims is to suppress the market in finds illegally recovered from the United Kingdom. This should mean that those dealers who have previously not asked any questions of vendors will, before buying objects, have to take greater care to establish that the vendor has a legal right to sell, although it remains to be seen whether this is in fact happening. However, as we have noted, eBay does not fall within the scope of the new offence. As at the time of writing in 2008, no prosecutions have so far been brought under this Act, which applies only to artefacts that can be shown to have been illegally removed after 30 December 2003.

Arguably the problems now lie not so much with the legislation but with its enforcement, which remains patchy, although there are some encouraging initiatives. HM Revenue and Customs now has an officer who specialises in cultural property issues. The United Kingdom has only one dedicated team of police officers who specialise in art crime, the Art and Antiques Unit at Scotland Yard, which consists of four full-time officers and three support staff.[12] Press reports in January 2007 (Copping, 2007) suggested that the Unit was threatened with a 50 per cent reduction in its budget unless it attracted outside sponsorship, although this has subsequently been denied by the Home Office Minister in response to a parliamentary question from Lord Renfrew (*Hansard*, House of Lords, 20 February 2007, cols 997–98). The Unit has recently launched an initiative, Art Beat, to recruit special constables from the national museums and related organisations (such as the Art Loss Register), and the first tranche of special constables (including Dr Michael Lewis, Deputy Head of Portable Antiquities) is now in place. Kent Police has launched an initiative to tackle illicit metal detecting as part of the wider anti-social behaviour and rural crime agenda, and this offers a

[12] This compares with the Italian art crime unit of the Carabinieri, which has 250 staff (CMS Committee, 2000, II: 151–58).

model that could be copied by other police forces where illegal metal detecting does not have priority.

Oxford Archaeology was funded by English Heritage and other UK national heritage bodies to carry out a survey of nighthawks and nighthawking in the United Kingdom, and this was published in February 2009 (Oxford Archaeology, 2009). This was intended to give the most thorough survey yet of the extent of illicit activity in the whole of the United Kingdom and to provide a baseline against which future surveys can be measured, as this is a necessary first step in persuading the law enforcement agencies (the police, HM Revenue and Customs, and the Crown Prosecution Service) to give greater priority to combating illicit detecting. As a first step, illegal metal detecting should be made a reportable crime so that accurate statistics can be kept, since we currently lack accurate figures on the scale of the problem.

Ultimately, however, the answer must be to raise public awareness on this issue and to educate those who buy and sell such finds on good practice. There is no doubt that the Treasure Act 1996 and the Portable Antiquities Scheme have achieved a great deal in improving public awareness of the importance of reporting archaeological finds. The DCMS's acquisition guidelines for museums provide more detailed and helpful guidance on these issues than has hitherto been available (DCMS, 2005). The PAS has also developed guidelines for people buying and selling archaeological objects from the United Kingdom, which are published on its website,[13] while the recently launched Cultural Property Advice website, funded by the DCMS and run by the Museums, Libraries and Archives Council,[14] is intended to provide comprehensive advice for dealers, collectors, and museums on buying and selling cultural objects.

This chapter reports mixed results in attempts to inhibit the trade in illegally removed archaeological objects found in the United Kingdom. The monitoring of eBay for potential treasure finds has had only limited success, and it is difficult for the Portable Antiquities Scheme to put as much time and resource into this as it needs. It seems that eBay, while profiting from the sale of these items, has no responsibility for ensuring that adequate checks are made on them before they are listed on its website. On the other hand, the emerging results of the nighthawking survey, which show that this is less of a problem in 2008 than it was in 1995, are encouraging and should probably be regarded as a testimony to the educational impact of the Portable Antiquities Scheme. There is no doubt that more could be done to suppress the trade in illegally removed antiquities from the United Kingdom and there is a need for legislation to extend the duty to report treasure finds to anyone who comes into possession of them and to require anyone who

[13] www.finds.org.uk/advice.
[14] www.culturalpropertyadvice.gov.uk.

deals in antiquities to keep adequate records on them. However, compared with the situation only 15 years ago, progress has been made in this area. It is clear that raising public awareness of the importance of provenance and due diligence is the key.

REFERENCES

Barford, P (2006) 'Metal detecting and the archaeological resource', 98 *Rescue News* 1–2.

Bland, R (1996) 'Treasure trove and the case for reform', 1 *Art, Antiquity and Law* 11–26.

—— (2005) 'Rescuing our neglected heritage: the evolution of the Government's policy on portable antiquities in England and Wales', 14(4) *Cultural Trends* 257–96.

—— (2006) 'Metal detecting and the archaeological resource: a response from the Portable Antiquities Scheme', 99 *Rescue News* 4–5.

Brodie, N, Doole, J, and Watson, P (2000) *Stealing History: The illicit trade in cultural material* (Cambridge, McDonald Institute for Archaeological Research, ICOM UK and Museums Association).

Copping, J (2007) 'Police seeks sponsors to tackle art crime', *Sunday Telegraph*, 14 January.

DCA (Department for Constitutional Affairs) (2006) *Coroner Reform: The Government's Draft Bill. Improving death investigation in England and Wales*, Cm 6849 (London, DCA).

DCMS (Department for Culture, Media and Sport) (2000) *Ministerial Advisory Panel on Illicit Trade Report* ['the ITAP Report'], authored by N Palmer, P Addyman, R Anderson, A Browne, A Somers Cocks, M Davies, J Ede, J Van der Lande, and C Renfrew, (London, DCMS).

—— (2001) *Report on the Operation of The Treasure Act 1996: Review and Recommendations* (London, DCMS).

—— (2002) *The Treasure Act 1996. Code of Practice (Revised) England and Wales* (London, DCMS).

—— (2005) *Combating Illicit Trade. Due Diligence Guidelines for Museums, Libraries and Archives on Collecting and Borrowing Cultural Material* (London, DCMS).

Dobinson, C and Denison, S (1995) *Metal Detecting and Archaeology in England* (York, English Heritage and Council for British Archaeology).

Faulkner, N (2003) *Hidden Treasure: Digging up Britain's Past* (London, BBC).

Hill, GF (1936) *Treasure Trove in Law and Practice* (Oxford, Oxford University Press).

House of Commons CMS Committee (2000) *Cultural Property: Return and Illicit Trade*, Seventhth Report, 1999–2000 Session, 3 vols (London, The Stationery Office).

Kusin and Company (2002) *The European Art Market in 2002: A Survey* (Helvoirt, The Netherlands, The European Fine Art Foundation) (executive summary available online at: www.kusin.com/publications_2.htm).

Lewis, M (2007) 'Watching the family silver', January–February *British Archaeology* 24–25.
Malvern, J (2004) 'Man on coin plunder charges walks free', *The Times*, 3 April.
Merryman, JH (1994) 'The nation and the object', 3 *International Journal of Cultural Property* 61–76.
Normand, AC (2003) *Review of Treasure Trove Arrangements in Scotland* (Edinburgh, Scottish Executive).
O'Connell, MG and Bird, J (1994) 'The Roman temple at Wanborough, excavation 1985-1986', 82 *Surrey Archaeological Collections* 1–168.
Oxford Archaeology (2009) *Nighthawks and Nighthawking. Damage to Archaeological Sites in the UK and Crown Dependencies caused by the Illegal Searching and Removal of Antiquities. Strategic Study. Final Report*, available at: www.helm.org.uk/server/show/nav.20434.
Palmer, NE (1993) 'Treasure Trove and Title to Discovered Antiquities', 2 *International Journal of Cultural Property* 275–318.
Priest, V, Hill, JD, and Leins, I (2006) 'Community, politics and sacrifice', July–August *British Archaeology* 34–39.
Punter, G (2004a) 'Man jailed after swoop at Treasure site', *Leicester Mercury*, 26 November.
—— (2004b) 'Anger as jail term is cut', *Leicester Mercury*, 29 December.
Saville, A (2002) 'Treasure Trove in Scotland', 76 *Antiquity* 796–802.

6

Crime Goes Underground

Crimes against Historical Sites and Remains in Sweden*

LINDA KÄLLMAN AND LARS KORSELL

THIS CHAPTER IS concerned with crimes against cultural heritage, here confined to historical sites and remains, as well as archaeological finds, located in Sweden. While not primarily focused on the trade in illicit antiquities, the chapter is still concerned with an aspect of the market—the finding of objects, which forms the beginning of the chain of 'supply', producing objects for the market: in this case Swedish archaeological finds. We also attend to the wider issue of damage caused to historical sites and remains, and place this damage within a market perspective. The research we report here compares, in the Swedish case, the incidence of damage to antiquities by looting, and damage by other incidental means. We argue that the latter seems more significant, in terms of incidence at least. It often takes the form of business activities in which certain neglect is shown to the cultural heritage. We suggest that the associated damage can often be explained by the urge to comply with economic rationality, or by the need to be a competitive actor in the market. The chapter is based on a recent study, which will be summarised and discussed.

THE THREAT AGAINST CULTURAL HERITAGE IN SWEDEN

In Sweden, as in many other countries, there is great concern over the threat that plundering may pose to historical remains and there is widespread interest in this question within the field of cultural heritage management. It has been noted that metal detectors are commonly used in illegal excavations (see Östergren, 1985; Hammarstedt, 1999; Gustafsson, 2000). Since 1991,

* This article is based on a report published by the Swedish National Council for Crime Prevention, 'Crimes goes underground', Bra 2006:5.

there has been a general prohibition against the use of metal detectors in Sweden, although it remains legal to buy, sell, and own a metal detector.

The problems have been most evident on the island of Gotland, abundant with Viking and medieval treasures, where plunderers have also been arrested and sentenced. Apart from this, there are few cases where crimes of this kind have been proven. The question, then, is how extensive such plundering is in Sweden. Andreas Hennius (2004) of the Uppland Museum states that, 'between 80 and 90 percent of the sites of finds of gold artefacts in Sweden have been searched by plunderers using metal detectors over recent years'. Hennius derives this figure from subsequent investigations conducted at known sites of gold artefact finds—a site was supposed to have been plundered if no metal was found during these investigations. In his licentiate dissertation Leif Häggström concludes that 2.5 per cent of the land investigated during the Vittene project[1] had been plundered with the aid of metal detectors (Häggström, 2001). In this case the investigations were not limited merely to sites of gold and silver finds, but instead covered specified areas of land. The two figures do not therefore allow for a comparison, but they do suggest a problem of widescale looting activity in Sweden.[2]

In Sweden, shipwrecks more than 100 years old are classed as historical remains and are thus protected under the Heritage Conservation Act (*Lag om kulturminnen m.m.*, SFS 1988: 950). In Swedish waters there is a unique wealth of wrecks as a result of the favourable marine conditions, which serve to conserve the wrecks. Besides the famous Vasa, the man-of-war that has become the most famous museum in Stockholm and Sweden, visited by thousands of tourists every year, there is also the man-of-war Kronan.[3] She sank in the Baltic Sea in the year 1676 during a sea battle against the Danish–Dutch fleet and is now subject to archaeological investigations.

The relatively few marine archaeologists share their interest in and knowledge of the shipwrecks with many sport divers. Most divers have an active interest in the preservation of the wrecks, and special societies have formed to this end, but there are also divers who remove souvenirs and trophies from such sites (Elwér, 2005; Brå, 2006).

Plundering and souvenir hunting are not the only offences that threaten historical remains. The remains can also be damaged in other ways, for example in connection with farming and forestry and other forms of land use. Unlike plundering, little attention has been focused on offences involving damage of this kind. Accidental or incidental damage lacks the

[1] The Vittene project was initiated subsequent to the discovery of a unique find of gold relics at Vittene in the region of Västergötland.

[2] It should be mentioned that this type of assessment have been challenged. See, eg, a 2006 discussion about looting with the aid of metal detectors on a Swedish Internet forum for archaeology (Arkeologiforum: Plundring med metalldetektor, www.arkeologiforum.se/forum/index.php/topic,809.0.html, accessed 27 March 2008).

[3] See www.regalskeppetkronan.se.

dramatic characteristics of plundering: it is a more mundane and, as we will show, common type of 'cultural heritage crime'.

There are 1.5 million recorded archaeological sites in Sweden, but there are still areas where nothing has been recorded. During the twentieth century extensive inventories have been recorded, but they do not yet exist for the whole country. What this means is that a substantial number of potential objects of crime have yet to be recorded, while many are yet to be discovered (Brå, 2007: 5).

SWEDISH LEGISLATION

Swedish historical sites and remains have been protected by law since the seventeenth century, when King Karl XI issued a decree on the inventory and protection of historical sites and monuments (Lundström, 2000). The Swedish legislative protection for cultural heritage is probably one of the oldest in the world. The remains were to bear witness to Sweden's role as a great power with an ancient and honourable history, an image that the ruling elite of the time wanted to enforce.

Today, cultural heritage crimes are defined in the above-mentioned Heritage Conservation Act of 1988. In different chapters, the care, use, and preservation of archaeological sites and remains, culturally significant buildings, and cultural heritage related to the church are regulated. There are also chapters on the protection against movement of certain older objects of cultural significance to other countries, and on the restitution from other EU countries of such objects illegally removed.

Consideration of cultural values is also incorporated in other legislative areas, concerning, for example, the environment, forestry, city planning, and so on. Not surprisingly, however, those with responsibility for cultural heritage management feel that cultural values often have to give way to economic or environmental values when weighed against each other. On the other hand, landowners or entrepreneurs often seem to think that the required considerations present obstacles for private or corporate enterprises.

Sweden signed the 1970 UNESCO Convention as late as 2002, but no legislative amendments were thought necessary. It is unclear how the Swedish legislation complies with the Convention; only restitution to EU member states is regulated in the Heritage Conservation Act. No ban on the import of stolen artefacts has been passed (restitution and bans on import are dealt with under Article 7b of the Convention); instead the importation of stolen artefacts is to be considered under legislation relating to receiving stolen goods.[4] Sweden has not yet signed the Convention on Underwater

[4] See memorandum from the Ministry of Culture prior to the ratification (Kulturdepartementet, 2002), as well as the report from the Committee of Culture (Kulturutskottet, 2003).

Cultural Heritage 2001, despite several parliamentary bills on ratification. Ratification of the UNIDROIT 1995 has been subject to consideration by a commission (SOU, 2005: 3), which approved the ratification and proposed necessary legislative changes, but no action has yet been taken.

The types of crime that will be discussed in this chapter are defined in chapter 2, section 21 of the Heritage Conservation Act. This chapter of the Act relates to historical sites and remains,[5] as well as archaeological finds. In short, the chapter states that sites and remains must not be altered or damaged in any way, and that permission must be applied for when remains might be affected by activities such as forestry or construction work.[6] Damaging or altering a site or remains constitutes a crime under section 21. Furthermore, it constitutes a crime to acquire, hide, damage, alter, or dispose of finds that should be reported to the state. This provision therefore makes looting a criminal act. Archaeological finds are defined as objects without an owner, found in connection to a historical site or remains, or found under other circumstances and at least 100 years old. The types of finds that must be submitted or offered to the state for redemption are: (1) all finds that are found in connection to a site or remains, and (2) finds that consist of gold, silver, bronze, or other copper alloys, as well as finds consisting of several objects that seem to have been buried together. These provisions for sites and remains apply to registered as well as unregistered sites, and even to sites previously unknown. As mentioned earlier, shipwrecks more than 100 years old are defined as historical remains.

The punishment for breaking the law is a fine or imprisonment of up to six months; for an aggravated offence the prison term might be up to four years. Intent is a necessary requisite only for the aggravated offence. The limitation period is two years; 10 years in the case of aggravated offences.

The following acts are also criminalised (under section 21a): failure to report the above-mentioned type of finds; not immediately putting a stop to the work and not reporting to the authorities when remains are found during land work; usage of a metal detector without a permit;[7] and breaching

[5] The Swedish original term corresponds to 'permanent remnant', and is defined by a list of different types of sites and remains, like the term 'monument' in UK legislation (the Ancient Monuments and Archaeological Areas Act 1979).

[6] While only scheduled monuments (sites of national importance) are protected in UK legislation, the Swedish legislation covers *all* sites—even those not yet discovered. A site might be removed after survey or excavation if exploitation of the land is needed, but only after permission from the county council.

[7] A total ban on the use of metal detectors was introduced in 1991, although permission can be applied for at the county council. The ban does not apply to military use, authorities' activities, or to the National Heritage Board.

conditions set up regarding a site or its surrounding. There is no aggravated offence for these acts, if they do not form part of the offences mentioned above.

CRIME GOES UNDERGROUND—THE STUDY

There is still very little substantial knowledge about cultural heritage crime in the Nordic countries. In 2004, the Swedish National Council for Crime Prevention initiated a Nordic project with the purpose of surveying the frequency and structure of crime connected to the cultural heritage. The term 'cultural heritage crime' was introduced instead of the commonly used 'art crime' in order to better encompass the broad variety of objects and contexts affected by these crimes. Part of the project resulted in an in-depth analysis of thefts from churches (Brå, 2005). The Nordic study made it clear that crime against historical sites and remains was a difficult area to investigate, and it was clear that more research was needed.

Objective of the Study

The central objective of the study was to develop and improve existing knowledge about the extent and structure of crime related to historical remains in Sweden. The focus was also to highlight the problem with these crimes and increase awareness. The research investigated factors associated with illegal excavations, damage to historical remains. and the plundering of shipwrecks in Sweden. Preventive measures to combat such crimes were also proposed and discussed.

The questions addressed in the 'Crime Goes Underground' study were as follows:

- What is the character of the crimes, which types of historical remains are targeted, and how are the offences committed?
- What are the motives for these crimes and who commits them?
- How are such crimes detected and which cases result in a prosecution?
- Is it a national problem or regional problem?
- Is the extent of this problem increasing or decreasing?
- How can these crimes be prevented?

The trade in historical remains, national or international, did not fall within the scope of this study. Instead, it dealt with crimes that are necessary for an illegal market to exist and crimes that in other ways erode the potential for archaeological research. Definitions of the crimes studied have been given below. The scope of the study was limited to crimes against historical remains in Sweden.

Definitions

This chapter is based on a study in which the different types of offences were divided into two main sub-categories, according to the offences defined under chapter 2, section 21 of the Act; these categories will be referred to as 'find offences' and 'damage offences'.

The typical find offence involves a perpetrator who has actively been looking for historical remains or by chance has found something that should be submitted or offered to the state, but fails to report the find and instead keeps it. Damage offences occur in situations where the activities of the perpetrator affect the historical remains in some way. It is often a question of damage occurring in connection with different kinds of land use (construction, forestry, agricultural work, and so on).

There are also a number of cases where an offence against the Act has been committed without causing any damage. Most often, these offences have had to do with breaching conditions set up in permits, or not applying for a permit when required to do so by law. In the study, offences of this kind were categorised as 'permit procedure offences'. This category primarily refers to offences that are not related to a find and that in addition have not entailed any real disturbance or damage to historical remains. Cases where a metal detector has been used and it is quite clear that the intention has been to search for archaeological finds have been categorised as find offences, irrespective of whether or not it has been possible to prove that any finds have been made. Other cases of unlawful use of a metal detector, however, have been classified as permit procedure offences.

Some of the sites and remains that were affected by these crimes were registered; others were discovered during inspections of construction work that was carried out—and the damage offence was thus discovered at that same time. In some cases the county administrations deemed the damage so serious that the site had to be excavated; in other cases the sites could be restored to their previous condition.

Method and Material

Offences related to historical remains are underground crimes in both the literal and figurative sense of the term. Such offences are difficult to detect and investigate. This is due to the fact that historical remains are often located in places that are rarely frequented by large numbers of people. When signs of plundering are detected, it is still impossible to know what might have been taken from the ground. In addition, many historical remains have yet to be discovered and recorded. This creates substantial difficulties for the development of a clear conception as to the extent and structure of the crime involving such remains.

In order to address these difficulties, the study employed several methods and sources of data:

(1) An analysis of the reviews of the court judgments of all crimes relating to historical remains that resulted in a conviction in Sweden between 1973 and 2005.[8] Of 39 court judgments issued in relation to these Acts, 36 concerned crimes related to historical remains.

(2) A questionnaire survey concerning suspected offences from the period 2001–05. The survey was primarily focused on county administrative boards, which constitute the relevant supervisory authorities in this area, and on county museums. The questionnaire was also sent to a number of other businesses and organisations active in the field of cultural environment protection and cultural heritage management. The idea was to reach those who supposedly had the best knowledge about crimes against historical remains. The total sample comprised 91 respondents, of whom 64 sent a reply of some kind and 59 actually completed the questionnaire.

    In the questionnaire respondents were asked about their knowledge of suspected crimes related to historical remains (under chapter 2, section 21 of the Heritage Conservation Act) and whether these suspicions had been reported to the police. Many respondents said they found it difficult to give specific figures on suspected crimes, and referred to the fact that no statistics are kept. There were also questions concerning the circumstances surrounding suspected crimes—the type of environment, the type of historical remains involved, as well as the suspected perpetrators and their motives.

(3) A number of interviews were carried out, both at the start of the project to serve as a guide for the subsequent work and later to acquire more detailed information. The interviewees included representatives of the supervisory authorities, interest organisations, the police, and divers interested in marine archaeology.

(4) When investigating the extent of a given type of crime it is common to use data on the number of reported offences. Even if not all crimes are reported, such data can provide an indication as to possible increases or decreases in the level of crime over time. However, reported crimes relating to historical remains are not registered under a unique crime code, which means that offences of this kind cannot be distinguished

[8] The existing legislation on cultural remains, the Heritage Conservation Act, came into force in 1989. The study also includes court judgments relating to offences against the Historical Remains Act (1942: 350), the Historic Buildings Act (1960: 690), and the Act on Protection against the Export of Certain Older Cultural Artefacts (1985: 1104)—ie the laws which preceded and have now been replaced by the present legislation.

in the official statistics.[9] Instead, a small study was conducted on the basis of a request for data on crimes reported to the police authorities in four counties (out of the total of 21 police authorities). Here too the sample was restricted to the period 2001–05. The police authorities in question had recorded a total of 26 reports relating to suspected offences involving historical remains.

Theoretical Model

The study was conducted from a criminological point of view, with an underlying market perspective as a theoretical framework. The model presented in Figure 6.1 was used as a map for the analysis and was extracted from a larger model, presented in the earlier Nordic study (Brå, 2006: 2). In that study, the market aspect and the interaction between the legal and illegal markets was more evident. Here the market is alluded to through issues relating to supply.

The model is divided into two parts. The upper section focuses on find offences, listing such factors as motive, opportunity, objects of crime, service functions, and market. Typically, the crimes referred to as find offences have economic motives, and the historical remains end up on a market; the motives may also be collector interest or a desire to acquire souvenirs or trophies. This is particularly common in relation to the plundering of shipwrecks. The opportunities for committing find offences are abundant, since the objects of these crimes are often unprotected and unsupervised. The targets of these crimes are most often historical remains, like burial sites, remnants from early settlements, or shipwrecks. The objects might be coins, jewellery, tools, black oak, or equipment from ships. Common service functions that serve to facilitate crimes of this kind include lists of historical remains, and equipment such as metal detectors and GPS.

In the lower section of the model the perspective is reversed. A different kind of market provides various incentives of a more or less economic character and leads to the perpetration of damage offences or permit procedure offences. The background to these offences may be the desire to be able to construct a building or to finish a building project before a certain date. There is often an element of ignorance or carelessness involved. This part of the model focuses on such factors as market, motive, opportunity, and the objects of crime. The term 'market' here refers to other aspects of the economy than the demand for different commodities. Farming and forestry are conducted in a rational way and this rationality comes into conflict with the preservation of historical remains. The same applies to society's needs

[9] Data on offences that are assigned unique crime codes are otherwise available in the official crime statistics, for which the National Council for Crime Prevention is responsible.

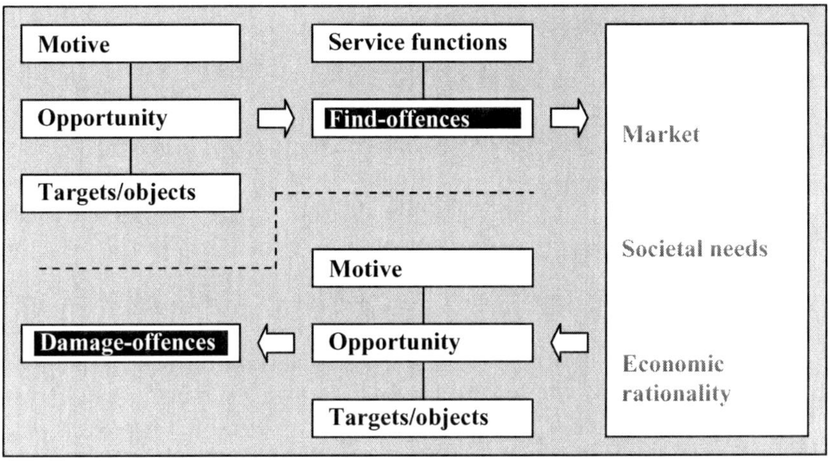

Figure 6.1. Schematic Model of Offences relating to Historical Remains

for housing, industries, and infrastructure. Thus, crimes are motivated by a desire to comply with this societal rationality and target historical remains in the ground/on land and under water. Opportunities to commit crime arise because the land is exploited to a high degree, historical remains can be difficult to identify (the use of the land itself does not attract any special attention, and no one notices that historical remains are being damaged), and there exists uncertainty as to the regulations that apply.

Damage to historical remains may also occur in connection with the commission of find offences. The labels proposed here are based primarily on the purpose of the act; deliberately seeking out archaeological finds is thus labelled a find offence, even if the act causes damage as well.

Results

Examination of Court Judgments

Over a period of 30 years, only 36 cases of crimes relating to historical remains have led to convictions. This number could either indicate that very few crimes are committed or that committed crimes have not led to convictions. The most likely explanation is that few crimes end up in court, primarily because they are not even detected. Additionally, as will be discussed below, detected crimes are not always reported to the police and when reported only a few lead to prosecution.

Among the offences that have both been detected and then resulted in convictions, damage offences of various kinds account for a large majority (26 cases out of the total of 36). Find offences, relating to illegal excavations or to the non-reporting of finds, account for six cases. The remaining cases relate exclusively to permit procedure offences. Five of the 36 court judgments relate to offences involving the use of metal detectors. Three of these were find offences; the fourth might be called an attempted find offence resulting in damage, while the fifth merely involved the unlawful use of a metal detector.

There may be several explanations for the fact that the detected offences that resulted in convictions more commonly involved damage or some other disturbance of historical remains than they did find offences. One explanation is that the offenders involved may more often be identifiable in cases involving damage, since they may be associated with various kinds of documented land development projects. Another explanation is that damage and disturbance are often visible and can be demonstrated after the event whereas it is difficult to prove that something has vanished when there is no prior knowledge of its existence and it has simply been lying concealed in the ground. It is also reasonable to assume that the number of landowners and land developers who may cause damage is much greater than the number of potential plunderers.

The court judgements were relatively evenly distributed across Sweden, although there are counties where no such court judgments have been issued. Gotland has issued more court judgments relating to find offences than the rest of Sweden (three of the six find offence judgments). No significant increase or decrease was noted in the number of court judgments over the period of slightly over 30 years covered by the study.

Table 6.1. Number of Court Judgments Distributed across Three-year Periods, 1973–2005

Period when court judgments were issued	Type of offence			Total
	Find	Damage	Permit procedure	
1973–75	2	0	0	2
1976–78	0	3	0	3
1979–81	0	2	1	3
1982–84	1	3	1	5
1985–87	0	4	0	4
1988–90	0	2	0	2
1991–93	2	3	0	5
1994–96	0	3	1	4
1997–99	0	2	0	2
2000–02	1	3	1	5
2003–05	0	1	0	1
Total	6	26	4	36

The most common types of crime location involved building land and various types of arable land. Roughly half of the cases involved damage to graves and burial sites. In four of the six cases the find offences had no connection with any previously known remains. One case involved the plunder of a shipwreck, although there was a suspicion of one further case of wreck plundering. This latter case illustrates the difficulty of linking objects to concrete find offences—it cannot be proven where the find was taken from, since it is impossible to know what was in the ground or in the water at different locations.

The offender was in most cases a private person, but the offence was in several instances related to some form of land use. There were also a number of farmers among the offenders. In most of the damage offence cases, the motive could be described as ignorance or carelessness, whereas the motives behind the find offences in all cases were interpreted as involving collector interest or economic motives.

In two cases, the sanction was a prison sentence; in all other cases, a fine. Compensation for damage was imposed in five of the judgments.

Reported Offences

Data on reported offences were requested from four police authorities—those in the counties of Gotland, Västernorrland, Västmanland, and Västra Götaland. During the period 2001–05 these authorities had together registered a total number of 26 reports of suspected offences against the Heritage Conservation Act. The largest numbers were recorded in the counties of Gotland (13 offence reports) and Västra Götaland (11 offence reports). Västmanland had registered one reported offence and Västernorrland two, of which one had been incorrectly categorised as an offence involving historical remains. During the same period, three court judgments were issued in these four counties—two in Västra Götaland and one in Västernorrland.

In eight of the cases the reports relate to suspected find offences. Seven of these cases—all of which took place in Gotland—involve the use of metal detectors; one case was linked to a shipwreck. However, if Gotland had not been included in the sample, only one of the 13 reports would have been related to a find offence. One of the suspected cases of damage offences is linked to forestry, whereas most of the other cases are linked to other types of land use. Some cases relate to pure vandalism. County administrative boards had filed just over half of the offence reports, sometimes after being contacted by private persons. In at least four cases, suspected plundering was reported by a landowner. In eight cases, the offence reports also include information on a suspected offender.

The find offences made up a greater proportion of the reported offences than they did of the offences that resulted in a court conviction. This could mean that find offences are more difficult to investigate than other offences and that investigations into these cases are more likely to be abandoned. In some cases we asked for more information about the results of the investigation into the reported offences. All of these investigations had been closed without leading to a prosecution, due to reasons such as: 'no leads for an investigation exist', 'offender unknown', or 'offence clearly impossible to investigate'.

Questionnaire Study

Compared with the studies of court judgments and offence reports, the questionnaire study may be viewed as an attempt to get closer to the real extent of crime involving historical remains. Special attention was given to the answers provided by respondents such as the county administrative boards and county museums, due to their central roles in this issue. We received replies from 20 out of 21 county administrative boards and from 19 out of 22 county museums.

Comparing proven criminality (resulting in a court conviction) and suspected crime (as measured in the questionnaire) strengthened the impression that damage offences are considerably more common than find offences (see Table 6.2). The proportion of damage offences was even greater among the suspected offences than among those that resulted in court convictions. Few of the respondents reported knowledge of suspected find offences. Only nine respondents—two county councils, four county museums, and three other respondents—reported such knowledge. Together they knew of 28 suspected offences (although note that the same suspicions may be shared by several respondents). A total of 40 respondents reported knowledge of damage offences. Find offences are undoubtedly more difficult to detect than damage offences. Nevertheless, it is striking that only two county boards claimed knowledge of any suspected find offence. Knowledge of suspected crimes among these respondents does not, of course, equate to the actual crime rate.

Table 6.2. Suspected Offences, 2001–05

Year	Find offences	Damage offences
2001	0 (1)	35 (41)
2002	2 (1)	25 (40)
2003	1 (2)	35 (53)
2004	3 (0)	53 (72)
2005	6 (2)	87 (51)
Total	12 (6)	235 (257)

Note: The figures refer to suspected offences that had come to the knowledge of county councils. The responses from county museums are presented in parentheses.

The answers to the questionnaire survey might be interpreted as indicating a certain increase in crimes of this kind over recent years. Alternatively, it may have been the case that it was easier to remember suspected cases from more recent years. As regards damage offences, part of the explanation is that Hurricane Gudrun (a hurricane that affected the southern parts of Sweden in the year 2005) resulted in the compilation of additional damage inventories, which also resulted in the discovery of suspected crimes. This also constitutes a good example of how the number of detected offences rises and falls in proportion to the amount of monitoring activity that is conducted, something that is also typical of certain other crimes, for example economic crime (*cf* Korsell, 2003).

The geographical distribution of the offences is shown in Figures 6.2 and 6.3 below. Whereas the damage offences were distributed across the entire country, the suspected find offences were concentrated in Gotland.

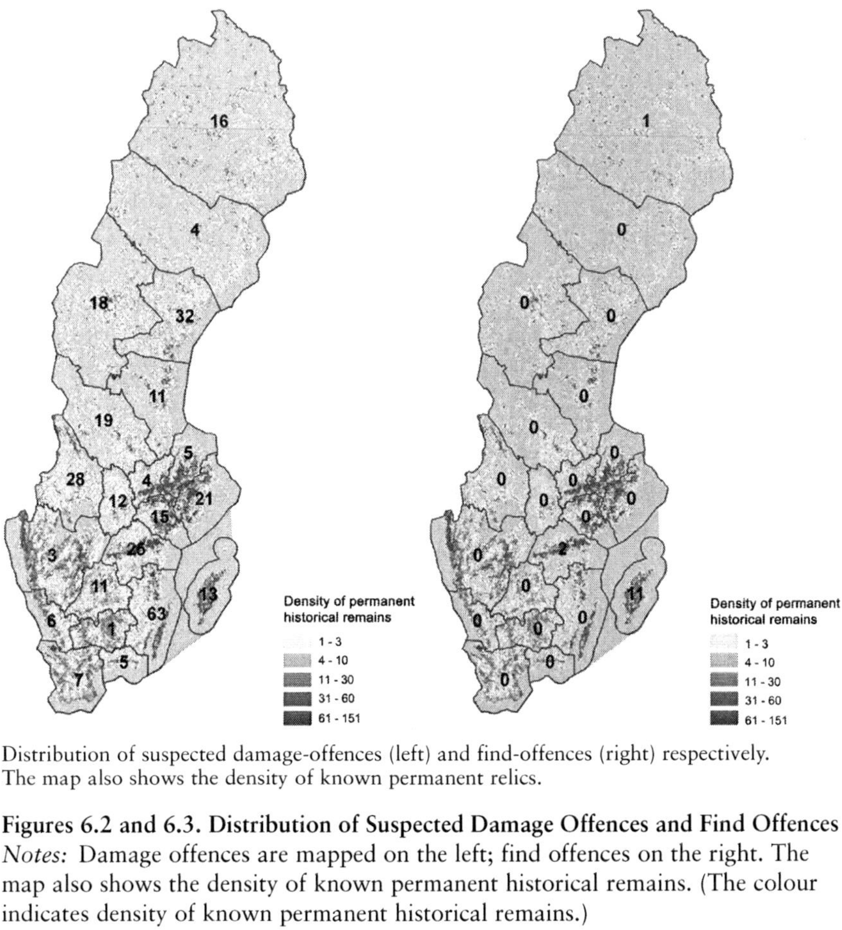

Distribution of suspected damage-offences (left) and find-offences (right) respectively. The map also shows the density of known permanent relics.

Figures 6.2 and 6.3. Distribution of Suspected Damage Offences and Find Offences
Notes: Damage offences are mapped on the left; find offences on the right. The map also shows the density of known permanent historical remains. (The colour indicates density of known permanent historical remains.)

The majority (over two-thirds) of suspected offences were committed on forestry land, which is linked to the fact that a large majority of the crimes involved damage offences and probably occurred in connection with forestry work. Other environments or types of land that were mentioned by more than just one or two respondents are building land and pastures. Graves were the type of historical remains most often subject to offences, with sites of settlements coming in second place (in slightly under half as many cases). The response 'other remains' was, however, reported as frequently as graves.

The fact that graves are most often subjected to crime corresponds well with the offences described in the court judgments. The connection found in the questionnaire survey between many of the offences and various types of forestry work did not show in the court judgments presented above. Only a few of the offences described in the judgments were related to forestry land. The questionnaire also dealt with the reporting of offences to the police, and it was found that a much smaller proportion of the suspected damage offences were reported to the police than were find offences, and this may apply to crimes related to forestry in particular. A possible explanation for this is that the authorities strive to maintain good relations with industry, and prefer to settle things without involving the judicial system.

Damage offences and find offences are, by their very nature, different kinds of offence and they have different dynamics. As regards find offences, the respondents described 'hobby collectors', 'plunderers with a profit motive' and 'foolishness on the part of private persons' as likely perpetrators and motives. With regard to damage offences, the responses were 'negligence on the part of forestry workers', 'ignorance or negligence on the part of a land developer' and 'carelessness on the part of farmers and other landowners', respectively. Different kinds of land developers and landowners were described as being frequent perpetrators of damage offences, whereas the court judgments referred mainly to 'private persons'.

The study's most important finding concerning shipwrecks was that the knowledge of supervisory authorities was very poor. A conclusion that could possibly be drawn from the questionnaire is that souvenir hunting and carelessness are more important factors than pure plunder for profit. The following were mentioned as probable motives and offenders: 'carelessness/foolishness on the part of both sport divers and boat owners', 'souvenir hunters/collectors' and 'plunderers with a profit motive'. Many of the responses indicated some uncertainty on the part of the authorities engaged in crime prevention.

As mentioned above, the questionnaire study showed that only a small proportion of the damage offences were reported to the police. During the period between 2001 and 2005, county administrative boards reported

38 of a total of 235 suspected damage-offences to the police, whereas 8 out of 12 suspected find offences were reported.

Several reasons were given for the lack of willingness to report these crimes: 'inadequate evidence', 'lack of time', 'the statute of limitations having expired', 'a settlement having been reached', and 'obscurities in the legislation'. Ignorance, 'a feeling that it is pointless', and a lack of clarity regarding the issue of responsibility were also given as reasons.

As explained earlier, some archaeological finds must be submitted to or offered to the state for redemption. Those finds that the state chooses to redeem are usually placed in a museum, and the finder is sometimes given compensation. If the state chooses not to redeem a find, the finder gets to keep it. Since archaeological finds that are for sale often awaken suspicions that plundering has taken place, it was of interest to examine how many finds are actually reported to the authorities and what sort of interest these actors have in the redemption of these finds. If finds are reported to but not redeemed by the state, it is difficult to argue that finds on sale are evidence that plundering has taken place. The willingness to report finds is also directly related to compliance with the law.

Whilst it is not possible to know how many finds are actually made every year, we can nonetheless verify that finds are reported to some extent. The questionnaire respondents were asked how many such finds had been reported to them. The question was answered by 31 respondents, of whom 20 had not received any such reports,[10] while 11 county museums and county administrative boards during the years 2001–05 had received a total of 98 reports of the discovery of archaeological finds. Half of these reports were, curiously enough, made to one single institution, a county museum in the south-east of Sweden. The respondents reported that there had been an interest in redeeming 19 of these objects.

This means that 79 objects were reported to the relevant authority but not redeemed and, thus, stayed in the hands of the finder. Furthermore, this means that Swedish archaeological finds, at least in theory,[11] can be found quite legally on the market. This creates ambiguity when claiming that archaeological finds for sale equals looting, and makes it difficult for buyers to make informed decisions.

[10] Finds that are to be submitted or offered to the state can be reported to a police authority, a county administrative board, a county museum, the coast guard (concerning shipwrecks), or the National Heritage Board. On request, the finder is then obliged to hand over the find against a receipt. In the legislation nothing is said about the issuing of a certificate when a find has been reported but not redeemed by the authorities.

[11] Even if it is not likely, it could be that some of the finds were simply rusty nails of no historical value.

General Conclusions

The overall impression given by the analyses and interviews can be summarised in a few points that will be expanded upon below:

- Damage offences constitute the major problem, and there is a tendency not to report these offences.
- Ignorance and carelessness are important causes of offences being committed, as is a lack of clarity regarding the regulations.
- Supervisory and heritage preservation authorities express uncertainty about how they should act and say that reporting crimes of this kind serves no purpose.
- The police rarely feel that they are given sufficient information to warrant starting an investigation.
- The overall impression in combination with data collected in the interviews is that the offences often fall between different actors' spheres of perceived responsibility as a result of ignorance and uncertainty on the part of the authorities concerned.

The accepted general view is that historical remains throughout the whole of Sweden are under threat from plunderers and that the country's cultural heritage is being dissipated by the hunt for these treasures (Gustafsson, 2000; Häggström, 2001; Hennius, 2004). This study provided almost no support to suggest that this represents a true picture of the actual threat. In fact, the major problem seems to be the damage that is constantly being done to historical remains in connection with various forms of land use. Damage occurs in connection with farming and forestry and other types of land development and land use.

There are only a few confirmed cases of plundering in Sweden, and there are not many suspected cases. Nevertheless, it is a fact that plundering is difficult to detect. A hole in the ground may be the only trace, and only the ground knows what may have lain there. Despite the difficulties in acquiring better knowledge of plundering offences, our assessment is that these offences constitute a smaller problem than damage offences. This is not to discount the seriousness of the plundering that does occur, nor to deny that certain areas and objects may be targeted by crime particularly often.

The reasons for damage offences are often inadequate knowledge and carelessness—common causes for crime that takes place within the framework of legal activities (Winter and May, 2001; Simpson, 2002). In addition, the offences are committed in connection with activities governed by economic considerations involving time pressure and a demand for efficiency. The upside is that motives or causes of this kind provide good opportunities for preventing these crimes.

Another aspect is that it might be difficult for the layman to recognise certain historical remains when they are encountered in the course of work. For many, it may also be difficult to navigate the various regulations and authorities involved.

By comparison with those who commit damage offences, plundering offenders have a stronger motivation for their crimes, varying from spontaneous souvenir hunting to planned looting operations.

The motives that emerged in the analysis signify that measures for crime prevention should be based on two components. With regard to landowners and land developers, the supervisory authorities should first of all adopt a collaborative approach in the prevention of damage, whereas more effective crime-combating measures are required in relation to motivated plunderers.

Collaborating with those who cause damage means that the authorities must establish active contacts with landowners and entrepreneurs. Historical remains will be protected more effectively if an increased emphasis is placed on preventive work rather than on responses and sanctions when the damage has already been done. Knowledge and clear guidelines are key aspects of successful preventive work. Improved collaboration between the different agencies involved is a necessary condition for this approach. Although the focus should be on prevention, legal enforcement where crimes have been committed remains important. Many of these perpetrators are commercial businesses, and as such, they are often sensitive to the negative publicity that will follow suspicions of criminal actions.

In order to deal effectively with suspected plundering offences, the crimes must first be detected. More crimes can be detected by increased surveillance of areas that are targeted and not least by means of improved contacts with landowners and others who can serve as the eyes of the authorities. Some of the reports made to the police in Gotland provide examples of this. Crime prevention and law enforcement can be made more efficient by improvements in the level of collaboration between supervisory authorities and the police. What should also be looked into is how to gather and make use of existing police competence in the area of crimes against historical remains and other cultural heritage offences. No special force exists to deal with these crimes.

Much of what has been said above also applies to shipwrecks. The most salient point to emerge from the study in relation to marine heritage is that official knowledge of crimes involving shipwrecks is almost non-existent. It is also clear that the agencies of crime prevention have poor knowledge of existing regulatory frameworks in this area. In view of the rich collection of well-preserved shipwrecks lying in Swedish waters there is much to be done in order to increase their protection. Serious sport divers could be important allies in this work.

Both looting and damaging have connections to market mechanisms. Economic considerations play an important role when some farmers and entrepreneurs see ancient remains more as obstacles that cause a loss of time and money than entities of cultural significance. This resembles what Mackenzie (2005) presents as the market actors' argument for dealing with chance finds; his interviewees argue that when a farmer (examples from Italy and Thailand are mentioned, see pp 180–81) finds something on his land, he risks having the farm closed without compensation for quite some time while the authorities make the necessary archaeological investigations—this creates incentives either to just destroy the finds or to sell them for a profit. While acknowledging that these arguments are sometimes well founded, Mackenzie's central point is that market participants make strategic use of arguments such as these in order to support their view that buying finds 'saves' them from destruction. This instrumental rationality serves to legitimise dealing with any object, regardless of origin, creating a grey zone in market dealings. This is an important point, but requires to be understood in the context of the findings of our research: destruction of cultural heritage results not only from the demand for artefacts, but also from a pervasive economic rationality that exists both in the often poor source countries and in market countries.[12] In other words, even without a market in antiquities, a certain level of cultural heritage destruction would persist, represented by incidental damage to sites in the process of economic activities by landowners, businesses, and other private persons. A true challenge for policy makers is to engage with the wider mechanisms of market activity—beyond the antiquities market—which our research suggests impact on the issue of preserving cultural heritage in Sweden. If cultural heritage preservation no longer equated to loss of profit for individuals and businesses, serious reductions in destructive practices might be seen.

This chapter has not dealt with the trade, as such, and just a few words will be said about it. Grey zones and loopholes often cause problems in regulation as well as in law enforcement. Swedish legislation contains a loophole that creates similar grey zones concerning the trade with Swedish artefacts to those described by Mackenzie. The issue lies in the availability of evidence that would show whether the artefact for sale was found in connection with a site or not. Was it found together with other artefacts or not? Was it offered to the authorities or not? (See the legislation referred to at the beginning of this chapter.) The answers are not written on the artefact, and there will be no other way of knowing the answers for sure, but nevertheless they will determine whether the artefact can be legally traded or not.

[12] There are also other causes, as described by the non-profit organisation Cultural Heritage without Borders (most of them less applicable to the richer countries): 'Time and time again we see how war, political conflicts, natural disasters, climate changes and neglect deprive people of their cultural heritage and history.' (Cultural Heritage without Borders website, www.chwb.org)

Dealing with the incentives created by the market for antiquities, the solution will probably entail some degree of compromise and pragmatism, as argued by Fincham (2007: 68): 'a pragmatic balancing of the values at stake ... is needed to bring all the disparate interest groups to the table and create a system which prevents theft, destruction of archaeological sites, and allows a robust and healthy trade'. Negotiated solutions reached by compromise and pragmatism can be problematic, however, if the processes are captured by trade interests (Mackenzie and Green, 2008).

REACTIONS TO THE STUDY

The results of this study have provoked some rather indignant reactions from a few archaeologists and others engaged in archaeology. Our conclusions were interpreted as a way of saying that 'it is OK to loot'. We were also accused of having omitted data on the true extent of these crimes, even though we never claimed to have such data—figures on the true extent of these crimes are quite impossible to obtain. One critic admitted that it was, of course, a correct conclusion that 'far more remains are damaged than looted', but maintained that one crime committed with intent is 'worse' than 10 crimes committed out of neglect.[13]

This is not to be read as a defence speech as there is obviously a lot more to be done in this field of research in order to cover different aspects of the problem. Instead, the criticism can serve as a starting point for a challenging discussion about the values at stake.

If we are to protect the cultural heritage, why is it worse that one site is possibly looted and stripped of one or more artefacts than that 10 sites are damaged? Is it because the issue in fact is more about morals than about protecting cultural heritage? That deliberately committing a crime because of the monetary value of an object is considered to be morally more condemnable than committing a crime out of neglect or disrespect for any kind of value that might be attributed to archaeological sites and artefacts? We could propose two explanations. The first is that we are all more concerned about *things* than context, while the second explanation proposed here has to do with *values*, a struggle between discourses.

The first explanation is a view that is reflected in the 1970 UNESCO Convention, which is clearly focused on things—*property*—that can be removed:

> CONSIDERING that it is incumbent upon every State to protect the cultural property existing within its territory against the dangers of theft, clandestine excavation, and illicit export. (From the preamble to the 1970 UNESCO Convention)

[13] E-mail correspondence.

According to this approach, cultural heritage cannot be destroyed, but it can be stolen or illicitly (re)moved (the expressions 'cultural property' and 'cultural heritage' are both used in the text of the Convention). Furthermore, *things* are easier to count, define, claim, and reclaim than more abstract environments—and maybe that is why they make better objects of crime, and looting a better target for crime prevention and combating than damaging. Alternatively, it could be that protectors of the cultural heritage themselves are more interested in things, as reflected in legislation that bears traces from a different view than that held today (*cf* Bland, chapter five, this volume, on English legislation on 'treasure', and the definitions in the Swedish legislation where only finds made from gold, silver, bronze, or other copper alloys must always be offered to the state).

The second explanation as to why the one intentional crime is considered worse than the 10 less intentional crimes (acts that nevertheless are just as criminal and cause damage to cultural heritage) has to do with *values*. An archaeological find probably represents a monetary value to the looter, while someone who damages an archaeological remain probably does not recognise any value whatsoever of the site. Could it be that the looter causes greater outrage because he challenges the establishment's monopoly in defining cultural heritage and its value (*cf* Ronström, 2005)? The value represented by cultural heritage is often described as universal and absolute, but Ronström (2005) broadens the perspective on value in an interesting way by analysing cultural heritage as *mindscapes* (p 91). He describes heritage production as a task assigned to 'especially approved professional experts' (p 99). In his analysis, cultural heritage is something that is being *produced*, and the production always entails selection. Thus, instead of providing objective knowledge about our past, 'heritage production is a way to exercise power' (p 104). From this perspective, much of the conflict concerning how best to protect the cultural heritage seems to be a struggle between discourses.

Discussing *things* and *value* from the standpoint of Simmel's sociology of value, Ward (chapter two, this volume) proposes that cultural objects have an intrinsic value, but his conclusion that 'some things are intrinsically valuable ... but only to human beings who, as a matter of contingent historical fact, are disposed to value them' seems to remind us more about the fact that human beings occupy very different positions in local and global society, and point back to a discussion on political power.

What on the surface looks like a very neatly formulated problem—'how can we best fight crime that threatens cultural heritage?'—is no longer neat once the surface has been scratched. Future criminological research on cultural heritage crime should continue to make use of expertise and experience from relevant fields in order to gain a better understanding of the subject, but should also be careful not to let the criminological problem be defined, or the conclusions influenced, by the different interests involved.

REFERENCES

Legislation, Policy Documents and International Conventions

Kulturdepartementet (Ministry of Culture) (2002) Memorandum, 10 March.

Kulturutskottet (Committee of Culture) (2003) *Kulturutskottets betänkande 2002/03: KRU2*, Report, 6 February, www.riksdagen.se/webbnav/index.aspx?nid=3322&dok_id=GQ01KRU2.

Lag om kulturminnen m.m. SFS 1988: 950 (Heritage Conservation Act).

Sveriges tillträde till 1995 års Unidroitkonvention om stulna eller olagligt utförda kulturföremål, SOU 2005: 3 (Stockholm, Fritzes).

UNESCO Convention on the Means of Prohibiting and Preventing the Illicit Import, Export and Transfer of Ownership of Cultural Property 1970.

Secondary Sources

Brå (Brottsförebyggande rådet) (2005) *Brottsplats kyrkan*, Webb-rapport, www.bra.se.

—— (2006) *Cultural Heritage Crime – The Nordic Dimension*, Report 2006: 2 (Stockholm, Brottsförebyggande rådet, Fritzes).

—— (2007) *Brott under ytan. En undersökning om fornminnesbrott*, Webb-rapport 2007: 5, www.bra.se.

Elwér, S (2005) 'Hesperus: En djupdykning', 3 *Apropå* 32–33.

Fincham, D (2007) 'Why US Federal Criminal Penalties for Dealing in Illicit Cultural Property are Ineffective, and a Pragmatic Alternative', 25(2) *Cardozo Arts & Entertainment Law Journal* 597–645.

Gustafsson, B (2000) 'Ligor skattplundrar de svenska fornlämningarna', 2 *Populär Arkeologi* 14–15.

Häggström, L (2001) *Några Lemningar Om Också Förstörda – en fornlämningsbiografi över Vittenebygden*, Ph Lic thesis, Göteborg University.

Hammarstedt, S (1999) 'Silverskatternas Gotland hemsöks åter av plundrare', 3/4 *Tidevarv* 3.

Hennius, A (2004) 'Plundring! Hotet mot vår historia' in H Liby (ed), *Uppland 2004. Årsbok för medlemmarna i Upplands fornminnesförening och hembygdsförbund* (Uppsala, Upplands fornminnesförenings förlag), pp 117–128.

Korsell, L (2003) *Bokföringsbrott – en studie i selektion*, PhD thesis, Stockholm University.

Lundström, L (2000) 'Kongl: Mayst:tz(!) Placat och Påbudh, Om Gamble Monumenter och Antiquiteter', *Svenskt tryck före 1700*, www.kb.se/F1700/Monumenter/Text.htm, accessed 15 January 2007.

Mackenzie, S (2005) *Going, Going, Gone: Regulating the Market in Illicit Antiquities* (Leicester, Institute of Art and Law).

Mackenzie, S and Green, P (2008) 'Performative Regulation: A Case Study in how Powerful People Avoid Criminal Labels', 48 *British Journal of Criminology* 138–53.

Östergren, M (1985) 'Metalldetektorn i praktiskt bruk', 57 *Gotländskt arkiv* 11–28.

Ronström, O (2005) 'Memories, tradition, heritage' in O Ronström and U Palmenfelt (eds), *Memories and Visions*, Studies in Folk Culture IV, Department of Estonian and Comparative Folklore & Department of Ethnology, University of Tartu (Tartu, Tartu University Press).

Simpson, SS (2002) *Corporate Crime, Law and Social Control* (Cambridge, Cambridge University Press).

Winter, S and May, PJ (2001) 'Motivation for Compliance with Environmental Regulations', 20 *Journal of Policy Analysis and Management* 675–98.

Part IV

Regulation and the Market in Looted Antiquities

7

The Paradox of Regulation

The Politics of Regulating Global Markets

DAVID WHYTE

> Prohibition was the dumbest law in American history. It was never going to work, not ever. But what it did was create the mob. These dummies with their books and investigations, they think the mob was invented by a bunch of Sicilians in some smoky place. Probably in Palermo. Bullshit. The mob was invented by all those self-righteous bastards who gave us Prohibition. It was invented by ministers, Southern politicians, by all the god-damned idiots who think they can tell people how to live. I know what I'm talking about on this one. I was there. (Frank Sinatra[1])

INTRODUCTION

THE PROCESS OF regulating the antiquities market, as Mackenzie (2005) has noted, contains some unavoidable paradoxes. In the context of recent UK regulatory reforms, law that is apparently aimed at controlling and restraining markets at best has failed to realise its intended aims, and at worst, is counter-productive. This chapter aims to excavate the deeper paradoxes that lie at the foundations of the regulatory relationship. It begins by unpacking the limiting hypotheses that characterise dominant theoretical understandings of the state and exploring what this means for understanding the regulatory process. The chapter then argues that the policing and regulation of global markets is best understood as a process that constitutes both 'legal' and 'criminal' markets. A series of 'criminogenic' paradoxes are then used to demonstrate how policing/regulation also act to constitute the conditions of existence for 'crimes' of the market.

[1] Cited in Smith, 2005: 74.

PLURALISM AND STATE POWER

In social science generally and criminology in particular, there is a tendency to conceptualise state power in pluralist, one-dimensional terms (Lukes, 1982) and to reify the state as a monolithic source of power. From the pluralist point of view, state power is enacted when one party (government institution) uses power directly to force another party (individual or civil society group) to do something it would not normally do. This view depends on the immediately visible manifestation of actual or observable conflict between the 'state' and the object of state power.

Pluralist approaches assume a concentration of power in a relatively fixed and closed state system dominated by institutions of government. In other words, states are self-referential, solely drawing on their own ideologies, logics, histories, policies, and so on, in an autopoietic sense (Luhmann 1990). One consequence of viewing states as relatively fixed and closed systems is that they can be viewed in isolation from an analytically separate system of social relations that exists independently from, and outside of, the state (Mann, 1984). The state is thus reified as a set of socially isolated, autonomous, and self-referential institutions. Power-brokering by states is therefore reduced to the internal dynamics of state institutions, obscuring the possibility that states play a key role in constituting, and are themselves constituted by, social relations. This is not to deny the centrality of institutional histories and logics to political outcomes, but it is to say that those histories and logics do not develop in isolation from broader social relations of power.

There is at the same time a tendency in the pluralist approach to conceptualise state power as the ability to exert 'power over' other interests. Pluralist understandings of power often assume that states compete for power with civil society groups and institutions. This is particularly pronounced in the globalisation literature, whereby states are juxtaposed in zero-sum terms against markets: the power of the state diminishes as the power of the market rises, and vice versa (Pearce and Tombs, 1998; Tombs and Whyte, 1998). The tendency to conceptualise state power purely in 'power over' terms arises from a narrow understanding—found in most criminology—of what Gramsci (1996) calls the 'state as policeman' (see also Coleman et al, forthcoming). By this he meant that what is normally understood in a formal sense as the 'state' (restricted to 'safeguarding of public order and of respect for the laws'—subordinates our understanding of the centrality of 'private forces' in the historical development of states. The problem with this focus is that it obscures the important interconnections between the policing/social control/criminal justice functions of the state and the broader social ordering functions of the state. Thus, for Gramsci, the 'state as policeman' approach is a 'limiting hypothesis' (1996: 261). Poulantzas had similarly acknowledged that a danger of delineating understandings of the state across the two resources of power that he was most concerned with (the repressive and ideological state apparatuses) is that the *economic* role of the state is downplayed (1978: 33–35). Gramsci counterposed the 'state as policeman' with the 'ethical' or 'interventionist' state and argued that 'the concept of the interventionist state is of economic origin, and is connected on one hand with tendencies supporting protection and economic nationalism and on the other ... the "protection of the working classes from the excesses of capitalism"' (1996: 262). In many advanced capitalist economies, positive state interventions in the lives of citizens provide basic health and welfare services and a minimum income, and so on. We can understand the 'ethical' state as an expression of the close coupling of its economic and ideological roles. Thus, the provision of health and welfare services themselves can be theorised both as a means of securing a hegemonic compromise with subordinate populations and as a crucial component of population and labour market regulation (Offe, 1984).

Even in critical views of the state–market relation, we find a fairly consistent assumption of this relation as purely antagonistic. Thus, the liberal commentator Noreena Hertz, in her widely acclaimed book *Silent Takeover*, argues that corporate power has become unassailable since 'Governments are now like flies caught in the intricate web of the market' (2001: 140). But if this truly were the case, if government institutions were paralysed by markets, then markets would really be in trouble, for markets cannot function outside of states. It is state institutions that constitute capital, commodity, commercial and residential property markets, help to produce different kinds of 'human capital', constitute labour markets, and regulate contractual relationships (see Whitfield, 2001: 16–18). In other words, regulation is a necessary function of a state even in the quintessential market economy, no matter that advocates of global neo-liberalism consistently deny such a role for the state and regulation (Coleman et al, forthcoming). Moreover, it is important to recognise in this context that businesses themselves often realise that regulation is in their long-term interest, even where the immediate impulse is to reject 'state intervention'. Large firms in particular are generally unwilling to subordinate themselves to the vagaries of the market (Pearce, 1976: 82–84). It is more than 60 years since Karl Polanyi—following the work of Marx and the classical political economists such as Adam Smith who together showed clearly how such a thing as the 'free' market never existed—documented the 'embeddedness' of markets, and their construction through economic, social, and public policy (Polanyi, 1962[1944]). Precisely because the state constitutes the terms and conditions upon which markets are sustained, a 'free market' existing wholly separate from and 'outside' the state simply could not exist.

In a counterbalance to the one-dimensional, fetished, understanding of the state as a force of restraint upon impulsive and 'free' markets,

Michael Mann (1984) more usefully distinguishes between the *despotic* and *infrastructural* capacities of states, whereby the former corresponds very broadly to the 'state as policeman' and the latter to the 'ethical' state and to the organisation of the economy. Despotic powers are those powers that the elite is empowered to take without routine, institutionalised negotiation with civil society groups. Infrastructural powers of the state, on the other hand, are those that enable the state to penetrate and centrally coordinate civil society. There are similarities here with the Foucauldian concept of 'power through' (as opposed to 'power over'), whereby state power in infrastructural terms is not merely a matter of crude domination of will, but is understood as a complex disciplinary process that acts through the social body, through professional disciplines, institutional discourses, and so on. Mann's analysis also has something in common with the Gramscian/Poulantzian approach to the state, for he views the state not merely as a set of government institutional assemblages that 'negotiate' or seek the approval of civil society, but as an arena in which we find the 'condensation, the crystallisation and the summation of social relations' (Mann, 1984).

There are three main points that we can derive from the reflections on pluralist approaches to understanding state power that have been outlined in this section. First, states have 'positive' ethical and interventionist capacities that are umbilically connected to their 'negative' coercive and control capacities. Second, the state has creative, infrastructural capacities that give form to markets and enable them to function (markets are always highly regulated by states, even in the most neo-liberal versions of capitalism). Third, it is the ethical, interventionist, and infrastructural capacities of states that enables the penetration of civil society and allows states to 'act', or deliver 'power through' civil society.

THE REGULATORY DIALECTIC

Put together, those features of state power tell us something important about the place of markets in capitalist states and provide us with a starting point for thinking about the *regulation* of markets. The apparent contradictions at the heart of the regulatory relationship (coercion vs consent; states vs markets; state as policeman vs civil society, and so on) are not merely contradictions. For in each of the dualisms noted here, there is a complex symbiotic relationship. Where we can identify contradictory and oppositional forces within this relationship, their character is dialectical, rather than one of binary dualism. The dialectical nature of the process is illustrated by exploring the well-worn dichotomy of state 'rollout' vs state 'roll-back' that has been used to characterise neo-liberal privatisation and deregulation strategies. The problem with posing a binary opposition between the two is, first of all, that (neo-liberal) arguments supporting the 'rolling back' of the state (the expression of anti-interventionist or anti-regulatory tendencies) could never lead to the eradication of states' role in constituting markets. 'Deregulation' policies always involve the withdrawal of the state from some spheres of activity, but at the same time they involve the active encouragement and empowerment of private actors in (state-organised) market spaces. This might take the form of restructuring tax regimes, commandeering public finance for the public sector in the form of public–private forms of financing public projects, or other forms of 'corporate welfare' subsidies (Nader, 2000). In other words, policies that appear to be deregulatory or concerned with reducing state interference always depend on some form of state action. Thus, according to Passas, the global inequalities that appear to result from a lack of state intervention:

> are the doing of national authorities. It is their economic policies that bear responsibility for relative and objective deprivation. It is their protectionism and subsidisation of domestic industries, while they preach 'free market' and 'liberalisation of trade' to others that impair the efforts of less developed trade to narrow the gaps. It is their monetary policies and control of international organisations that preserve asymmetric development and growth. It is authoritarian regimes that cause ethnic and political violence. It is their hegemonic policies and support for dictatorial regimes overseas that provoke international terrorism and fundamentalism. It is their selective control and promotion of domestic military industries that fuel armed conflicts. (2001: 40)

To describe such policies as 'state rollback' or 'state retreat', then, is highly misleading. By definition they involve the reframing or rescaling of the form that state intervention takes, rather than its eradication.

If we think about struggles around the regulation of markets—for example struggles for tighter environmental standards or controls over the importation of illicit antiquities—the outcome of struggles between business and issue-based social movements is never a complete victory of one over the other, and never could be. Rather, because the regulatory relationship is a dialectical one, the contradictions that are apparent in the relationship between 'states' and 'markets' can be understood as dynamic, producing new regulatory outcomes and new forms of market activity. 'Deregulation' then, in a dialectical sense, is better described as an ongoing process of 're-regulation' or 'state rescaling' (Jessop, 2002). It is particularly important to grasp the dialectical nature of this process, especially in the context of sociology and socio-legal studies which remains fixated upon the limited hypothesis of 'power over' relationship, whereby regulation is something one set of actors (regulatory agents) *does* to others (regulated individuals and organisations).

The impulse to re-regulate (not deregulate) can be found in the contradiction between the promotion of law observance on one hand, and market values that are consistent with routinised offending on the other.

Neo-liberals have been remarkably successful in promoting a value system that gives primacy to entrepreneurialism and the pursuit of self-interest above other social values. For McLennan (2005: 158), 'the increased elevation of corrosive corporate market values over those of democratic civil society' in contemporary America has precipitated the normalisation and institutionalisation of law-breaking and corruption in the US corporate sector. Neo-liberalism creates the ideological conditions for profit accumulation to be projected as a morally defensible end. A key feature of neo-liberalism, then, is that it *ideologically* undermines socially protective laws by promoting the values of profit accumulation and maximisation above all other values. It is important to think about this ideological dimension to regulation, both in terms of how particular ideas and discourses act to discipline the targets of regulation (individual and corporate participants in markets) *and* in terms of how they target regulators (Whyte, 2006). Thus, we can say that neo-liberalism as a set of ideas and practices, aims to reconstitute markets by influencing and shaping the 'habitus' of market actors, regulatory policy makers, and regulatory agencies in a way that consolidates rather than distances or weakens state power (Snider, forthcoming).

Regulation in capitalist social orders, then, is characterised by a contradictory relationship between a practical need to observe the laws that structure, and place restrictions on, economic activity on the one hand, and, on the other, an ideological impulse and normative structure which places the values of 'free enterprise' above values of law observance. This contradiction manifests itself in the creation of new market spaces which often provide fertile locations for the production of socially harmful practices involving private enterprise. Thus, the destruction of the Ecuadorian mangroves for the shrimping industry, or the mangroves of the Niger Delta as a result of oil exploration and production (Green and Ward, 2004), is made possible only because of a regulatory balance that promotes the productive and profiteering goals of foreign oil firms above the protection of local communities and their habitats. Similarly, markets in, say, arms, minerals, or indeed antiquities flourish in market spaces that privilege the promotion of particular forms of commercial activity over socially protective regulation.

Neo-liberalism's tendency to produce liminal or anomic market spaces (Passas, 2000; Whyte, 2007a) can destabilise the economy and, in extreme cases, expose large sections of the population to market exigencies (causing, in the case of the banking collapse of 2008, job losses and loss of pension funds on a devastating scale). This feature of neo-liberalism creates the risk that counter-movements will emerge to give momentum to popular demands for regulatory intervention, which may in turn result in political strategies aimed at imposing tougher regulatory controls on market actors. Witness, for example, the emergence of new movements against corporate killing in the United Kingdom,[2] which resulted in a new law, and current NGO campaigns for corporate *legal* responsibility[3] and for a climate change law.[4]

The relationship between criminal markets and neo-liberal policies is a complex one that will be returned to later in this chapter. For the time being it is important to understand how the contradictory dynamic between the need to maintain a legal order and the need to promote neo-liberal values of free enterprise causes problems for the stability of social orders and therefore creates the need for regulatory interventions (Mahon, 1979). Regulation is a process that acts as a necessary control on the self-destructive tendencies of unchecked market activity. We see this principle in action at every moment of economic crisis when states intervene to bail out banks, ensure the liquidity of markets, impose capital controls, and so on. Those are extreme regulatory responses in the face of crisis that rips the *faux* mask away from the myth of the powerless state. Regulation as a process is therefore necessary to stabilise and reproduce the conditions of development in a system that always has the potential to self-destruct. This point was made in rather different terms by Marx in his commentary on the emergence of the nineteenth-century Factory Acts:

> These Acts curb the passion of capital for a limitless draining of labour power, by forcibly limiting the working day by state regulations, made by a state that is ruled by capitalist and landlord. Apart from the working class movement which daily grew more threatening, the limiting of factory labour was dictated by the same necessity which spread guano over the English fields. The same blind eagerness for plunder that had in one case exhausted the soil, had, in the other, torn up by the roots the living force of the nation. (1954[1887]: 229)

The legal protections for workers enshrined in the Factory Acts therefore originated in the need to resolve a contradiction in the relentless demand for greater profit that threatened to exhaust the capacity for sustaining profits in the long term. This is perhaps the most generally applicable paradox that we can identify in the regulatory process: that the state must intervene and constrain individual capital for the general benefit of capital. In terms of what this means for understanding the process of regulation, Marx argued that the general impulse to regulate is not simply the result of a consensual or philanthropic decision to make industrial progress humane, but that it arises out of the conditions of the factory itself—conditions which need to be regulated to secure the general interests of capital (1954[1887]: 252–57). Of equal importance here is that regulatory outcomes are crucial to

[2] For example, the Centre for Corporate Accountability, www.corporateaccountability.org/, and Families Against Corporate Killers, www.hazardscampaign.org.uk/fack/.

[3] For example, the CORE coalition, www.corporate-responsibility.org/.

[4] For example, Friends of the Earth's Big Ask Campaign, www.foe.co.uk/campaigns/climate/press_for_change/email_mp/index.html.

providing the motivation for technological advancement and rationalisation of industrial production.

It is in the process of creating the very spaces necessary to achieve the aims of capital accumulation that we find its irresolvable contradiction: the need to enforce a rule of law that preserves the viability and legitimacy of the economic system whilst reproducing an economic order that preserves the primacy and autonomy of market actors. What is being revealed here is the central paradox of regulation, a paradox that can be summed up in no more complex terms than: *regulation controls at the same time as it enables*. In terms of the socially protective role played by environmental or health and safety regulation, we find that regulatory interventions have two connected effects: they limit the harms created by corporations to enable those same corporations to continue being harmful in a more controlled manner.

CONSTITUTING MARKETS

Although it is rarely described in this way, the preceding discussion allows us to redefine 'regulation' in capitalist social orders as a process by which states attempt to sustain a social and economic order that is intrinsically self-destructive. Regulation can be seen as a process that maintains the conditions of existence of productive and market 'forces'. We can make precisely the same point more generally about the role of policing in capitalist social orders. Policing is necessary to provide both ideological and material supports to structures of inequality as they are realised through unequal property relations and racialised social divisions, for example, and to impose social discipline as the self-destructive aspects of capitalist social orders manifest themselves in various forms of 'crime' on the streets (Hall et al, 1978; Choong, 1997; Neocleous, 2002). The purpose of policing/regulation, then, in its most fundamental sense, is to produce and reproduce social relations of power. The production and reproduction of particular forms of market is part of this more general role.

Findlay (1999: 54) points out that regulation is not merely a strategy of control; the form that regulation takes also reproduces 'boundaries of permission'. And it is in the process of drawing out of the boundaries of permission that policing/regulation reproduces the conditions for both legal and illegal markets to exist. Thus, there are 'legal' and 'illegal' markets in arms, just as there are 'legal' and 'illegal' markets in drugs. Beyond the superficial level of 'moral panic' discourse or ideology, the boundaries of permission here are not related to the intrinsic properties of the 'criminal' or the properties of the commodity or the service being bought and sold; neither are they related to anything intrinsic about the market itself. The constitution of the legal status of markets itself depends on a contradictory normative structure. After all, the side effects of many licensed pharmaceutical drugs (for example, tranquillisers and drugs for the treatment of psychological conditions) are every bit as harmful as 'recreational' drugs, and many are equally addictive; the arms that are traded on grey markets are precisely the same as the arms that are bought and sold 'legitimately'. If we analyse their intrinsic qualities, it is virtually impossible to establish a conceptual separation between illegal and legal commodities. And very often we can say the same for the forms of organisation that produce and distribute them (Ruggiero, 2000).

Rather, policing global markets has to be understood as an intensely politicised activity (Brodeur, 1983) where the legitimate scope of intervention is being continually contested. And often we see the rawest expressions of state power in such activities. Take the example of the relatively new movement to criminalise alternative remittance systems that are used in financial transactions. *Hawala* is a traditional Islamic system of remittance which is—amongst other traditional systems of remittance—currently facing a regulatory assault led by the IMF (International Monetary Fund Monetary and Financial Systems Department, 2005). This assault, supported by an ongoing CIA investigation, was given force by the post-September 11th political climate. The *Hawala* system is under suspicion as a breeding ground both for corruption and, relatedly, for the financing of international criminals and terrorists. In fact, the evidence to support this is sketchy at best. A more plausible explanation for the regulatory assault is that *Hawala* is not amenable to control by the global banking system of regulation. The problem with *Hawala* for the International Financial Institutions is that it does not comply with international reporting rules and does not charge interest as other banking systems do. It therefore presents a real alternative to capitalist forms of financial administration. This is not to deny that those involved in investigating or developing policy that targets *Hawala* vendors see their work as part of a war against terror or corruption, but it is to say that by continuing to stand outside the world economic system, *Hawala* is positioning itself in opposition to 'good' markets. If it is to survive, the *Hawala* system will either have to find ways of resisting and surviving in the grey market, or will have to reconstruct itself in a way that is approved by the IFIs and their constituent states. In this sense, the movement against *Hawala* is a very clear movement to reconstitute this section of the financial market. Setting the boundaries of permission in markets—the process of delineating legal and illegal goods and services, different forms of legal and illegal market activity, different forms of legal and illegal conduct within markets, and so on—is a decisive stage in the constitution of markets.

The delineation of the 'legal' from the 'illegal', then, might be called a process of creative destruction, whereby some markets are pushed to the margins to allow others to flourish. This, at least, is the *economic* dynamic that we find at the core of policing/regulation. But it is by no means the only dynamic (Arlacchi, 1998; Gill, 2002). The control of criminal markets undoubtedly has its origins elsewhere, for example in moral opposition (the control of some drugs) or in a commitment to the application of universal standards of human rights (the control of exploitative forms of people smuggling). There is an interesting disjuncture here between the *effects* of forms of market policing/regulation and the political reasoning behind those forms of policing/regulation. Thus, police/border authority clampdowns on people smuggling may be justified on the basis of protecting the 'victims' and preventing exploitation in the workplace. Such clampdowns may, on the other hand, be justified by racist or exclusionary discourses. But in so far as the effect of policing and regulatory interventions in criminal markets is to reconstitute those markets in particular ways, they produce a whole set of (both intended and unintended) consequences that are often not present in the rationalities or justifications that support them.

In this context it should not be surprising that we should find market actors arguing in favour of new forms of regulation even if this observation does not fit comfortably with a schematic view of state–market antagonism or of state intervention always acting to constrain free markets. The Gangmasters (Licensing) Act 2004, for example, was introduced in the wake of the Morecambe Bay disaster in the United Kingdom, which killed 23 Chinese migrant workers on 5 February 2004. The Act was supported by the government, the trade unions, all of the major supermarkets, and the National Farmers Union. The new law stipulated that 'gangmasters' (employers who organise gangs of casual labourers, normally paid on a piece-work basis, in the agricultural industry) must register with a new Gangmasters Licensing Authority before they can operate. In so far as the Act created a skeleton regulatory structure for gang labour, but it did not specify a legal minimum for safety conditions, training, or housing for immigrant workers, 'gangmasters' who had previously operated underground were able to shed their ambiguous legal status and at the same time avoid any added costs of provision for workers. At best, the new licensing regime will remove some of the more unscrupulous employers from market regulation and will bring others to the attention of the Inland Revenue and other regulatory authorities. The most likely result of this form of regulation is to stimulate the supply of casualised migrant labour that remains concentrated in grey markets. In other industries we can observe a similar dynamic. The UK trade association for armed private security companies, the British Association of Private Military Companies, is a case in point. This organisation is currently involved in concerted campaign *for* a regulatory structure to be imposed upon its members (Whyte, 2007b). This, of course, will limit its ability to engage in some activities. But at the same time a 'light touch' regulatory structure will consolidate its commercial position in the world market and its position 'inside' the British state apparatus, both essential for opening up new market opportunities. And a similar pattern of regulation legitimising previously legally 'grey' areas has been observed by Mackenzie and Green (2008; chapter eight, this volume) in relation to the United Kingdom's recent regulation of the illicit market in antiquities.

To accept that policing/regulation is used as a means of transforming illegitimate markets into legitimate ones tells us that in order to understand the processes at work here, it is not enough to follow a simplified empirical division between 'legal' and 'illegal' markets. And there are good theoretical reasons not to automatically accept this division. We might argue, for example, that the rapid expansion of both is rooted in global asymmetries caused by economic and cultural globalisation (Young, 1999; Passas, 2000). We will return to this discussion below. Yet official reasoning behind the emergence of new forms of policing/regulation is always *ostensibly* to create new forms of criminal category, to produce new forms of crime control (or intensify those that already exist), or to organise popular opposition to particular forms of social activity and to redefine those as 'anti-social'. But the discussion here allows us to draw a preliminary conclusion that begins to turn received wisdom on its head: *just as policing/regulation constitutes the conditions of existence of markets, policing/regulation also constitutes the conditions of existence of the 'crimes' of the market.* It is this point, only alluded to so far, that will now be more fully developed.

PROJECTING POWER THROUGH CRIMINAL MARKETS

Karl Marx asked in the *Economic Manuscripts* of 1861–63, 'would the world market ever have come into being but for national crime? Indeed, would even the nations have arisen?' The dialectical oscillation between 'outlaw' and 'legal' status that we find in particular market relationships has been a central dynamic in state building and in the realignment of state sovereignty. Criminal markets have historically been used by governments and private corporations—and by 'deviant' elites within those institutions—to extend their sovereign reach, to assert authority over contested territories, and to consolidate domestic political power.

As Thomas Gallant (1999) has documented, from around the sixteenth century onwards, groups of 'military entrepreneurs' and 'bandits' at the 'periphery' and 'semi-periphery' of the emerging state system played a crucial role in the process of state formation. 'Criminal' markets were crucial to the formation of states in the sense that they hastened capitalist penetration of rural and remote locations. In particular, the illegal activities of military entrepreneurs and bandits (smuggling, robbery, and so on) provided the basis for the penetration of markets into the most remote geographical areas; it was markets in illegal goods and the proceeds of banditry that elevated the level of marketisation in rural economies. Criminal markets, then, were 'the connecting tissue that articulated rural hinterlands to developing economic zones' (Gallant, 1999: 37). Their incorporation into alliances with regular state military and security forces allowed the most remote, outlying geographical boundaries of states to be secured. In the absence of state monopoly of violence, they allowed a vacuum of state power to be filled. In a hegemonic sense, campaigns against 'outlaws' also allowed states to establish a physical presence in the hinterlands.

Criminal markets, then, have historically played a key role in state power-brokering; used instrumentally to strengthen sovereignty and authority. This point is illustrated clearly in the way that criminal markets are used to project state power beyond the boundaries of the nation state.

First, this is a process by which foreign governments and power brokers and international criminal networks are used to extend the reach of state 'by proxy' when it has exhausted its capacity for direct intervention. As Chambliss (1989) famously pointed out, the use of a range of 'private' agents by proxy made states in the sixteenth and seventeenth centuries the primary consumers and sustainers of markets in piracy. He explains that precisely the same 'state-organised crime' relationship endures in contemporary states. In particular, he identified drug- and arms-smuggling as activities engaged in routinely by US government and CIA personnel. This, for Chambliss, occurs as a result of the belief held by a small but key elite that it is incumbent on them to act autonomously in defence of national security. This belief, combined with the apparent lack of legitimate means to achieve this goal, creates a strain that results in their participation in illegal forms of power-mongering. Illegal markets allow state security personnel to raise funds and redistribute them and to smuggle and distribute weapons in relatively hidden and therefore unaccountable spaces. In other words, it is precisely their illegal status that makes some markets valuable to some organised interests and groups of elites.

Second, criminal markets are used as a means of policing and projecting military power directly. The emergence of private forms of war-making in alliance with transnational corporations and states, particularly in the mineral industries (oil, diamonds, cobalt, and so on) of sub-Saharan Africa and some parts of South America in recent years can be understood as a process of 'state re-formation', whereby military entrepreneurs or paramilitary militias emerge to fill the security vacuum that is created as the hegemonic authority of the state is weakened. This, of course, creates an ongoing challenge to the ability of states to maintain sovereignty, but also produces alliances between regular military forces and legally ambiguous military entrepreneurs and paramilitaries. In Colombia, for example, the US and Colombian governments (and indeed some transnational corporations; Stokes, 2005) deploy a combination of private security companies and right-wing paramilitaries to reassert authority over borders and territories that are dominated by left-wing guerrillas. The assertion of 'legitimate' government authority is, in those contexts, dependent upon markets in violence that—whether in the form of private military corporations or paramilitaries—routinely involve violations of human rights and humanitarian law (Whyte, 2003).

Criminal markets, then, in those contexts, can be understood as having a functional role for the projection of state power. But this is not merely a matter of functionality for states. For, in all of the cases referred to in this section, we can observe how intrinsically criminal relationships develop organically between state and market players. In *Crimes of the Powerful*, Frank Pearce (1976) outlined how interlinked interests between politicians, corporate elites, and organised crime syndicates allowed the latter to thrive, and at the same time expanded the ability of the former to project power. Those interconnections, for Pearce, are not merely a pathological flaw in the system of power, but, as we can also see from the brief review here, are long-standing and ever-present characteristics of state power.

CONCLUSION

This brief, selective, review of evidence reveals much about the underlying relation between markets and crime and impels us to reject any simple relationship between 'enforcement' and 'crime reduction.' By stressing the complexities of its effects it also impels us to reject a pluralist perspective on the regulatory process. In other words, it is those criminogenic features of policing/regulation discussed here that lead us to reject the idea that there is a necessarily antagonistic relationship between 'states' and 'markets' or that either can exist completely autonomously from the other, wholly disconnected from social conditions of inequality.

It is power-mongering by states *and* market players acting together that creates the conditions for criminal markets to flourish. Economic asymmetries are bolstered—and often multiplied—by the regulatory process. In this context, how can it make sense to disconnect the command-and-control or coercive capacities of policing/regulation from the capacities or techniques of infrastructural power, if both are used as means of projecting power? Criminology gets tied up in the contradictions of explaining, analysing, and dissecting 'crime'. But 'crime' is never the point. Foucault in relation to his study of the internment of the insane, noted: 'the bourgeoisie is interested in power, not in madness'" (1976: 102). Following Foucault, what concerns elites (whether we are talking about politicians, business leaders, or crime bosses) in the process of policing/regulation is *power*, not crime. To reiterate, the purpose of policing/regulation, then, in its most fundamental sense, is to produce and reproduce social relations of power.

If there is a broad conclusion that we might draw from this review of the dynamics of policing/regulation, it is that regulation often acts as an accessory to the grotesque inequalities that are currently being reproduced and widened in neo-liberal capitalist social orders. In this sense, the regulation of capitalist markets can never adequately guarantee our protection from crimes and harms that arise from and reinforce social inequalities, since, invariably, regulatory interventions do not—even on their own terms—seek a transformation of the institutional structure of neo-liberal capitalism.

It is important, then, not just to understand the regulation of markets as boiling down to a choice between 'command-and-control' and 'compliance' strategies, or a mixture of the two (Alder and Polk, 2005), or indeed to a choice between targeting either 'supply' or 'demand' (Polk, chapter one, this volume). It is the relative power of the various players involved: dealers, buyers, enforcement agencies, regulators, and the agents of supply and demand, all participating in a 'market' (in which, not incidentally, the cultural value of an object has been externalised) that will allow plundered antiquities to remain highly lucrative for the foreseeable future. Polk in chapter one of this volume outlines the failures of deterrence targeted at the supply side. And there can be no doubt of those failures in the context of US Prohibition of the 1930s and the 'war on drugs'. There, are, however, two problems with what has now become an orthodox dilemma: the posing of a dualistic choice between 'persuasion' or 'bargaining' strategies and 'strict enforcement' strategies.

First, although the failure of deterrence when applied to those of relatively low social status is undeniable, its failure is not so clear when applied to relatively high status offenders. A guiding principle in the criminal justice systems of market societies is that deterrence is reserved for the relatively weak, whilst the relatively powerful should be persuaded and assisted to observe the law. Of course, this is not an absolute principle, and at times some very powerful individuals are sent to jail. Nonetheless, this orthodoxy endures despite the lack of either theoretical substance or empirical evidence to support it. Moreover, it is the latter half of this guiding principle (that the relatively powerful should be persuaded and assisted to observe the law) that has now become an article of faith in John Braithwaite-influenced criminology.

Second, were there no structural inequalities between buyer and seller, then perhaps a simple dualistic strategy of regulatory enforcement (strict enforcement *or* gentle persuasion) might be viable (and this point is indicated in the conclusion reached by Källman and Korsell, chapter six, this volume). At the moment, neither appears viable, since it is those structural inequalities, organised around an intensely objectified form of commodity value, where power is concentrated in a group of powerful market actors (Mackenzie and Green, chapter eight, this volume), that ensures that the market will most likely remain vibrant. And it is the persistence of those structural inequalities that also provides the most convincing arguments for a deterrence strategy to curb the ability of the most powerful players in the market to do as they choose.

A much more profound question in relation to the eradication of this illicit trade is how do we eradicate the conditions of inequality or the global asymmetries that underpin the market (see also the conclusion reached by Lobay, chapter four, this volume)? How can the 'hypertrophy of objective culture' (Ward, chapter two, this volume) be replaced with human values of empathy or solidarity? And, in a practical sense, how can state regulation play a role in those processes? These are questions that require a response that goes beyond mere tinkering with enforcement policy or posing hypothetical choices between enforcement styles.

All of this does not mean we should abandon regulation. An understanding of the complexities of the relationship between states and markets does not imply a relativist opposition to any form of regulation as pointless (this merely allows states to absorb conflict, reconstitute markets and reproduce social inequalities from a stronger position). Rather, the analysis here demands that regulatory systems must always be subject to scrutiny on the basis of how they reshape or manipulate market relationships, rather than their symbolic injunctions to 'control' or 'eradicate' this or that.

REFERENCES

Alder, C and Polk, K (2005) 'The Illicit Traffic in Plundered Antiquities' in P Reichel (ed), *Handbook of Transnational Crime and Justice* (Thousand Oaks, CA, Sage).

Arlacchi, P (1998) 'Some Observations on Illegal Markets' in V Ruggiero et al (eds) *The New European Criminology: Crime and Social Order in Europe* (London, Routledge).

Brodeur, J P (1983) 'High Policing and Low Policing: Remarks about the policing of political activities', 30 *Social Problems* 507–20.

Chambliss, W (1989) 'State-Organised Crime', 27 *Criminology* 183–208.

Choong, S (1997) *Policing as Social Discipline* (Oxford, Clarendon Press).

Coleman, R, Sim, J, Tombs, S, and Whyte, D (forthcoming) 'Introduction', in Coleman, R, Sim, J, Tombs, S, and Whyte, D (eds) *State, Crime, Power* (London, Sage).

Findlay, M (1999) *The Globalisation of Crime: Understanding transitional relationships in context* (Cambridge, Cambridge University Press).

Foucault, M (1980) 'Lecture, 14th January 1976', in C Gordon (ed) *Power/Knowledge: selected interviews and other writings 1972–1977* (New York, Pantheon).

Gallant, T (1999) 'Brigandage, Piracy, Capitalism and State Formation' in J Heyman (1999) *States and Illegal Practices* (Oxford, Berg).

Gill, P (2002) 'Policing and Regulation: What is the Difference?', 11 *Social and Legal Studies* 523–46.

Gramsci, A (1996) *Selections from the Prison Notebooks, Vol 1* (London, Lawrence and Wishart).

Green, P and Ward, T (2004) *State Crime: Governments, Violence and Corruption* (London, Pluto).

Hall, S, Critcher, C, Jefferson, T, Clarke, J, and Roberts, B (1978) *Policing the Crisis* (Basingstoke, Macmillan).
Hertz, N (2001) *The Silent Takeover: Global capitalism and the death of democracy* (London, Arrow).
International Monetary Fund Monetary and Financial Systems Department (2005) *Regulatory Frameworks for Hawala and other Remittance Systems* (Washington, DC, International Monetary Fund).
Jessop, B (2002) *The Future of the Capitalist State* (Cambridge, Polity).
Luhmann, N (1990) *Essays on Self-Reference* (New York, Columbia University Press).
Lukes, S (1974) *Power: A Radical View* (London, MacMillan).
Mackenzie, S (2005) 'Dig a Bit Deeper: Law, regulation and the illicit antiquities market', 45 *British Journal of Criminology* 249–68.
Mackenzie, S and Green, P (2008) 'Performative Regulation: A Case Study in how Powerful People Avoid Criminal Labels', 48 *British Journal of Criminology* 138–53.
McLennan, C (2005) 'Corruption in Corporate America: Enron—before and after' in C Shore and D Haller (eds), *Corruption: Anthropological perspectives* (London, Pluto).
Mahon, R (1979) 'Regulatory Agencies: Captive agents or hegemonic apparatuses?', 1 *Studies in Political Economy* 162–200.
Mann, M (1984) 'The Autonomous Power of the State: Its origins, mechanisms and results', 25 *European Journal of Sociology* 185–213.
Marx, K (1954[1887]) *Capital: Volume 1* (London, Lawrence and Wishart).
Nader, R (2000) *Cutting Corporate Welfare* (New York, Seven Stories Press).
Neocleous, M (2000) *The Fabrication of Social Order: A Critical Theory of Police Power* (London, Pluto Press).
Offe, C (1984) *Contradictions of the Welfare State* (London, Hutchinson).
Passas, N (2000) 'Global Anomie, Dysnomie, and Economic Crime: Hidden Consequences of Neoliberalism and Globalization in Russia and Around the World', 27 *Social Justice* 16–44.
—— (2001) 'Globalisation and Transnational Crime: Effects of global asymmetries' in P Williams and D Vlassis (eds), *Combating Transnational Crime: concepts, activities and responses* (London, Routledge).
Pearce, F (1976) *Crimes of the Powerful* (London, Pluto).
Pearce, F and Tombs, S (1998) *Toxic Capitalism: Corporate Crime and the Chemical Industry* (Aldershot, Ashgate).
Polanyi, K (1962[1944]) *The Great Transformation: The political and economic origins of our time* (Boston, Beacon).
Poulantzas, N (1978) *State, Power, Socialism* (London, New Left Books).
Ruggiero, V (2000) *Crime and markets: Essays in anti-criminology* (Oxford, Oxford University Press).
Smith, M (2005) *When Ol' Blue Eyes Was a Red* (London, Redwords).
Snider, L (forthcoming) 'Accommodating Power: The "common sense" of regulators', *Social and Legal Studies*.
Stokes, D (2005) *America's Other War: Terrorising Colombia* (London, Zed Books).
Tombs, S and Whyte, D (1998) 'Capital Fights Back: from Cullen to Crine in the Offshore Oil Industry', 57 *Studies in Political Economy* 73–102.

Whitfield, D (2001) *Public Services or Corporate Welfare* (London, Pluto).
Whyte, D (2003) 'Lethal Regulation: State–Corporate Crime and the UK Government's New Mercenaries', 30 *Journal of Law and Society* 575–600.
—— (2006) 'Regulating Safety, Regulating Profit: Cost cutting, injury and death in the North Sea after Piper Alpha' in E Tucker (ed), *Working Disasters: The politics of recognition and response* (New York, Baywood).
—— (2007a) 'The Crimes of Neo-liberal Rule in Occupied Iraq', 47 *British Journal of Criminology* 177–95.
—— (2007b) 'Market Hegemony and the War on Terror', 34 *Social Justice* 111–31.
Young, J (1999) *The Exclusive Society* (London, Sage).

8

Criminalising the Market in Illicit Antiquities

An Evaluation of the Dealing in Cultural Objects (Offences) Act 2003 in England and Wales

SIMON MACKENZIE AND PENNY GREEN*

THE 2003 ACT

AS OUR EDITORIAL introduction to this volume suggests, source country legal controls have only been proven of significant value in relation to their place in an international network of control, and it has gradually become apparent to commentators on the illicit market in antiquities that there are other points in such an international network of control where intervention may be more effective than at source (O'Keefe, 1997; Polk, 2000). Strategies of regulation at the demand end of the chain of supply have been thought potentially capable of achieving a sanitising effect on the market, and it is under this broad philosophy of demand-reduction as applied to illicit antiquities that the 2003 Act appears.

The 2003 Act, an apparent attempt to confront the illicit element of the London antiquities market, was put before Parliament as a Private Member's Bill, taking effect as law on 30 December 2003. The Act, in section 1, provides for a sentence on conviction on indictment of up to seven years' imprisonment and/or a fine, where a person:

> dishonestly deals in a cultural object that is tainted, knowing or believing that the object is tainted.

* This research was funded by the Economic and Social Research Council (ESRC), grant reference RES-000-22-1074. The authors are very grateful to the ESRC for its support. Research assistance was provided by Dr Gordon Lobay, who also features as a contributor to this volume.

Under section 2 of the Act, a cultural object is 'tainted' if it is excavated, or removed from a monument or other building or structure of historical, architectural or archaeological interest, and such excavation or removal constitutes an offence. It is stated to be immaterial whether the excavation or removal took place in the United Kingdom or elsewhere. The intended effect of this legislation is therefore to criminalise (and by implication deter) the knowing possession or trade in the United Kingdom of antiquities looted either here or abroad.

The purpose of the present research was to evaluate the impact of the Act on the UK market and its role in the international illicit market. In approaching this research question we chose to focus on the market in London due to its prominent place in the international trade. While we have gathered some data outside London, both within the United Kingdom and abroad, our data are predominantly London-based. This focus was based partly on the need to effectively allocate research resources, attempting to achieve some depth of inquiry, which would have been lost if we had attempted greater breadth in approach. It was also based on jurisdictional legal issues such as the absence in Scotland at the time of the research of parallel legislation to the 2003 Act, which obviated the possibility of a UK-wide study. Where, therefore, we may sometimes talk of 'the UK market' in what follows, this extrapolation represents generic points that, based on our extra-London research and our study of the literature on the looting issue, we have no reason to think conceal major differences between market practices in London from those elsewhere in the United Kingdom.

CONDUCT OF THE RESEARCH: DATA COLLECTION

The first phase of the research was a postal survey, conducted during the summer of 2005. Using Internet searches, phonebook and other business directory searches, observation of suitable business premises, and recommendations from contacts in the market and among observers of the market, we identified in the London market all possible potential suitable recipients for the survey. This amounted to a sample frame of 102 persons/institutions. Of these, 13 were excluded from the mail-out due to either: (a) being impossible to find, (b) having indicated at an early stage that they did not want to receive a survey, or (c) having been included in the sample frame but for whom the survey was not thought appropriate or useful: these were generally research participants we knew, or knew of, from previous work and wanted to interview in depth and/or pursue informal discussions with. The number of survey recipients was therefore 89.

The number of responses we received to the survey was 24; a response rate of 27% of the 89 mailed out. This is a low response rate for a social survey, but should be considered in context. That context consists in a necessarily rather blunt initial probe into a highly sensitive subject through an unsolicited approach to members of a community whose main public characteristic is its private nature and its reserve, and which has become rattled over recent years by academic and legal attacks on its way of doing business, the latter of which have resulted in the high-profile prosecutions of some of its members.[1] Further, some of the 'non-responses' we received were in respect of survey recipients who had died, or who had been incorrectly targeted as being specialists in antiquities. In this latter respect, we took an inclusive approach with our survey mail-out which meant that where research revealed an ambiguity over whether a person or institution fell within the remit of our sample population we erred on the side of caution and included them in the sample frame, sending them a survey. This inclusive approach tends to exaggerate non-response.

Against this background a response rate of 27% in relation to a survey which had the relatively modest aims described below does not, we would suggest, indicate methodological deficit or generate untrustworthy data. We would accept that, on the face of it, it would appear hazardous in the absence of supporting material to argue that a quarter of the surveyed respondents accurately represented the views and experiences of the whole market under study. That supporting material is, however, available in the form of the expanding literature surrounding the problem of looting—some of which is based on empirical investigation. The answers we received in the survey fit well with the picture of the market, and its relationship with the question of regulation, drawn by this literature, and this provides triangulation for our survey data which supports their validity. We must also bear in mind the small sample frame from which the survey population was drawn. That is, our 102 targeted respondents represented *everybody* we considered to be in possession of relevant information on the question of the regulation of London's antiquities trade: a list put together building on known key players and supplemented by several weeks of research into market participants, commentators, and regulators. We also, of course, allowed for some snowballing during the project based on recommendations and introductions by current respondents, but the point we should make clear is that our response rate effectively represented over one quarter of the London market and its attendant spectators.[2] Put that way, and in light of the other arguments presented above, a low survey response redeems itself with a validity particular to the circumstances of the research area and design.

[1] eg *United States v Schultz* 178 F Supp 2d 445 (SDNY 2002), 333 F2d 393 (2d Cir 2003), 147 LEd 2d 891 (2004).

[2] To put the size of our sample in proportion, the Department for Culture, Media and Sport (DCMS) has informally estimated that 'there are around 20 large dealers in the UK dealing in antiquities and a further 100 or so smaller dealers who deal, to some degree, in antiquities. Furthermore, there are around 80 museums around the country that regularly purchase treasure items and so have an interest in purchasing antiquities' (personal communication).

The survey was designed to allow anonymous response, and many of the respondents chose this route rather than identifying themselves on the return. The short survey had several aims. One of these aims was to gather some 'foundational' information on the reactions of key market players to the legislation under study, in order that we might adopt a suitable interview strategy in the second phase of the research. Another aim of the survey was to invite participation in the interviews. The major rationale for the survey was, however, to elicit information from hard-to-reach respondents, who viewed the issue as too sensitive to warrant their volunteering for interview but who were, in fact, perhaps the most interesting subset of the market we wished to study. Previous research into the antiquities market (Mackenzie, 2005), combined with a review of the other research literature in the field, suggests that certain central figures participate repeatedly in opinion-forming opportunities relating to the question of regulation, and that while some of these 'vocal minority' are certainly high-profile market participants, they do not necessarily represent unproblematically the views of other dealers who operate, or try to operate, with a lower profile.

In the second phase of the research, interviews were conducted with targeted key respondents in London, Oxford, Cambridge, Cairo, and Bangkok. The total number of interviews was 38. The interviews were qualitative in method, meaning that their goal was less to elicit quantifiable data than to gain, in an interpretive vein, insight into what the 2003 Act means to actors 'on the ground'. While attempting to secure the anonymity of our informants where possible, we can provide a general breakdown of the actors we interviewed:

- five dealers from a selection of the most prominent dealerships in London;
- five 'specialists' with expertise in observing, researching, and commenting on the illicit market;
- three specialist law enforcement representatives, including representatives of police and customs;
- four respondents in senior positions drawn from the United Kingdom's museums sector, including prestigious museums, their major funding sources, and associations established to provide collaborative spaces for discussions of matters of museum governance;
- two key actors in the legislative process who played central influential roles in the design and/or passage into force of the 2003 Act;
- five respondents in Thailand, including a senior figure in the National Museum, a senior figure in the legal arm of the Fine Arts Department, a dealer, and two archaeologists (one local, one foreign);
- 13 respondents in Egypt, including senior representatives of the Supreme Council of Antiquities, foreign and local archaeologists, specialist academics, and a senior representative of the Egyptian Museum.

FINDINGS OF THE RESEARCH: DATA ANALYSIS

Survey Data

The survey responses provide a contextual framework within which to further analyse the importance of the 2003 Act in regulating the illicit part of the trade in antiquities in London. A list of the survey questions used is provided as an Appendix to this chapter. Trade survey recipients were asked all of the questions, while non-trade survey recipients were asked questions 1 to 6 only. The survey produced the following data:

— *Respondents*: What was the balance of trade/non-trade response to the survey? The survey was designed to be filled out anonymously if the respondent so desired, with the result that we cannot categorise respondents in this way unless they identified themselves on the form or otherwise made clear their affiliation in their answers. In fact, the vast majority of respondents were identifiable in this way. Therefore, we can say that 58% of respondents were definitely from the trade, 29% were not (that is, they fell into the categories of regulators, commentators, archaeologists, and other specialists), and in respect of the rest (13%), affiliation is unknown.

— *Self-regulation*: 75% of respondents thought the trade required formal regulation, and that self-regulation was not adequate to prevent the purchase of illicit antiquities by the trade. This compares with 25% who thought that the trade could effectively self-regulate.

— *Knowledge of the 2003 Act*: 71% of respondents reported familiarity with the requirements of the 2003 Act, 17% reported no such familiarity, and 12% did not answer this question on the survey.

— *Effect of the 2003 Act*: Asked if they thought the impact of the Act on the trade in antiquities in London 'has been or will be positive or negative', the majority of answers were neither. 17% thought the effect positive only, and 8% thought it negative only. 12.5% thought the effect to be both positive and negative, while the greatest proportion, 29% of respondents, declined to answer the question as it was put but instead wrote that they thought the Act had been and/or would be 'neutral', 'minimal' or 'little' in its effect, or would be 'ineffective'.

— *Perceived change in market*: Asked whether they had noticed a change in the way dealers operate as a result of the Act, 50% of respondents said they had seen no change; 21% said they had noticed a change, and 29% did not respond. The 21% that had noticed change represents five responses, of which one suggested any change noticed was 'purely cosmetic' and had in effect driven the market 'more underground or more under the counter than it was before', one simply noted that the *Art Newspaper* had reported a small number of dealers relocating abroad, and another claimed to perceive 'less activity' in the market due to 'despondency'. None of these responses would seem to accord with the aims of the 2003 Act to 'protect small business from the illicit trade, which threatens their commercial position through unfair competition' (DCMS, 2004a: 1). 'Purely cosmetic' adaptation, dealer relocation, and 'despondency' have occurred precisely because the DCMS's characterisation of the trade as bifurcated between 'legitimate' and 'illegitimate' dealers is in error. Illegitimate objects pass through the 'legitimate' trade, and therefore any regulatory attention paid to such objects will, rather than support 'legitimate' dealers by eliminating their 'illegitimate' peers, directly affect the business of the trade generally.

In fact, however, the Act appears to have been ineffective in achieving any substantial effect on the trade: the most important finding here for an evaluation of the Act is that half of respondents, and a significant majority of those who responded to this specific question, had seen no change in market routines as a result of the passage of the Act.

— *Change in personal routines*: This question was asked only of trade respondents. Asked whether their knowledge of the Act had affected the way they carried on business, or whether it would in the future, 64% said no, 22% said yes (although in some cases only 'formal' change was planned), and there was 14% non-response. The detail of these responses is important to understand their character within this statistical distribution. The majority 'no change' group generally saw no reason to change their routines, which they saw to be adequate to constitute legitimate dealing and therefore most unlikely to trigger an offence under the 2003 Act. That the majority of traders surveyed have not and do not intend to alter their activities in light of the Act must be seen to be a significant failing of the legislation unless the 'bad apples' market story (see below) is believed.

There is considerable evidence that there are bad apples in the antiquities trade, as there are in any business enterprise, in the sense of individuals or organisations who willingly break the law or violate social or moral norms of behaviour. There is also, however, considerable evidence that the problem of dealing in illicit antiquities is an issue that affects the 'legitimate' trade in so far as looted antiquities are bought and sold as part of the general routine dealing activity of the open trade, often, it seems, without direct knowledge of the illicit nature of an object due to a lack of provenance information (Mackenzie, 2005). The absence of thorough and effective provenance investigation has become routinised in the trade, in the United Kingdom as elsewhere, and as such in some deals made on the 'legitimate' market, illicit objects are traded with no direct knowledge as to whether they have been looted or not. Importantly, although perhaps obviously, this means that these objects could have been looted, and that the trade either lacks interest in sanitising its procedures (in which case it requires incentive and/or supervision), or that it lacks the capacity to do so (in which case it requires the support of mechanisms of object identification such as databases).

The DCMS has not helped the cause of effective regulation here, having declined to use the legislation to spur the trade with incentive to change, supporting the reluctance of the market to adopt stringent and energetic provenance investigations upon contemplated purchase by stating in the guidelines accompanying the Act that 'the Act does not necessarily oblige dealers to take steps to ascertain provenance or to exercise due diligence to avoid committing the offence' (DCMS, 2004a: 1).

It also seems the DCMS has abandoned the idea of a UK database of illicit artefacts, recommended by the Illicit Trade Advisory Panel (ITAP) and briefly considered by government (DCMS, 2004b), but now dropped. In fact there are good reasons to doubt the efficacy of a database of illicit objects in addressing the problem of looting. Predominantly, looted objects are excavated and exported without coming to official attention in source countries, and therefore give rise to no precise information which might be entered on such a database. Indirectly, then, an illicit object database might have the perverse effect of serving to legitimate purchases of looted antiquities, as dealers could argue that, having checked the database and found no record of their intended purchase, they had no knowledge or belief of its illicit status.

— *Bad apples*: There was no specific question asking whether respondents were of the opinion that problems relating to looted antiquities in the trade were the work of a perceived minority of 'bad apples' or whether the problem infected the trade as a whole. However, responses to the survey questions are noteworthy in that 25% of respondents (six in number) attributed problems in the trade to 'bad apples', suggesting that a small sector of the trade was untrustworthy and should not be associated with the legitimate trade. Of these six respondents, five were from the trade. Thus, 36% of the trade respondents associated the problem of looting with 'bad apples' without being prompted by a specific question to that effect. Given that this response was unprompted, we suggest that the 'bad apples' opinion carries significant weight in a diagnosis of the trade's relationship with the looting problem. In light of previous research (Mackenzie, 2005), we suggest that this represents a somewhat pious and complacent view on the part of dealers who may well themselves be dealing in illicit antiquities, perhaps unwittingly.

Interview Data

The conceptual starting point for an analysis of the data is the market reduction model of crime reduction strategy in relation to markets in illicit commodities, as developed by Sutton and colleagues and published by the Policing and Reducing Crime Unit at the Home Office (Sutton, 1998; Sutton, Schneider, and Hetherington, 2001). Jacqueline Schneider, an early proponent of the market reduction approach (MRA) with Mike Sutton, has very recently published a paper in which she explores the potential of the MRA to apply to commodity markets that are more exotic than domestic stolen goods markets, focusing on the international market in illicit wildlife. She notes that she has previously suggested at the UN Crime Congress 2003 that the MRA might be useful in tackling the property markets which are the concern of the UN Convention on Transnational and Organized Crime, including (as well as wildlife) weapons and ammunition, humans and body parts, and cultural heritage (Schneider, 2008). The 2003 Act, on the face of it, would seem to fit with a market reduction philosophy: in a simplified model of the movement of goods from source to market, that criminal sanctions applied to the purchase of illicit material in the market will reduce the uptake of such purchase opportunities; that this reduction in sales will filter back to the 'suppliers' of the market, the middle-men; and that the reduction of demand among the customers of these middle-market traders will result in a concomitant reduction in their demand for illicit antiquities from the looters who take objects from the ground in source countries. Sutton, Schneider, and Hetherington summarise the MRA as follows:

> The general theory of the MRA—that reducing dealing in stolen goods will reduce motivation to steal—means that all MRA theft reduction strategies will begin with the following 2 aims:
>
> — instil an appreciation among thieves that transporting, storing, and selling stolen goods has become at least as risky as it is to steal goods in the first place
>
> — make buying, dealing and consuming stolen goods appreciably more risky for all those involved (2001: vii).

The MRA is broader than this simplified model, however. It speaks, for example, to the variations in the dynamic of supply and demand relations; conventional wisdom has held that demand stimulates supply in markets, but the MRA notes that thieves or fences can create markets by their offers of stolen goods for sale and that therefore supply can sometimes lead to demand. The MRA also discusses at some length the benefits of inter-agency approaches to tackling illicit markets—a trend which is increasingly popular across all fields of criminal justice presently (Hughes, 2006) and which seems particularly sensible in relation to markets such as that in antiquities, which crosses borders and which is policed by a small squad with resources that are severely limited even by comparison to policing resources in general.[3]

The MRA also acknowledges the structural parameters within which certain property crimes occur, for example the 'strain' experienced by consumers who cannot afford products heavily advertised as fashionable or otherwise desirable. Sensibly, the model proposes that attending to the provision of alternative legitimate routes to the realisation of these goals for individuals or businesses will reduce the incentive to find or accept illegal means of goal-satisfaction. This might be characterised as a 'harm reduction' component to the regulation of illicit markets and can be seen to form a complement in the model to the more traditional 'penal deterrence' component outlined above and which, in our analysis, informs the 2003 Act. Our research suggests that the penal deterrence part of the MRA philosophy, in which conceptual location we see the 2003 Act, is fraught with difficulty in its application to the antiquities market, and that there may be other more productive approaches that a market country like the United Kingdom can take to tackling the problem of the international market in looted antiquities (see Polk, chapter one, this volume, for a similar view more broadly stated).

Dealers are apparently out of touch with the reality of the problem of illicit antiquities. As has been argued elsewhere (Mackenzie, 2005), while cases of high-level smuggling are given high profile in the media and therefore provide the most readily-available graphic case studies of the illicit transit of looted antiquities, these cases must be seen in the context of a market which operates in a routine manner to circulate illicit antiquities in much less remarkable ways. To be successful in sanitising the market the 2003 Act must require dealers not only to be averse to accepting offers of goods which are clearly illicit, but also to take serious steps to investigate the provenance of the objects they routinely purchase, from sources they might historically have assumed to be 'trustworthy'. The MRA predicts that it is the disruption of this routine lack of reflexivity in seeing oneself *qua* buyer as a generative part of the chain of supply of illicit commodities that will have the greatest effect on the supply chain, and we might add that in the antiquities market this routine lack of reflexivity manifests itself as an assumption that open market dealing equates to lawful dealing in objects which are not tainted. In light of the evidence we have from sellers on the open market as to the depth of their investigation into object provenance (or general lack thereof), this faith

[3] The Art and Antiquities Squad of the Metropolitan Police is the unit which has responsibility for the specialist policing of the market under discussion here. It is staffed by a detective sergeant and three detectives, together with a small number of analysts and researchers.

in the open market, typified by comments such as that quoted below, appears to be misplaced:

> Well, what I do for instance, is only buy on the open market. I don't buy from any individuals or anyone like that. I buy on the open market, which is basically an auction house—somewhere like Bonhams where they publish the object's description and it's been in a published catalogue, which could have been looked at by the people at the British Museum or the Police's Art and Antiques Branch, it has been illustrated, it has been up on the Internet and if there is any objections to its sale I would imagine that it would have been raised at that point ... So, there is no need to buy looted antiquities. When I looked at the Cultural Offences Act I thought, where would I go to buy looted antiquities? I mean how would you do it? ... I mean, this [the 2003 Act] doesn't really concern me because everything that I do is in the public domain and I think everything that most of other dealers do is in the public domain. Unless someone can show me that I am acting illegally then I cannot see where the question of problems are. (London dealer)

The 'problems' become apparent when we see the antiquities market as a 'grey market'. This signifies that the flows of licit and illicit objects are intermixed and therefore that, rather than being a market characterised by a 'clean' public trade and a 'dirty' private or 'underground' trade, the supposedly clean public trade in antiquities is tainted 'grey' by the circulation therein of illicit antiquities (Polk, 2000). This is not to say that there is no private or underground trade in illicit antiquities, of course. Rather, it is simply to observe that the public antiquities market is in this sense a 'grey market', and indeed was described in precisely these terms by one of our specialist interviewees. Characteristic of such a grey market, dealers who would describe themselves as 'legitimate', while at times expressing (usually publicly) concern about looted artefacts in the market, are, at other more private moments, surprisingly complacent about the issue of dealing in stolen goods. In a market which functions without the serious transmission of provenance, such dealing is seen as a standard risk, and remains so despite the creation of the offence in the 2003 Act:

> So, stolen goods, yes, they must be here. Possibly over the course of time 10% of my stock has probably been stolen at one time or another ... I don't know, but it would not surprise me if it was that high, ..., either stolen in China, or wherever, you just don't know. (London dealer)

The 2003 Act is perceived by dealers and regulators alike as an ineffective control mechanism. A law enforcement respondent put it pithily: 'they passed a dead duck there'. We can identify the failings of the 2003 Act in terms of a series of 'problems' which are given clear form by the data, and which come together to undermine the impact of the legislation. These include:

(1) the problem of proof;
(2) the problem of national self-interest and political will;
(3) the problem of power.

(1) The Problem of Proof

The problem of proof in relation to the 2003 Act arises in relation to:

(a) the non-retroactivity of the operative provisions of the Act;
(b) the absence of provision for enforcement of breach of foreign export prohibition;
(c) the difficulty of availability of evidence in relation to the central 'knowing or believing' provision.

We shall examine these in turn.

(a) The Non-retroactivity of the Operative Provisions of the Act

The 2003 Act came into force on 30 December 2003. It is not retroactive and therefore a 'tainted' object is only such if it has been stolen after that date. This clearly restricts the application of the Act in respect of objects already in circulation in the market on that date. More seriously, in any successful prosecution it must be proven that the object in question was stolen after the above date. This perpetuates a problem of proof that existed for prosecutors under the law prior to 2003. The sites from which antiquities are stolen are often isolated, their contents are known only to the finders, and looted antiquities cross national borders without being recognised or recorded. In these circumstances, it is very difficult indeed to establish proof of the date of theft of an object which has appeared on the market without accurate accompanying information relating to its date of finding.

(b) The Absence of Provision for Enforcement of Breach of Foreign Export Prohibition

Objects which have been exported in breach of a foreign export restriction are not included in the definition of 'tainted' under the 2003 Act and, as such, a considerable proportion of illicit antiquities are excluded from its scope. This could have been an effective site of intervention into the illicit market for the 2003 Act, had it been decided to follow examples of international illicit market regulation for other commodities, such as the CITES regulation of the international movement of protected wildlife, which encourage countries to sight export documentation from source before allowing import. The opportunity to tie import into the United Kingdom with licit export overseas was not taken for antiquities, however.

As well as declining to engage with the import into the United Kingdom of objects illegally exported from other countries, the 2003 Act exists within a context of difficulty in the control of illicit objects within the United Kingdom which are to be exported. EC Regulation 3911/92 applies to the export of cultural goods outside the EU (export within the EU does not require an export licence). EC Regulation 3911/92 in Article 2 creates in the United Kingdom the obligation to provide an export licence for cultural goods to be exported outside the EU where 'the cultural object in question was lawfully and definitively located [in the United Kingdom] on 1 January 1993' or if it is presently located within the United Kingdom 'following … lawful and definitive dispatch from another Member State, or importation from a third country'.

In other words, where an object has been imported into the United Kingdom after 1 January 1993 then, unless it has come from an EU Member State, its 'dispatch' from that importing country does not have to have been 'lawful' in order for it to be entitled to grant of an export licence from the United Kingdom. Even if an object is known to have been looted in a country outside the EU, in contravention of a state vesting statute, it appears contrary to the EC Regulation for the United Kingdom to refuse it an export licence. This creates a situation of conflict between the EC Regulation and the 2003 Act. The latter defines 'deals in' under section 3(1) to include export. Therefore, putting the two rules together, if a person dishonestly deals in (here, exports from the United Kingdom) a cultural object that is tainted, knowing or believing that it is tainted, and where that taint has occurred by virtue of its theft from a non-EU state, the person commits an offence in terms of the 2003 Act, but the United Kingdom is powerless to refuse the grant of an export licence under the terms of the EC Regulation. This unfortunate situation looks unlikely to be resolved in the near future:

Lord Renfrew of Kaimsthorn asked Her Majesty's Government:

> What progress there has been with the proposed amendment of the European Community regulations governing the refusal of export licences for illicitly removed cultural materials that have entered the United Kingdom (a) from another member state of the European Community; and (b) from outside the European Community?

Lord Davies of Oldham replied:

> No amendment is required to Council Regulation EC 3911/92 to enable the UK to refuse an export licence in relation to an item that has been illegally exported from another member state. In such cases, the UK will not be the competent authority as defined in Article 2 of that regulation to issue a licence in relation to such an item and would, therefore, have to refer the matter to the member state in question.
>
> The UK has made a proposal for the amendment of Council Regulation EC 3911/92 which would allow the UK to refuse an export licence in relation to an object that had been illegally exported from a third country to the UK. However, this proposal does not yet have sufficient support from other member states (*Hansard*, 2006).

This is a considerable lacuna in the legislation, since an application for export licence is clearly a point of legal 'surfacing' at which many artefacts will come to the attention of the UK authorities; a 'pinch point' in the MRA crime reduction jargon. The export licensing system was considered by ITAP to be a productive potential site of application of the 2003 Act, but has been proven ineffective in this regard by the conflict that has emerged with EU legislation.

(c) The Difficulty of Availability of Evidence in relation to the Central 'Knowing or Believing' Provision

Proving that a defendant was aware, to the extent of 'knowing or believing', that an object he or she dealt in was tainted in practical terms renders unworkable, in three words, the offence the Act creates. At the same time, this wording serves to undermine the basic message that unites all critics of the market: that effective due diligence in relation to object provenance needs to become an essential component of any purchase of antiquities. As the DCMS guidelines state:

> The burden of proving knowledge or belief that an object is tainted rests with the prosecution and such proof must be beyond all reasonable doubt. *This means that a failure by the accused to carry out adequate checks on the provenance of an object will not constitute knowledge or belief* (DCMS, 2004a: 8, emphasis added).

This major failing of the 2003 Act is well known to market participants. Through the 'publicity vacuum' which has surrounded the non-enforcement of the Act since its inception, the problem of proof even acts as a kind of 'pre-emptive' neutralisation of the MRA approach of the 2003 Act, in that 'capable guardians' (Cohen and Felson, 1979; Felson, 1994) in the chain of supply remain unlikely to report suspicious behaviour. Thus, a museum respondent reported that if offered a cultural object he suspected to be tainted, he would in all likelihood simply refuse to purchase the object and send the seller on her way rather than report her to the police. This fits with the findings of prior research on the most common reaction of conscientious trade figures to offers suspected of being illicit (Mackenzie, 2005). In the case of the museum respondent, the prospect of reporting a suspicious offer to the police 'never occurred to me'. Even after prompting on the matter, the interviewee suggested that you would have to be 'pretty damned sure of your ground before you ... summon the police'.

We have accumulated considerable evidence of the 'don't ask, don't tell' culture in relation to provenance in the antiquities market. This culture of ignorance in relation to the origin of objects is no longer a fresh revelation, having been raised in almost all of the literature on the illicit market. Given that it was precisely this aspect of 'the problem of proof' that the panel recommending the offence which would be enshrined in the 2003 Act purportedly wanted to encourage (DCMS, 2000), namely due diligence in provenance-checking by dealers when purchasing antiquities, it is instructive here to reproduce some extracts from the transcript of a prominent dealer in London as illustration that the culture of secrecy remains little affected after the 2003 Act:

> *Dealer*: The people in Hong Kong don't tell you [about provenance] because the people who smuggle the goods out of China are not the sort of people you want to talk about. When I've asked about odd pieces, you know, 'Are there any excavation notes? Can you find where something like this came from? It would be fascinating to know' they just say, 'You don't ask those questions; you don't want to get a reputation for asking questions.' It wasn't me saying that; that's what they say. That's the way presumably, if you're a Hong Kong dealer, to end up in the harbour.
>
> *Interviewer*: So, when you bring things back here there is no culture of people wanting to know where they came from ...
>
> *Dealer*: No, as far as I know in that field, there is no particular question. They're more concerned with the objects rather than any sort of cultural history attached.

Dealers remain more concerned with the question whether they can recover their outlay if an object purchased turns out to be stolen than they do with the new penal consequences of such a purchase under the 2003 Act. In this way, then, the market reduction deterrence penny is still to drop with respect to illicit purchases, and trustworthy sellers are seen as removing the need even to ask about provenance, since if title turns out to be defective the buyer knows he will get his money back from the seller. The same dealer reports:

> A dealer friend could walk in any minute now and put something on the table in front of us and say, 'It's £70, do you want to buy it?' I like the thing and say, 'OK, yes, I want to buy it, where does it come from?' He's going to sit there and say, 'You think I'm going to tell you where I got this, get out of here!' He's never going to disclose a source. That's your biggest problem, you can't get a source, all you can do is trust that person. And with my friends I wouldn't even dream of asking them; I would know that if it's stolen you don't have a problem [ie they will refund the price]. Other dealers are not quite so good.

International transport compounds the problem of the difficulty of proving dealers' knowledge or belief. One can find in the literature, and even in the case law, lively reports of dealers smuggling artefacts from source to market using inventive scams (see, for example, Gerstenblith, 2002, in relation to the *Schultz* case) or organised criminal networks (Mackenzie, 2002). There is also a considerably more mundane side to the international transportation of illicit antiquities, which is symptomatic of and contributes to the lack of provenance information in the market. From the dealer's perspective, the mechanism of transport of illicit commodities is rather straightforward, even to the point of being unworthy of great attention. One dealer in our sample reported never to have been approached by any law enforcement officials 'with any hostility as it were—certainly Customs has never said anything; they never seem to ask any questions'. When asked a more detailed question about his dealings with customs and the mechanism of getting his goods through the customs barrier, he revealed an extraordinary lack of knowledge; indeed, it was as if he were being asked to think about the question of import and legal barriers for the first time. One is left with an impression of a market in which goods just unproblematically turn up at the office door:

> I don't personally take it [the shipment], it just comes in and our shippers deal with it. I don't know exactly what Customs does, I suppose they inspect it ... I mean there is a shipping invoice that says what everything is, so they look at that, but it pretty much just comes here (London dealer).

This dealer acknowledges that, at least until the passage of the 2003 Act, he specialised in excavated material, and we can be sure that some of that material will have entered the United Kingdom and been dealt with in breach of domestic law prior to 2003. The 2003 Act does not seem to have seriously altered this position, and, as we will discuss later, it is the dealer's reluctance to break the law rather than any successful enforcement activity making use of the new law's provisions which have reduced his demand for illicit objects.

We can offer a practical example of the 'knowing or believing' provision in the 2003 Act as it currently affects the routine activity of the market. This example, provided by a law enforcement source, illustrates the powerlessness of the authorities to restrict illicit activity in the market using the offence in the Act, consequent upon the inability of officers to prove, or even gather evidence on, *mens rea*:

> I got called in last week by one dealer who said, 'Right, these are the objects, can I sell them?'
>
> I asked 'Do you think they're stolen?'
>
> He said, 'No!' [laughs]

Such interaction with the authorities is not uncommon in the trade in London. Dealers sometimes ask the police for a certificate stating that the cultural objects they wish to buy or sell are not on the police's database of stolen objects. Obviously this does not in practice mean that these objects have not been looted. This level of superficial formality in the legitimation of transactions is symptomatic of a sophisticated market operating under ineffective legal controls. These ineffective legal controls have left police disaffected:

> *Interviewer*: What proportion of your work is in antiquities?
>
> *Police respondent*: This year, 5%; two years ago, 34%.
>
> *Interviewer*: Why is that?

> *Police respondent*: Because there is no point; we're not getting any convictions. You have to accept that we have to get convictions and we have to arrest people and prevent crime, and I can't do any of that at the moment in the antiquities world ... I'm rarely getting any arrests ... so you've got to look and see where our time is best deployed ... because I'm not getting any results there, so what's the point of carrying on?

The problem of proof is so severe that when the 2003 Act is held up alongside other avenues of prosecution that permit a greater chance of success in court, the offence in the 2003 Act finds itself languishing at the bottom of the toolbox available to the police, the Crown Prosecution Service (CPS), and Her Majesty's Revenue and Customs (HMRC).

At the time we conducted our fieldwork for this study, there had been no prosecutions in terms of the offence in the 2003 Act, and this remained the case at the conclusion of the study in 2007 (see Baroness Scotland's reply to Lord Renfrew's question in *Hansard*, 27 October 2007, col WA143, where she confirms that at that date no prosecutions had been recorded either by the CPS under section 1 of the Act or by HMRC under section 4). Asked to expand upon this, a law enforcement respondent said:

> I'll tell you that there haven't been any because we don't consider it [the Act] of any real value. There are so few lacunas in the law that we considered that it would fill, that I don't foresee us ... we've estimated that we may pursue one charge under it every five years. That's a view that was supported by CPS opinion at the time. The only scenario that we actually envisage using it for is if a person is stealing property from their own premises, if it is a listed property. That is the only part of law that we think isn't filled by some other statute and most particularly the Proceeds of Crime Act, money laundering. That is where we pursue nearly all charges now, we don't use 'handling in stolen goods'; that is nearly always a secondary or alternate charge. The primary offence is the Proceeds of Crime Act because of its burden, the elements of proof required compared to the 'Dealing in Tainted' Act, which has the double-non-retrospective problem as we foresee it. I don't see it as being of any value at all.

(2) The Problem of National Self-interest and Political Will

The 2003 Act is designed to play a part in the control of London's part in the international market in illicit antiquities. As London is a central market for the sale of antiquities which originate, and in some cases have been stolen from, overseas, this mission involves the acceptance by the UK government of a role in policing crimes which predominantly affect the interests of foreign powers. The idea of the protection of the interests of humanity generally—'the world's history', 'our common cultural heritage' and other such emotive terminology—is lost in the practical implementation of a system of resource prioritisation which inevitably occurs in the routine conduct of policing in the context of limited funding and manpower, and a climate of public and political accountability and attention to targets encouraged by the risk-management paradigm which characterises contemporary law enforcement (at least at the level of central government; see Hughes, 2006). A law enforcement respondent is clear on this point:

> Also, you have to look at the fact that most of our use of this Act would be to help other countries and now you have to say that we as a [law enforcement] service don't really even want to help the other countries because our responsibility is to make London safer, it's not to protect the cultural heritage of Iraq or Afghanistan. And that's where our efforts are focused. Even on our very small team my primary role is not to recover Iraqi or Afghani or other antiquities and send them back, my primary objective is to arrest people in London and send them to prison and stop them dealing in art work stolen in London, that's my primary role. Very much my secondary role when we have spare time I can try to do the other side of it.

There is in our research interviews evidence of a widely held perception that the government no longer attributes much importance to the question of the market in looted antiquities. The 'flurry of activity' represented by the ITAP report, accession to the UNESCO Convention, and the 2003 Act is now perceived in many quarters to have ceased, and the government appears to have no firm plans to follow up on this period of regulatory focus through pressing for application of the offence in the 2003 Act or otherwise. DCMS representatives since Alan Howarth are thought by our sample to have little interest in the issue, and their occasional statements of concern are seen as performative and superficial by market-watchers.

(3) The Problem of Power

At issue here is the capacity that 'powerful' constituencies have to protect their interests. In our study, the powerful constituency is the antiquities market, including some museums[4] and collectors, but particularly comprised of a core of active dealers and their lawyers. This group has managed to achieve such a high level of representation in official circles that their interests have become fused with the more 'controlling' elements of

[4] Some representatives of museums in the United Kingdom present similar attitudes to dealers. Generally, however, the museums sector in the United Kingdom appears considerably more sympathetic to archaeological concerns than the trade, and certainly the sector is public and visible in its attempts to address the illicit trade through such measures as the Museums Association Code of Ethics. In the United States the position is different, with museums in general being closer to the market than they are in the United Kingdom. In a parallel to the 'bad apples' argument we have discussed in respect of dealers in London, a museum respondent suggested in the present research that 'most museum opinion in this country is firmly on the side of the archaeologists in deploring the illicit trade and in taking a strong stand against it', but that against this general stance there were 'a few mavericks' (personal communication). This suggestion would usefully be the subject of further research by way of an independent review of attitudes in the sector.

the 2003 Act. We have explored the history of the 2003 Act elsewhere, tracing the influences on its structure and content from inception to passage into force (Mackenzie and Green, 2008). In that work, we show how the incorporation into the legislative process of the interests of the more powerful spokespeople in the antiquities market has served the end of control dilution. Market interests were in fact in considerable degree constitutive of the 2003 Act, and in this way a picture emerges of a market taking a leading role in its own regulation. This is not self-regulation, however. Rather, it is a form of legislative influence corrosive of the regulatory mechanism; a purposive and forceful watering-down of the laws that govern a certain market sector through a process of inclusion in discussions around appropriate levels of control at the time the law was drafted. As with other historical examples of market influence on the laws which govern harmful market activity, for example in the automotive industry (Lee, 1998) and the asbestos industry (Calhoun and Hiller, 1988; Tweedale, 2000), what on the face of it might appear to be benign consensus-based policy and legislation is on the basis of our findings more properly construed as the sabotage of formative mechanisms of control through tactical legal and discourse-based manoeuvres by affected parties with the power to do so.

In the case of the 2003 Act, a significant site of market influence on the process of governance of its activities was the ITAP panel, which brought representatives of the trade lobby together with archaeologists and lawyers with the aim of achieving a consensus as to the most appropriate regulatory way forward. The DCMS view is that ITAP 'was representative of all the stakeholders that have an interest in combating the illegal trade in cultural property' (personal communication). Such a stakeholder view of the formation of criminal legislation is at odds with the top-down model generally adopted in criminal justice legislation and, particularly in questions of regulation of a grey market, can set business interests against effective criminal legislation. In this forum, as members of the ITAP panel have reported to us, the question of what the dealers would 'acquiesce to' (specialist interviewee) became the measure of how tight the legislation would become, and once ITAP's recommendation for an Act came to fruition by way of a Private Member's Bill, the matter of acquiescence became all the more important. The 'knowing or believing' wording—which significantly diminishes the reach of the 2003 Act—was a central plank of the bridge which had to be built between the trade and its archaeological critics, and its dilution of the *mens rea* attached to the offence was important in achieving the acquiescence we have mentioned.

Ultimately, dealers are currently—and wish to continue to be—lightly regulated. In practice this boils down to forms of self-regulation. 'Self-regulated' in this market takes on an even more insular meaning than its use in the compliance and regulation literature would suggest, however. While there are professional bodies such as the Antiquities Dealers Association

(ADA) in the United Kingdom which provide, amongst other things, a code of ethics for their members, a very small proportion of dealers have chosen to join such organisations. One dealer described his reluctance to pay a £300 per annum membership fee to join the ADA when he was 'confident that my [personal] code of ethics is better'. He also adverted to the observed deviance of some members of professional organisations, which activity suggested to him that the ethical commitments of members were formal rather than substantive:

> [T]here are a few members of the ADA who in my view have also acted unethically. There is one dealer who has in the past acted almost like a supermarket, if there was a catalogue and you wanted to buy one object, he has one of a type illustrated and he's got no end of them. I suspect some of that supermarket-style selling might have dubious sources, but again that is doing the trade a lot of harm. Again, this individual is a member of the ADA, so in my view the ADA needs to police their activities better than they do. (London dealer)

Of course, the trouble with individual self-regulation is that, when coupled with a view of the market as generally unproblematic in its relation to the issue of looted antiquities, it results in inadequate due diligence and the perpetuation of the problem the 2003 Act was intended to address.

POSITIVE EFFECTS OF THE 2003 ACT

The data are not uniformly dismissive of the effect of the 2003 Act, however. Despite the lack of prosecutions and the other problems, theoretical and practical, with the Act, listed above, there is evidence that some members of the trade have been affected by the new legislation.

Generally, the reaction from the trade which we have distilled from our interviews and our observations of the market more generally has been one of a cautious and more reflexive 'business as usual'. As one of our specialist informants euphemistically put it: 'the impact of the Act is not instantly evident!' Dealers generally appear to engage in the same transaction routines as before the implementation of the 2003 Act, encouraged by the general (accurate) perception of a culture of non-enforcement around the new legislation. They remain conscious that at this relatively early stage in the aftermath of legislative activity this period of non-enforcement might come to an end, but we might hypothesise that the longer the period of enforcement inactivity continues, the more confident the market will become in the permanence of this state of affairs and the more likely it is that old dealer routines will persist.

That said, some dealers have reportedly begun to implement changes in their patterns of dealing as a result of the 2003 Act. One dealer in our sample in particular asserted that he was taking the new legislation very seriously and that his office had 'cut down dramatically on things we buy from Hong Kong'. He suggested that on his construction of the Act, 'you can buy there [in Hong Kong, with particular reference to the large auction houses], but you can't sell what you've bought there!' In criminological terms, this reaction might be interpreted as the self-control of an individual particularly susceptible to criminal justice deterrence.

> *Dealer*: You mean, why am I self-policing in this manner?
>
> *Interviewer*: Yes.
>
> *Dealer*: Well, I just think that the law ... I mean, the general view in the trade is that the law is difficult to enforce and a bit toothless ... although obviously the penalties are quite large, essentially. My own view is that laws might start off like that, but you never know, they might change one day! You just need a couple of zealots to go around trying to enforce it and the whole aspect of it changes quite rapidly. I don't like the idea of dealing with that sword of Damocles hanging over my head.

It would be mistaken, on our reading of the market, to take this extreme self-policing as common among market actors, although some level of self-policing is characteristic of the 'semi-conscious state of siege' (London dealer) which typifies the current market reaction to the new Act. The deterrence-susceptible dealer cited above has considered relocating to America or continental Europe, where he perceives the legal constraints on purchase are less stringent. Whether they are in fact less stringent 'on the books' and in practice is a matter for debate which we shall not address here, other than to note that despite the high net worth of many of the community of dealers in the United Kingdom, few have yet actioned any such relocation plan, and even this dealer who considers himself obliged to comply with both the letter and spirit of the law 'may yet [relocate abroad], but the current plan is to try to deal in things that don't contravene the Act'.

While we did obtain reports of dealers relocating to jurisdictions perceived to display less regulatory interest in the market, these dealers were thought to be those whose merchandise was suspect enough to demand a retreat from the heightened climate of control in the United Kingdom. While displacement does not 'solve the problem' of the international market in looted antiquities, it does suggest that if other jurisdictions follow the United Kingdom's lead in implementing controls, the bar may be internationally raised in relation to the segment of the dealing community who are able and willing geographically to follow the path of least resistance to their activities:

> A number of dealers and collectors panicked, of course, and some dealers moved to Brussels, which doesn't have any laws like this and actually is one of the most liberal countries in that sense because Belgium doesn't even have any worries about export licences. I know some people moved there who deal in material that might be at risk. But, there are lots of antiquities dealers that are still operating in London. (London dealer)

Importantly, for such a general raising of the bar to occur, the United Kingdom would have to begin to set an international example by taking seriously its regulation of the market, and building a more effective structure of control on the platform of the moral sentiment contained in its currently half-hearted and flawed attempts to control the flow of illicit antiquities into and through its jurisdiction by means of the 2003 Act.

In this vein of optimism, perhaps the most important latent potential the Act has is its cumulative effect. Leaving aside problems of drafting and other issues with the practical workability of the legislation as it stands, the problem of non-retroactivity becomes less of a restraint to prosecution as time passes. It is harder to break the law put in place by the 2003 Act now than it will be in five years' time, simply due to the increased number of objects which will be excavated in that time, and therefore which will fall foul of the Act. However, in the absence of mechanisms of object provenance identification it will remain very difficult to prove date of excavation. Therefore, in the final section we will offer some constructive suggestions as to how to capitalise on the opportunities a sustained focus on the market might bring as the 2003 Act increases its reach over objects in the market over time.

IMPLICATIONS FOR POLICY

The MRA works where buyers of stolen goods feel that they are under a level of law-enforcement scrutiny such that an illegal purchase will have adverse consequences for them. Deterrence theory traditionally has comprised three elements (Nagin, 1998): certainty (that is, likelihood of being caught); celerity (swiftness of punishment); and severity (a punishment of a level that is thought sufficient to provide a disincentive to law-breaking). The offence in the 2003 Act has failed to have a market reduction effect because, although it may satisfy the severity test—and possibly the celerity test, although without cases to study this is difficult to say—it falls down on the most basic premise of deterrence: likelihood of detection and punishment. The dealers in our sample were well aware that the police are largely unable to detect the crime of dealing in tainted cultural objects, for the various reasons set out above. This absence of relevant, irrefutable evidence leads dealers to maintain the view that they are not breaking the new law by continuing 'business as usual':

> I don't think I am under threat from the law personally, so I feel pretty relaxed about it. I don't want to break any law, but I don't feel that I will. (London dealer)

It must also be recognised that the prohibition of dealing in tainted cultural objects is in effect a prohibition on an unknown, but clearly considerable, part of the trade as it currently functions. While estimates have been put on the size of the illicit trade (DCMS, 2000; Brodie, Doole, and Watson, 2000; House of Commons Culture, Media and Sport Committee, 2000), it is acknowledged on all sides that these figures are in fact educated guesses as to the extent of the problem rather than hard facts. In addition to general studies, individual case studies have catalogued the extent of looting in a given area, on the one hand, and the amount of unprovenanced material appearing in auction catalogues, on the other, which in combination give quantitative analysts grounds for assessing the scale of the international illicit market (Gill and Chippindale, 1993; Chippindale and Gill, 2000; Elia, 2001). We have not entered into such a quantitative analysis here, but our qualitative market data lead us to assert that, *in the view of some of the most prominent and successful traders in the market*, trafficking in looted artefacts is central to its activity. These market actors equate the cleaning up of the market's activities with its inevitable demise:

> I suppose the other thing where the individual is concerned is that the standards have tightened over time. Whereas 20 years ago no one really cared what they were selling, so they'd find themselves in a profession earning a livelihood, it is now almost impossible to do it legitimately if you start asking all of the questions, I think. (Museum interviewee)
>
> I mean if you envisage a situation where no new material has been acquired by the British Museum in the world of Greek, Roman, or Mesopotamian cultures for 50 or 60 years, then people will say 'What is the point of having these frozen collections?' because it has always been axiomatic in the museum community that a collection that doesn't flow is one which will fossilise and wither on the vine. (Another museum interviewee, from a different museum)

We put this proposition to a major dealer in London:

> *Interviewer*: I think it is a noble proposition for an antiquities dealer to make, to say that 'I don't agree with looting', because although in the abstract we may say that we disagree with looting, in actual fact, what the current realities of the national situations mean is that if an antiquities dealer says 'I don't agree with looting' that is the end of the trade in new objects ...
>
> *Dealer*: Oh yeah.
>
> *Interviewer*: There is nothing new, there's only old things to circulate around ...
>
> *Dealer*: Absolutely.
>
> *Interviewer*: So, it must be a very difficult thing to come to terms with.
>
> *Dealer*: Professionally, it's suicide.

In this context, the MRA as currently operationalised in the antiquities market, albeit in a deficient manner in the case of the 2003 Act, calls for the end of the antiquities market as it has traditionally functioned. Where most source countries have passed vesting legislation, taking ownership of undiscovered antiquities, and where UK dealers are prohibited from dealing in these antiquities if they are discovered, excavated, and exported, the UK market may only deal in the corpus of artefacts which were in circulation prior to 30 December 2003. This is a finite class of objects, and a proposition which market actors see as 'professional suicide'. Objects new to the market may be discovered uncatalogued in attics and basements as time goes on, but these are thought, by the market at least, not to provide sufficiently interesting opportunities for profit when compared with freshly excavated archaeological material. 'Option 1' then, as we might call it, is to tighten up the law—perhaps by amendment to the generous wording of the offence in the 2003 Act—so that the deterrence component of the MRA works more effectively in this market: and to kill the market in antiquities in the United Kingdom as we know it.

Option 2 might involve working towards a compromise between the market and source countries. This would involve a shift in the weight attached to internal components of the MRA. The MRA component currently prioritised in UK policy approaches to the market, and embodied in the 2003 Act, is, as mentioned above, punishment-based deterrence, focused on market purchase. The problem of looted antiquities in the market is transnational, however, and, as such, somewhat more complex than domestic stolen goods markets. In addition to the penal component of the MRA—which focuses on reducing the number of stolen goods passing into a market—is the desire of the MRA model to attend to structural 'strains' which underpin stolen goods markets. Thus we might consider mechanisms to maintain the market while reducing the damage it causes. This is a 'harm reduction' approach to stolen goods markets, which asks: 'What is the harm that this market causes, and what can we do about it?' Harm-reduction has come to form a core mode of contemporary intervention into criminalised markets, illicit drugs markets being a notable reference point here, and given some of the successes of the approach (often in the face of political opposition and the challenge of deeply embedded social problems), it would seem worthwhile to consider the philosophy of harm reduction as it might apply to the looting problem.

In the antiquities market the damage caused by looting is predominantly to the archaeological record, and secondarily to the financial and patrimonial interest of source countries in their heritage. Several examples of schemes for the sponsored excavation, cataloguing, division, and sale of antiquities have been practised over the years, and many market participants support the idea of such schemes, which can in theory involve benefit for all: for archaeologists who conduct the digs and can gather their data; for the market, which receives a share of the finds (in some models in return for sponsorship); and for the source state, which exercises control over proceedings and decides which objects to release to the market and which to retain. The suggestion that these schemes may provide a panacea for the current problems in the antiquities market often meets with disapproval from archaeologists, however, who argue (among other things) that legitimating a section of the market will not discourage illicit dealing, and may indeed provide opportunity and motive for greater illicit activity. There are in fact many serious objections to such a model of market sanitisation, and clearly the application of a harm-reduction strategy through this mechanism is problematic on many fronts. Yet the structure of regulation we have now is not working, and further thought about alternative models of engagement with the problem remains a useful activity. The emergence of initiatives such as the United Kingdom's Portable Antiquities Scheme operating alongside the Treasure Act 1996 is interesting in this regard. Bland, in chapter five of this volume, has suggested that this model and its possible variants can encourage reporting of finds, and such strategies can fit the harm-reduction philosophy in their capacity to address the problem of the grey market by marking out legitimate markets in reported goods.

The regulation of the international market in antiquities does not have to be a zero-sum game, and to achieve the mutual benefits which can occur from market reconstruction, a shift in the philosophy of the United Kingdom's intervention is required so that the structural dictates of the MRA model are given due weight alongside its more penal dictates. International cooperation towards worthwhile harm reduction approaches, combined always with an effective deterrent for dealing outside any such cooperative schemes as are erected or revived, appears a more productive route to market sanitisation than the bare implementation of the penal part of the MRA model which currently informs the philosophy of UK intervention into the market. It is hoped that the DCMS will turn its attention to exploring possibilities for such harm-reduction approaches, perhaps through funding research in this direction, rather than investing further in the 'pseudo-crackdown' approach which has been shown here to be so problematic. In respect of what precise form a harm-reduction model for the antiquities market might take, further research is needed.

APPENDIX: SURVEY QUESTIONS

(1) What do you think of current market regulation? Should the trade be left to regulate itself?

(2) Do you think that looted antiquities are a problem for the trade? If so, what is the scale of the problem? If not, why not?

(3) Are you familiar with the requirements of the Dealing in Cultural Objects (Offences) Act 2003?
Yes
No

(4) If yes, do you think its impact on the trade in antiquities in London has been/will be:
Positive
Negative?
(5) Please take a few moments to explain the reasons for your answer below:
(6) Have you noticed a change in the way dealers operate as a consequence of the Act?
(7) Has your knowledge of the Act affected the way you carry on your business, or will it?

REFERENCES

Brodie, N, Doole, J, and Watson, P (2000) *Stealing History: The Illicit Trade in Cultural Material* (Cambridge, The McDonald Institute for Archaeological Research).

Calhoun, C and Hiller, H (1988) 'Asbestos Exposure by Johns-Manville: Cover-ups, Litigation, Bankruptcy and Compensation' 35 *Social Problems* 162.

Chippindale, C and Gill, DJW (2000) 'Material Consequences of Contemporary Classical Collecting', 104 *American Journal of Archaeology* 463.

Cohen, LE and Felson, M (1979) 'Social Change and Crime Rate Trends: a Routine Activity Approach', 44 *American Sociological Review* 588.

DCMS (Department for Culture, Media and Sport) (2000) *Ministerial Advisory Panel on Illicit Trade Report* ['the ITAP Report'], authored by N Palmer, P Addyman, R Anderson, A Browne, A Somers Cocks, M Davies, J Ede, J Van der Lande, and C Renfrew (London, DCMS).

—— (2004a) *Dealing in Tainted Cultural Objects—Guidance on the Dealing in Cultural Objects (Offences) Act 2003*, DCMS Cultural Property Unit Publication PP639 (London, DCMS).

—— (2004b) 'Government Response to "Cultural objects: developments since 2000" (HC 59), Report of the Culture, Media and Sport Select Committee, Session 2003–2004 (Norwich, HMSO).

Elia, RJ (2001) 'Analysis of the Looting, Selling and Collecting of Apulian Red-Figure Vases: a Quantitative Approach' in N Brodie, J Doole, and C Renfrew (eds), *Trade in Illicit Antiquities: The Destruction of the World's Archaeological Heritage* (Cambridge, MacDonald Institute for Archaeological Research).

Felson, M (1994) *Crime and Everyday Life* (Thousand Oaks, CA, Pine Forge Press).

Gerstenblith, P (2002) '*United States v Schultz*",' 10 *Culture Without Context: The Newsletter of the Illicit Antiquities Research Centre*, Cambridge: University of Cambridge.

Gill, DJW and Chippindale, C (1993) 'Material and Intellectual Consequences of Esteem for Cycladic Figures' 97 *American Journal of Archaeology* 602.

Hansard (2006) 'House of Commons Written Answers for 18 December: Cultural Goods: Seizures', www.parliament.the-stationery-office.co.uk/pa/cm200607/cmhansrd/cm061218/text/61218w0022.htm, accessed 13 February 2007.

House of Commons Culture, Media and Sport Committee (2000) *Cultural Property: Return and Illicit Trade*, Seventh Report, 1999–2000 Session, 3 vols (London, The Stationery Office).

Hughes, G (2006) *The Politics of Crime and Community* (Basingstoke, MacMillan).

Lee, MT (1998) 'The Ford Pinto Case and the Development of Auto Safety Regulations, 1893–1978', 27 *Business and Economic History* 2.

Mackenzie, S (2002) 'Organised Crime and Common Transit Networks', *Trends & Issues in Crime and Criminal Justice No 233* (Canberra, Australian Institute of Criminology).

—— (2005) *Going, Going, Gone: Regulating the Market in Illicit Antiquities* (Leicester, Institute of Art and Law).

Mackenzie, S and Green, P (2008) 'Performative Regulation: A Case Study in How Powerful People Avoid Criminal Labels' 48(2) *British Journal of Criminology* 138–53.

Nagin, DS (1998) 'Criminal Deterrence Research at the Outset of the Twenty-first Century' in M Tonry (ed), *Crime and Justice: A Review of Research, Vol 23* (Chicago, IL, University of Chicago Press).

O'Keefe, PJ (1997) *Trade in Antiquities: Reducing Destruction and Theft* (London, Archetype).

Polk, K (2000) 'The Antiquities Trade Viewed as a Criminal Market', September *Hong Kong Lawyer* 82.

Schneider, JL (2008) 'Reducing the Illicit Trade in Endangered Wildlife: the Market Reduction Approach', 24(3) *Journal of Contemporary Criminal Justice* 274–95.

Sutton, M (1998) *Handling Stolen Goods and Theft: a Market Reduction Approach*, Home Office Research Study 178 (London, Home Office).

Sutton, M, Schneider, J, and Hetherington, S (2001) *Tackling Theft with the Market Reduction Approach*, Crime Reduction Research Series Paper 8 (London, Home Office).

Tweedale, G (2000) *Magic Mineral to Killer Dust: Turner and Newall and the Asbestos Hazard* (Oxford, Oxford University Press).

Index